ALEXANDER HAMILTON
AND THE
BATTLE OF YORKTOWN
OCTOBER 1781

ALEXANDER HAMILTON

AND THE

BATTLE OF YORKTOWN

OCTOBER 1781

THE WINNING OF AMERICAN INDEPENDENCE

PHILLIP THOMAS TUCKER

Skyhorse Publishing

Skyhorse Publishing books may be purchased in bulk at special discounts for sales promotion, corporate gifts, fund-raising, or educational purposes. Special editions can also be created to specifications. For details, contact the Special Sales Department, Skyhorse Publishing, 307 West 36th Street, 11th Floor, New York, NY 10018 or info@skyhorsepublishing.com.

Skyhorse® and Skyhorse Publishing® are registered trademarks of Skyhorse Publishing, Inc.®, a Delaware corporation.

Visit our website at www.skyhorsepublishing.com.

10 9 8 7 6 5 4 3 2 1

Library of Congress Cataloging-in-Publication Data is available on file.

Cover design by Kai Texel

Print ISBN: 978-1-5107-6935-9
Ebook ISBN: 978-1-5107-6936-6

Printed in the United States of America

Contents

Contents

Introduction

In one of the great ironies in the annals of American history, Alexander Hamilton's special roles—especially as General George Washington's invaluable chief-of-staff for nearly four years—that he played during the American Revolution and in the making of America after the war have left one of the important ones in relative obscurity. Although a recent immigrant to America, Hamilton made the most important and memorable contributions by far of the thirty-two members of Washington's staff.

Most glaringly and surprisingly, the long list of Hamilton's accomplishments at the nerve center of Washington's headquarters, and earlier in the war—including at the Battles of Trenton and Princeton, New Jersey, during the 1776–77 Campaign as a young commander of a New York artillery battery—have cast a giant shadow to this day over his all-important role during the crucial Yorktown Campaign, in part because this was the last major campaign of the American Revolution. This relative obscurity in the historical record has been especially the case in regard to Hamilton's stirring role in leading the attack that captured strategic Redoubt Number Ten, which anchored the left flank of Lord Charles Cornwallis's lengthy defensive line on the York River, on October 14, 1781, not long after the autumnal sun had dropped over the western horizon.

But more than in the case of nearby Redoubt Number Nine, which was overwhelmed by French troops at the same time, the capture of Redoubt Number Ten by Lieutenant Colonel Hamilton and his storming party of Continental light troops was key to turning Cornwallis's left flank of his sprawling siege line, which shortly forced his surrender. Only five days later and thanks to the fall of Redoubt Number Ten and also Redoubt Number Nine, to a lesser degree, Lord Cornwallis surrendered his British, Hessian, and Loyalist Army in a broad field situated along the Hampton Road just outside Yorktown: the decisive turning point of not only the American Revolution but also of world history, ensuring that the infant United States of America won its struggle for independence and gained a lengthy life as the newest people's republic in the world.

Clearly, Hamilton's special day of destiny came on Sunday October 14, 1781, when a great deal was at stake in this war for America's liberty because Cornwallis was expecting the arrival of reinforcements from New York City as promised by his superior, Sir Henry Clinton. At that time, Hamilton audaciously tempted fate as never before. He lived to tell the tale of the harrowing experience in having led the headlong charge on formidable Redoubt Number Ten and having been the first American to scale the parapet and leap inside the earthen fortification, surviving numerous close calls at a time when his pregnant wife, Elizabeth Schuyler-Hamilton in Albany, New York, was praying for his safe return home.

Hamilton led the charge of his Continental light troops over a broad stretch of open ground at a time when he had nothing to prove to anyone but himself because he had already demonstrated an abundance of courage as a gifted commander of a New York artillery unit. Nevertheless, he was so passionate about winning glory during this last chance that he risked all: an incredibly bright future; a beautiful, loving wife who hailed from one of America's leading families and carried his first child, Philip; an extremely supportive family of politically influential, wealthy in-laws who fully accepted him in every possible way despite his shadowy Caribbean background; and the high opinion that he enjoyed with General Washington and the Continental Army. His risk of all he had gained since migrating to America in 1773 reflected Hamilton's complex and paradoxical nature of enthusiastically embracing great challenges, even at the peril of his life. than high hopes during the summer of 1773: all part of Hamilton's complex and paradoxical nature in which he enthusiastically embraced the greatest challenges, even at the risk of his own life.

The unfortunate and almost unthinkable oversight by generations of historians and Hamilton scholars of Hamilton's role in the Revolution, and the Yorktown Campaign especially, has partly stemmed from his service time. Hamilton served as a combat officer for only a few months during the war's final campaign, after having served on Washington's staff.

Ironically, the importance of Yorktown; the brilliance of the combined offensive effort of the allied Generals Washington and Jean-Baptiste Donatien de Vimeur, Comte de Rochambeau, age fifty-six; and the vital contributions of the French Navy that won superiority at sea have overshadowed the key moment—estimated at only twenty minutes—that it took Hamilton and his crack light troops to capture Redoubt Number Ten.

Generations of historians have seemingly believed that Hamilton could have achieved relatively little of real importance on the war's last major battlefield in such a short time during the most important siege in the annals of American history, fostering the misconception that his military service was relatively undistinguished at Yorktown—the antithesis of the actual situation. But in fact, from the beginning of the American Revolution to the end, young Hamilton excelled as a battlefield commander and leader of men as both an artillery and infantry officer on the field of strife when not serving on Washington's staff.

Indeed, the young native West Indian played key roles not only at Yorktown but also as the commander of a New York artillery command before he joined Washington's staff on March 1, 1777—an impressive list of military contributions in leadership roles when not serving with distinction as a member of Washington's staff, remarkable for such a young officer and recent immigrant only in his twenties. In fact, very few, if any, Americans during this war possessed a more distinguished and impressive military record both on and off the battlefield or were at center stage of the most stirring events of the American Revolution, especially at Washington's headquarters, than Hamilton. Hamilton's rise both on and off the battlefield was meteoric, especially in regard to his vital role on Washington's staff from 1777 to 1781.

With America's storied past, and even the lives of the founding fathers, in the process of being reanalyzed and reinterpreted in the United States as never before during the third decade of the twenty-first century, it is now time to reexamine the life of America's most controversial and gifted founding father, the only one not born in America. Alexander Hamilton was a product of the Caribbean, having been raised on the island of Saint Croix in the Danish West Indies. In fact, he was far more of a West Indian than an American by the start of the American Revolution in April 1775.

However, many American biographers, especially pro–American exceptionalism scholars, have portrayed Hamilton as a true-blue American without acknowledging the significance of his deep immigrant roots, in no small part because his West Indies past was a dark one. Hamilton possessed the most tragic background of any founding father, with poverty, illegitimacy, and a Scottish father's abandonment. Most founding fathers hailed from largely stable and wealthy backgrounds.

Despite his lowly beginnings, Hamilton was a man of destiny, whose intelligence and achievements shone brightly throughout the years of the American Revolution, when he truly rose like the proverbial phoenix as Washington's invaluable right-hand man in the important role of chief-of-staff and all the way to his stirring role at Yorktown. From early 1777 to early 1781, no member of General Washington's personal staff was more important and indispensable than Hamilton. And no star shone brighter than that of Hamilton both on and off the battlefield year after year.

However, the meteoritic life of this remarkably gifted man from the West Indies was tragically cut short on July 11, 1804, by a small-caliber bullet fired from a dueling pistol of Aaron Burr, who was also a distinguished veteran of the Continental Army and a short-time member of Washington's staff, during the most famous duel in

American history. Most notable as President George Washington's secretary of the treasury from 1789 to 1795—before tragedy struck because of Burr's steady aim on a New Jersey day at Weehawken on the Hudson River's western shore across from New York City—Hamilton had emerged as the chief ultranationalist and brilliant architect of a robust system of capitalism that laid the central foundation of modern America. Actually, Hamilton was the chief architect behind the nation's spectacular economic growth and dramatic rise to power that continued for generations and well into the twentieth century.

Quite simply, in both war and peace, Hamilton was the most gifted founding father despite his youth and relative inexperience. Hamilton's dramatic rise had been nothing short of spectacular, considering that he had first migrated to New York City on a sailing ship from the West Indies during the summer of 1773, less than two years before the start of the American Revolution. At that time, he had no place in America, a land of strangers and the largest region he had ever seen. Here, in a new land of limitless potential, he almost immediately fully embraced the great dream of America and what it promised to a young immigrant. For Hamilton, the outbreak of the American Revolution was a godsend, allowing greater opportunities for young man of many unique talents without the usually required wealth, status, or family background, because of the dramatic rise of the spirit of republicanism and a new sense of equality. The gifted West Indian and former clerk of a large mercantile house from the small island of Saint Croix was not only a prodigy but also a genius who excelled with remarkable ease in multiple arenas.

In this book, I have provided a detailed look at the dramatic course of the ever-eventful life of Alexander Hamilton primarily in the Yorktown Campaign. No previous book has been devoted to Hamilton's vital role during the most important campaign of the Revolutionary War. He seemed to have led multiple lives of importance in only a remarkably short time and, unlike most, is actually more relevant today than ever before in many ways. His story is that of the American Dream and limitless opportunities, which still applies to hard-working and industrious immigrants to the United States to this day. His story is a truly timeless lesson about the core meaning and overall importance of America.

Indeed, the incredible story of Hamilton's life, which reads almost like a novel of historical romance created from an imaginative mind, has revealed a good many life lessons that still remain valid today for men and women around the world, especially to seize the day. A wise saying that first originated from a respected ancient Roman philosopher, *carpe diem*, or seize the day, has emphasized the wisdom for people, especially youth from disadvantageous backgrounds, to aggressively and boldly exploit opportunities to succeed. After he had escaped from his own Caribbean dead end, Hamilton seemed to have been blessed by fate and the gods to which the ancient Romans had often paid their sacred devotion in return for their benevolence and favor in all areas of life.

Throughout Hamilton's life, in which there never seemed to be a dull moment, he repeatedly demonstrated the timely wisdom of this ancient Roman philosophy to seize the day. This was a golden rule by which Hamilton lived and one that repeatedly paid immense dividends to him in both war and peace. The fact that Hamilton repeatedly risked his life on battlefields from New York to Virginia, especially during the climactic showdown at Yorktown, to fulfill his ambitions and personal destiny revealed the depth of the young man's character and commitment to his republican vision of America. But although an intellectual, he was never an idle dreamer but a man of action, which set him apart from all of the other founding fathers except Washington. For years, Hamilton struggled to make his grandiose vision of America become a reality by his own sacrifices and achievements. And he succeeded in the end.

Because of today's political climate in the United States during the nation's most unheroic age, the America as originally envisioned by Hamilton has seemingly grown out of favor among many Americans with the rise of a mild brand of twenty-first century American socialism that has been naively thought to be preferable to Hamilton's envisioned style of capitalism, which had reaped so much national success and wealth. That's an entirely unimaginable political development in America only a few years ago, which has partly reflected the process of the overall dumbing down of America for generations in an inferior educational system that has become increasingly politicized and polarized.

In idealistic terms combined with naiveté and an exuberant innocence, some active socialists in the United States today have embraced idealistic political concepts that are far too utopian and devoid of reality, especially in regard to history's timeless lessons, to be practical for the real world, which has been fully demonstrated throughout the course of history, especially during the twentieth century and most famously in the Soviet Union. If alive today, diehard nationalist and capitalist Hamilton would have been absolutely appalled by the recent fast-paced developments in America. And in the ultimate irony, the political movement to change America by gradually moving toward the left occurred not long after the play *Hamilton* became the most successful and popular in the long history of Broadway plays, which especially appealed to people of a younger generation. However, it seems that while most people loved the music of *Hamilton*, they missed his long list of military achievements, especially at Yorktown, and his role as the primary creator of the American capitalist system.

What has been often most minimized by generations of American historians, especially of the nationalist school of history, was the fact that he was a West Indian and a lowly immigrant to America. Hamilton's dramatic rise to prominence was nothing short of miraculous, a true Horatio Alger story. The fact that the West Indies consisted of largely a black population has caused the lack of focus on Hamilton's Caribbean background, long somewhat of an embarrassment to white nationalist historians, especially in regard to rumors that Hamilton possessed black blood from his mother's side because racial intermixing was so prevalent in the West Indies.

But unlike any other founding father, Hamilton made his American dream come true by way of his own abilities and intelligence.

The people's revolution that overturned the old social order on the English model bestowed a host of new opportunities for Hamilton to make a name for himself in the military realm: first as a dynamic New York artillery commander of his own unit during the New York Campaign and the Trenton-Princeton Campaign, then as Washington's indispensable chief-of-staff for years, and finally as the leader of his own command, a full battalion, of Continental light infantry troops, who were the crack fighting men of the Continental Army.

However, like a classic Greek tragedy in the end, this remarkable man of such incomparable talents and abilities needlessly threw his life away in the Aaron Burr duel that he did not have to fight. He was philosophically against the concept of dueling, especially since dueling had caused his teenage son Philip's death in November 1801. But, of course, a cruel destiny had deemed otherwise by backing him into a corner to preserve his reputation and causing him to engage in what he never desired to do, ordaining an early end to his life in July 1804—a tragedy of immense proportions. Ironically and as a strange fate would have it, Hamilton had survived dozens of close calls on the battlefield during the war years only to be fatally cut down in a New Jersey dueling field at Weehawken, by an equally talented man and the sitting vice president who had once been his comrade in arms during America's struggle for liberty.

Like the throngs of immigrants who still eagerly come to America's shores today from around the world with visions of a better life for themselves and their families, so Hamilton had early viewed the immense potential and seemingly endless possibilities of this new land. As Hamilton learned when he first disembarked from a sailing ship on American soil in the summer of 1773 with little prospects or expectations, the thirteen colonies were the antithesis of what he had known in the past. By the slimmest of margins and thanks to sympathetic patrons, he had narrowly escaped the severely limited opportunities on Saint Croix, where he had labored for years without prospects in the Cruger family trading firm of Cruger and Beekman.

In the boundless expanse of America that was as big as its endless opportunities that existed during both peace and wartime for a smart, enterprising individual, Hamilton gained the chance to soar to unprecedented heights both during the war years and afterward. But the most opportunities came for the young West Indian because of the overturning of the old order by a revolution that was the first successful people's revolt against a powerful European monarchy. Quite simply, Hamilton was at exactly the right place at the right time to boldly seize the opportunities to rise higher in life, transforming himself from an outsider to an insider in record time, when on American soil.

When he had lived on the tiny island of Saint Croix in the sweltering tropics and without future prospects at age fourteen, Hamilton wrote in a heartfelt letter (his earliest surviving letter) to his close friend Edward "Ned" Stevens in New York City on November 11, 1769, "I wish there was a War." Penned barely half a dozen years after the end of the Seven Years' War (known as the French and Indian War in America), his fondest wish eventually proved prophetic, because war was the key to his future recognition and fame, including the stirring role that he played during the dramatic showdown at Yorktown, Virginia, in less than a dozen years in the future.

Strangely, Hamilton seemed to somehow know that his reputation would be made because of war and that he was bound for greatness in the military realm far more than anyone, including himself, dared to imagine possible. Of course, Hamilton wrote his prophetic letter to Ned more than half a decade before the beginning of the American Revolution, when the redcoats and a small band of Massachusetts militiamen clashed on Lexington Green on April 19, 1775, and he had no idea what lofty heights he would reach in faraway America.

Indeed, in the end, Hamilton found not only his adopted home, destiny, and future in America, but also the conflict—nothing less than a world war after the French joined the American revolutionaries in 1778 with the signing of the Franco-American Alliance—that he had once so desperately desired to free him from a miniscule island in the West Indies.

He boldly maneuvered behind the scenes, including with General Washington, to win the coveted assignment of leading one of the most dangerous and the most climactic assaults of the American Revolution at great risk to himself on the night of October 14, 1781, when so much was at stake.

With the full strength of the French naval and land forces under the experienced and talented Comte de Rochambeau, France's best general who had been specially dispatched by King Louis XVI, now working closely together with Washington in Virginia, the general feeling in the army was that the revolution could be won at Yorktown. After years of faithful service to Washington on his staff, Hamilton jumped at the opportunity to secure the coveted role of leading the key attack in a position of honor on one of the most formidable British defensive positions at Yorktown.

However, Hamilton's ambition to lead the attack on strategic Redoubt Number Ten was much more than a selfish and greedy ambition. To young Hamilton and his revolutionary generation, nothing was more noble than the enlightened concept of republicanism—the political foundation of the infant American nation and the basis of his enlightened, idealistic thinking during the war years, which fueled his risky actions on the battlefield. As a young man who had been educated in America since his relatively recent arrival from Saint Croix in 1773, Hamilton had learned a good many historical lessons from the ancient classics, including the greatness of ancient Greek and Roman republicanism and democracy.

In this sense and like so many of the educated Continental officers, including fellow officers on Washington's staff like Tench Tilghman of Maryland, Hamilton not only saw himself as a New World man, but also the very embodiment of a republican hero on the battlefield, like an ancient Greek or Roman warrior. These historical notions fueled Hamilton's motivations, while gaining for him the moral high ground by way of appropriate republican analogies in a common people's righteous struggle for liberty. At Yorktown on the Virginia Peninsula beside the York River where Lord Cornwallis's army was trapped, Hamilton finally gained his long-awaited opportunity to emulate those ancient heroes of the distant past, his idols and models of true republican virtue. In a special fusion seen nowhere else to such an extent but in America among Washington's young Continental officers, the ancient Greek and Roman classics and the new sense of republicanism were interwoven to a degree almost unimaginable to the thinking of modern Americans.

Symbolically, the once imposing Redoubt Number Ten on the Yorktown battlefield long ago eroded, washed away by time and the weather until nothing was left as a reminder. However, the people of the National Park Service have reconstructed the strategic, though now smaller and less imposing today than it appeared to Hamilton and his men at the time. And a visitor to the battlefield in today's York County, Virginia, will look in vain for an appropriate memorial or statue to Hamilton for his notable tactical achievement on the most decisive and important day of the siege of Yorktown.

Ironically, today on the eve of the national celebration of the 250th Anniversary of the American Revolution, an ever-increasing number of Americans, who have become more cynical and politicized to a degree unimaginable only a few years before, generally look unfavorably upon the founding fathers for primarily racial reasons, especially because two of the most prominent founders were large Virginia slave owners: George Washington and Thomas Jefferson. Even more, it has become increasingly popular, if not fashionable, today for young protesters of social injustice to commit criminal acts of defacing and even tearing down memorials to the founding fathers, especially those of Virginia slave owners, including Jefferson and Washington, because they had only fought for white liberty and not black liberty more than two centuries ago when the world was altogether different.

However, what has been forgotten is that this ugly reality of a firm embrace of slavery stemmed from a calculated original Machiavellian decision of the founding fathers that was an absolute political necessity for the infant republic to guarantee a successful uniting of North and South so that all the states would come together as one to fight against the world's strongest imperial power from the Atlantic's other side—the new Rome. Unfortunately, this absolute political necessity for national survival of a weak republic compromised the revolution's most enlightened principle, as emphasized by Jefferson, that "all men are created equal."

This unfortunate development was the high price of going to war against a powerful Old World monarchy that ruled a vast empire and sought to impose its imperial will and autocratic authority on the American people. Generations of the unfortunate people of African descent paid the ultimate personal price for the fulfillment of America's liberty, sacrificed on its altar in the very beginning. Quite simply, there would have been no successful revolution if slavery, a basic foundation of the national economy, had been abolished early according to the egalitarian principles of the Age of Enlightenment.

In today's increasingly popular and widespread condemnation of the founding fathers for having betrayed fundamental egalitarian principles of the American Revolution because they failed to promote the cause of black liberty, even Hamilton has been most recently targeted by politically correct advocates of what has become a fashionable popular movement supported by the mass media and Hollywood, because it is today's most trendy form of demonstrating moral outrage and indignation, especially on the internet, based on a sense of self-reconfirming righteousness. In 2019 and 2020, even the popular Broadway play *Hamilton* came under fire because of its lack of sensitivity toward the ugly truths of race and slavery in colonial and revolutionary America. Ironically, *Hamilton* became the most popular in Broadway history in part because it had skirted such political and emotionally charged issues like slavery. As part of this sharp backlash, the *Washington Times* released a hard-hitting story on February 7, 2019 entitled, "Lin-Manuel Miranda's 'Hamilton' under Fire for Ignoring Founding Fathers' 'Complicity in Slavery.'"

However, this glaring omission of a much-needed focus on the institution of slavery in the Broadway play *Hamilton* has been most ironic. When it came to slavery, Hamilton was actually the least deserving of all the founding fathers to have today come under any kind of criticism. Indeed, what has been most overlooked about Hamilton, when he was serving on Washington's staff, was the key role that he played in promoting the recruitment of black slaves to fight for their own liberty, when America faced a manpower crisis during a war of attrition. War weariness and apathy among whites had grown extremely high across America, after so many defeats and ever-increasing battlefield Losses. Two distinct liberation efforts of the common people—one black, one white—of America were closely intertwined as Hamilton early realized, because the love of liberty knew no color and this struggle was one that naturally erased color lines and prejudice in the name of freedom for all. Along with his friend Lieutenant Colonel John Laurens who had also served on Washington's staff, Hamilton was one of the leading advocates for the use of black soldiers, or slaves, who would fight for their own freedom and that of America.

Then, after the war, Hamilton fought politically against the Jeffersonian vision of an agrarian society of yeoman farmers, who were also slave-owners, especially in the South but also in the North where slavery had not been abolished in some cases. He promoted the concept of a prosperous nation based on a strong industrial base instead of a robust institution of slavery. To criticize the play *Hamilton* today because of its shortcomings in regard to the subject of slavery is the greatest irony of all because Hamilton was the biggest abolitionist of the founding fathers, which reveals the lack of historical insight of the critics today.

Indeed, Hamilton was an abolitionist at an early date to a degree unimaginable to Washington and Jefferson, who were two of Virginia's largest slave owners to the end of their lives. After the war, Hamilton was one of the founders of the New York Manumission Society and was more open-minded about race than most founding fathers, especially those men from the South. He advocated for the use of black soldiers because of the *equality* of black abilities and intellectual capabilities to whites, long before the first gun was fired in anger at Yorktown. In Hamilton's words from a mid-March 1779 letter, "I have not the least doubt, that the negroes will make very excellent soldiers." Ironically, Hamilton won his greatest battlefield glory in America's largest slave state and on behalf of one of the world's largest slave-owning nations at a time when he was an abolitionist at heart by way of his own words and actions to a degree rarely seen from any American at the time. Hamilton and best friend John Laurens, another gifted member of Washington's staff, not only led the charge together at Yorktown but also earlier advocated a bold plan, which was formally presented to the Continental Congress, for black freedom and equality during the war years, one of the boldest emancipation plans before the Civil War. Clearly, Hamilton was more forward-looking, enlightened, and egalitarian about race than any other founding father, and his actions and words over the years revealed as much.

Ron Chernow's highly acclaimed 2004 masterpiece, *Hamilton*, upon which the popular Broadway play *Hamilton* was based and which was the finest Hamilton biography yet written, devoted less than five pages to the important story of Hamilton's role at Yorktown—in consequence, this book will thoroughly explore the subject.

To his great credit, Chernow is today's leading biographer and historian of Hamilton because his book is nothing short of brilliant on multiple levels, but the all-important Yorktown story was surprisingly minimized and neglected in this fine work of more than eight hundred pages. However, this highly-acclaimed Hamilton biography has provided an example of how the significance of Hamilton's role at Yorktown has been given a relatively light touch even by one of America's most gifted biographers and writers. This omission has motivated the writing of this book, to fill the missing gaps in the historical record as much as possible.

More than half a decade ago when I had the privilege of writing the 2017 book *Alexander Hamilton's Revolution: His Vital Role as Washington's Chief of Staff* for Skyhorse Publishing, which became a selection of the History Book Club, the dramatic story of Hamilton at Yorktown was minimized by this current author, but only because it was outside his chief-of-staff role. However, this current book tells the full story of Hamilton at Yorktown to a degree unlike any previous book because it is so important to be fully understood and appreciated on the eve of the 250th anniversary of the American Revolution.

This current book was also written because Hamilton's story is still important and relevant to this day for a variety of reasons. What the young West Indian demonstrated at Yorktown was not only heroic in the traditional sense but also a remainder of the high cost of liberty and how difficult it was to obtain and keep it—a valuable lesson that still applies not only in America but also around the world today. All in all, it was most fortunate for the United States that Hamilton survived leading the daring charge on formidable Redoubt Number Ten, because he was more responsible for the making of modern America as we know it today any other founding father, as President Washington's brilliant secretary of the treasury.

The overall purpose of this book has been to bring Alexander Hamilton to life as much as possible, especially by relying on his own words to reveal the real person. In many ways and especially because of his prolific writings that were penned with an unparalleled eloquence, intelligence, and honesty, he can be seen today as the most human and accessible of all the founding fathers. In his revealing letters, Hamilton displayed a mixture of wit and wisdom not seen in the words of any other founding father except Benjamin Franklin, which has made him come alive more than any other founding father.

Too often the founding fathers have been portrayed as "marble men" poised on the Mount Olympus of American icons, impossible for the average person today to get to understand. Fortunately, such is not the case with the multitalented Hamilton, a true Renaissance man. The extent of Hamilton's writings was so wide-ranging that it is now possible for readers to almost feel like they know Hamilton not only as a person, but also intimately. Therefore, this current book will quote Hamilton's own words as much as possible, including before and especially during the Yorktown Campaign.

And Hamilton accomplished so much during the war and afterward despite, or because of, possessing inner demons from a murky and shadowy Caribbean past—some false rumors even maintained that he had black blood because of his illegitimate birth in a land dominated by slavery and where the black population far outnumbered the white population—and a distinct penchant for high drama seemingly wherever he went and far more than any other founding father. Despite his prolific writings, however, Hamilton was still very much Sphinx-like, because he was a man without a past who was unknown in America, and this dark obscurity of his Caribbean days primarily fueled his spectacular rise to prominence.

Despite having been a man of rare genius at a relatively young age, he was still very much a common man—one example of his contradictory personality. Because of what he accomplished at Yorktown on October 14 and thanks to major colonial newspapers, especially those located in the capital of Philadelphia, Pennsylvania, Hamilton's name finally became well-known across America for the first time.

The twenty-first century has become America's most unheroic age partly because of the widespread and growing influence of political correctness and the dominance of the self-serving personal and political agendas of the Internet Age; the older values of a more heroic age, which had long defined the course of human history in many cultures around the world, have been largely erased, thanks partly to the comfortable convenience of looking at history in hindsight through a tainted politicized lens entirely out of focus, because of today's fashionable political agendas and popular partisan politics. Not only the United States flag but also decorated military veterans, who have fought to preserve America's freedoms and risked their lives in foreign lands, have been routinely mocked because partisan politics and political agendas have become so popular today. Even the Congressional Medal of Honor and their proud winners have been recently dishonored by people who know little, if anything, about the military or history, because of political falsehoods, a failed American educational school system that has been politicized, and the influence of morally corrupt political leaders motivated by self-serving agendas.

Compared to today and as noted, the period of the American Revolution was America's most idealistic heroic age on multiple levels as embraced by the Revolutionary War generation, especially Age of Enlightenment leaders and the founding fathers, including Hamilton. And none of these revolutionary leaders were more thoroughly imbued with the concept of the meaning of republicanism found in the ancient classics than the founding fathers, who modeled their infant republic upon the political and social lessons learned from the ancient classics. Founders like Jefferson and Washington's young staff officers, including Hamilton, knew all about the stories of famous republican leaders and institutions of ancient Greece and Roman and Homer's ancient Greek heroes of the *Iliad* and the *Odyssey*. Indeed, Alexander Hamilton, like his equally idealistic young friends John Laurens and Tench Tilghman who also served on Washington's staff and were educated at leading colleges, had studied and learned about the ancient classics at King's College (today's Columbia University) and other institutions of higher learning in the northeast.

It is certainly now time to not only look anew at Alexander Hamilton and the Yorktown Campaign in greater detail but also to explore the generally minimized French role, especially in regard to the supreme importance of naval superiority, which was the key to decisive victory.

For a wide variety of reasons including that he was the most dynamic and controversial founding father both on and off the battlefield, the remarkable story of young Lieutenant Colonel Hamilton and his key role at Yorktown will be explored and analyzed more thoroughly than in any previous book to enlighten readers about one of the vital architects to decisive victory at Yorktown during the most important chapter of American history. Most of all, Hamilton's.

What should not be forgotten was the belief in divine intervention. Hamilton had seemingly been sent to America in 1773 at exactly the right time by a benevolent and kind Providence, especially at Yorktown. Above all other factors, Washington sincerely believed that a kindly Providence was most of all responsible for the creation of the United States of America and the winning of the American Revolution for the benefit of all mankind. In fact, the entire people's revolution was based on the unique popular concept that America needed no king in Europe, because it already had a king and higher authority to guide it—God. Because Hamilton played so many vital roles, it almost seemed to many people—perhaps even Washington— as if he had been heaven-sent to America from the West Indies.

Clearly, at this late date, Alexander Hamilton must be viewed from an entirely new and fresh perspective, especially because he was the foremost abolitionist of all the founding fathers. He utterly rejected the Jeffersonian vision of a thriving American agricultural economy based on a vibrant institution of slavery, which darkly tainted the idealistic egalitarian vision, the promise of the infant republic, and the overall American experiment conceived in liberty.

In much the same way, so a new view of Lieutenant Colonel Hamilton's distinguished role at Yorktown needs to be looked at because he successfully orchestrated and conducted nothing less than the most climactic and vital assault on a strategic position during the course of the American Revolution on the night of October 14, 1781, that forced Lord Cornwallis to surrender his entire army and changed the course of history.

—Phillip Thomas Tucker, PhD

Chapter I

Frustrated Young Man of Scottish-French Descent from the West Indies

Ever the contrarian and maverick after having been born on the tropical island of Nevis and raised as an orphan on the island of Saint Croix in the Danish West Indies, young Alexander Hamilton had become heartily sick and tired of the most popular and esteemed military man in America by early 1781. This revered individual had become world famous because he symbolized America's revolutionary war effort and commanded the Continental Army, while Hamilton was saddled with the demons of a dark past, including an illegitimate birth in the Caribbean. Idolized around the world, General George Washington, a former Virginia militia officer before the war and veteran of the French and Indian War, was lionized by not only the American people but also much of the freedom-loving world, especially France.

However, young Lieutenant Colonel Hamilton had seen considerable shortcoming in the commander-in-chief, including how he treated subordinates shabbily, like he was still the master of Mount Vernon and a large number of slaves. Hamilton had seen the sudden and unpredictable outbursts of his fierce temper, especially in times of high stress, which Washington sought to control his entire life but often failed miserably.

As Washington's top staff officer and indispensable chief-of-staff who had performed brilliantly from early 1777 to early 1781 while only in his mid-twenties (at a time when he looked younger because of his boyish handsomeness, unbridled enthusiasm, and endless energy in having danced for hours at fashionable balls with some of the day's most beautiful women), Hamilton faced a serious dilemma for which had no solution. He had labored long and hard in the shadow of America's greatest hero and now seemed trapped.

As long demonstrated at headquarters, no one could speak more intelligently about so many diverse and complex subjects, especially those that were economicly and politically related, than the gifted Hamilton. And Washington fully realized as much, knowing that Hamilton, who was overflowing with ideas and solutions to problems, was crucial as the head of his staff in almost too many ways to count. The commander-in-chief of the Continental Army wisely knew that he needed Hamilton by his side throughout much of the war—a realization that ran in direct conflict with the talented native West Indian's ambitions, including a well-deserved promotion denied by Washington because it might free him from Washington's group of hard-working, young staff officers.

However, by early 1781, Hamilton thought much differently from almost all other patriots about America's most revered leader whom everyone called "His Excellency." Daily contact with Washington had changed his opinion. Despite having become the most famous man in America, Washington was quite provincial in many fundamental ways and still very much of a common Virginia plantation owner, but a rich one. This situation especially applied to Washington's inferior education, both military and civilian, which was duly noted by Hamilton because it was so glaringly obvious.

After all, Washington was a former Virginia militia colonel and large tidewater planter who had only once departed America's shores when he had journeyed to the West Indies, whereas Hamilton, familiar with different cultures and languages of Western Europe, was far more sophisticated, erudite, and cultured. The young man knew the tricky and complex ways of the international world from his years of working with the Cruger international trading firm on Saint Croix, which was located at the center of a booming international trade. Despite his youth, therefore, Hamilton was far more worldly than the tall planter and aristocratic gentleman farmer from Mount Vernon, which stood on the bluffs of Fairfax County overlooking the Potomac River and southern Maryland on the river's west side. Even more, Hamilton was nothing short of a genius, whose intellectual abilities towered above those of Washington, which allowed him to make key contributions and bestow sage advice to the commander-in-chief about political, economic, and military matters. He assisted Washington immeasurably at headquarters in a variety of ways, helping him to make the proper decisions and sage judgements in leading America's war effort.

Despite his many achievements as Washington's invaluable chief-of-staff, Hamilton was virtually unknown outside of the staff and top leaders of the Continental Army, because he had been a recent immigrant (1773) to America from the Caribbean and a former commander of a New York artillery unit—the "Provincial Company of Artillery." He had led his New York gunners with tactical skill and aggressiveness since March 1776 and played key roles during the dreary retreat south from the evacuated New York City and then during the Battles of Trenton and Princeton, New Jersey. These were Washington's first battlefield victories in late December 1776 and early January 1777, respectively.

Even more, Hamilton was an open-minded internationalist and brilliant economist and political thinker far beyond the knowledge of an average top staff officer, overflowing with innovative ideas and novel concepts that were generally alien to military men. He had long expressed his own well-defined thoughts in masterful writings in the form of official army orders and documents to which Washington readily gave his approval. For instance, during Washington's first meeting with the leader of France's expeditionary force, General Jean-Baptiste Donatien de Vimeur, Comte de Rochambeau, at the Hartford Convention in Connecticut in September 1780, the commander-in-chief brought an eight-page draft, written by Hamilton in French, for Rochambeau that proposed a joint attack on New York City.

Another simmering source of inherent friction and unease, albeit unconscious, existed between Washington and Hamilton, which has been overlooked by generations of American historians. Young Lieutenant Colonel Hamilton believed in freeing slaves if they fought for America in all-black battalions with white officers and had boldly put those thoughts in writing in 1779, while Washington was one of America's largest slave owners and a member of Virginia's upper class planter elite. And after nearly four years, Hamilton had also certainly tired of always addressing Washington as "His Excellency" like he was King George III himself on his throne, while watching the commander-in-chief being treated by all like some kind of a deity. Because of his past subservient clerking position for the wealthy Cruger family on Saint Croix, Hamilton especially detested the excessively deferential role that he had long played in Washington's shadow while serving on his staff, and only did so for so long for the overall good of America, while making Washington a much better and more insightful general in the end.

Therefore, Hamilton gradually grew to resent Washington, especially during some of the most stressful periods of the war when the patriots were losing. This was especially the case in the South after the British, under Sir Henry Clinton, captured Charles Town (later Charleston), South Carolina, in May 1780. This port city on the Atlantic was the largest and most strategic of the South, and its surrender was the largest patriot disaster of the war.

Especially vexing to the young man, Lieutenant Colonel Hamilton had failed to gain eagerly sought after positions of importance, including the adjutant-general position under the highly-capable General Nathanael Greene, who was Washington's top lieutenant and as a prestigious special minster to France by appointment of the Continental Congress. Because of his fluency in French, his keen intelligence, and his well-honed diplomatic qualities, Hamilton would have been an ideal choice for the crucial effort to gain additional French assistance for the sagging war effort. However, Hamilton was an unknown to the politicians of the Continental Congress, and he failed to gain the coveted diplomatic position, to his great disappointment and unfortunately for the overall war effort.

And Washington gained all the fame and glory for being America's savior and republican idol, while Hamilton had long continued to work hard behind the scenes and make important contributions without recognition for nearly four years.

Hamilton could never forget how, as commander of a New York artillery unit prior to becoming Washington's chief of staff, his trained gunners from New York had protected Washington's retreat south near New Brunswick in central New Jersey, to keep the pursuing redcoats and Hessians at a distance, while the reeling Continental Army moved steadily south toward Trenton, New Jersey. The long and miserable retreat south to safe Pennsylvania set the stage for Washington's surprise attack on the Hessian brigade of three regiments at Trenton on the snowy morning of December 26, 1776.

At this time, Washington's Army was extremely vulnerable because of a series of recent losses and humiliating defeats around New York City, including the city's loss, which had eroded morale and caused widespread desertions in the ever-dwindling ranks of the reeling patriot army. Hamilton's distinguished role on west side of the Raritan River, the largest river located entirely in New Jersey, in protecting the army's withdrawal toward Trenton first brought him to Washington's attention. Most important, he helped to ensure that Washington's Army would survive to fight another day by keeping Cornwallis at arm's length: ironically, the same commander who Hamilton was destined to face at Yorktown.

Captain Hamilton's vital last stand at the Raritan River was additional evidence that this talented young officer was actually more of a battlefield commander than just another desk officer in the traditional sense, not only because of his aggressive nature but also his tactical skill and natural instincts. Worst yet in Hamilton's way of thinking, Washington had personally thwarted the young man's repeated bids to depart headquarters and take a field command to get back to doing what he loved: leading men once again into action from the front and by inspiring example, when he was more qualified for those coveted field positions now filled by other Continental officers of less ability.

Lieutenant Colonel Hamilton realized that the idea to deny promotion was shared by high-ranking officers and his friends, especially members of Washington's staff, who were in the know. Of course, there was nothing malicious about Washington's repeatedly thwarting Hamilton's ambitions. After all, Hamilton was simply too invaluable to Washington on multiple levels to be allowed to leave his headquarters to seek glory on the battlefield, when so much work remained to be completed and a war had to be won.

No Continental officer had accomplished more significant milestones in dual roles both on and off the battlefield in the desperate bid to win a new nation's independence since 1775 than Hamilton. This was a striking paradox, because he seemed to have been the most unlikely of American heroes because of his lowly social standing, illegitimate birth, impoverished beginnings, and miserable boyhood in the West Indies. All in all, the haunting memories of this dark legacy from the West Indies propelled him to over-achieve in seemingly every single endeavor that he enthusiastically embarked upon in America, especially in the military realm but also in the field of economics. Despite his youth, Hamilton was an economic genius. He quickly understood the complex and intricate dynamics of the new republic's economics. He was correctly convinced that a much stronger national government and economic foundation than provided by the Articles of Confederation were badly needed not only to win the war but also for the nation's development and growth in the future.

It was only a matter of time before an eruption of some sort created a permanent rift between the commander-in-chief and his top staff officer. This clash—incredibly short and over only a trivial matter of no importance whatsoever—finally happened on dreary, cold February 16, 1781, at Washington's busy headquarters in the John and Catherine Ellison House in New Windsor, New York, on the Hudson River. Here, Hamilton's pent-up dissatisfaction with this subservient role finally rose to the fore, when Washington's temper got the best of him. Worn down by a mountain of pressures, recent mutinies of New Jersey and Pennsylvania Continentals, the British invasion of southeast

Virginia, and a high level of stress and overwork that had seen the two men laboring together late into the previous night and into the early morning hours, Washington exploded at Hamilton over an extremely minor issue of little significance. After having been refused twice for field commands, Hamilton was not in the most charitable mood by this time. This relatively minor incident began when Hamilton took about two minutes to return to Washington's side to resume work at headquarters, which the commander thought was too long. Before he could return upstairs to resume work with Washington, Hamilton had unexpectedly encountered his good friend the Marquis de Lafayette, the young aristocrat who had been one of the first Frenchmen to volunteer to serve in America and was basically Washington's surrogate son. This naturally resulted in an exchange of pleasantries, including words in French that were expected and customary.

General Washington believed that he waited a full ten minutes at the top of the stairs for his top staff officer's return, but the truth lies closer to Hamilton's estimation of only two minutes. Hamilton, at age twenty-six and with a healthy ego like Washington, took offense when the austere Virginian sharply accused him of having lingered much too long with Lafayette and displaying open disrespect toward him! Likewise losing his temper, Hamilton then departed the scene in outrage, after a sharp exchange of only a few words between the two men in an unfortunate incident that should have never happened. Hamilton, who was under comparable pressures like Washington and who had recently married a young woman whom he sorely missed, had not unleashed an angry outburst comparable to that of Washington.[1] As Washington's longtime eloquent "written voice" and principal sage advisor on his staff at the army's nerve center for years, Lieutenant Colonel Hamilton had finally stood up to the most revered man in American and in protest to his "snappish and overbearing" ways for which he was well known.[2]

As mentioned, only a relatively few words at a highly stressful time in the hectic headquarters environment caused the rift when an angry Washington had raised his voice and yelled in indignation:

"Colonel Hamilton, you have kept me waiting at the head of the stairs these ten minutes. I must tell you, sir, you treat me with disrespect." A stunned Hamilton replied with his own temper rising, "I am not conscious of it, Sir, but since you have thought it necessary to tell me, so we must part."[3]

No one had ever spoken to "His Excellency" so boldly since he had gained worldwide fame as the leader of America's war effort, which naturally shocked Washington to the core. Such directness was overdue, as Washington needed to hear straight talk more than the endless fawning that was not healthy for either Washington or his staff officers in the long run. If anything, this brief explosion of tempers at his New Windsor headquarters was a stunning wake-up call for Washington, highlighting his shabby treatment of his chief-of-staff-Washington's almost total lack of awareness in this situation had finally driven Hamilton to the point of exasperation. To his credit, General Washington learned a lesson from the unfortunate experience.[4]

On February 18, 1781, wrote of the incident to his father-in-law, General Philip Schuyler, who had accepted the native West Indian like a son:

> For three years past, I have felt no friendship for him and have professed none. The truth is our own dispositions are the opposites of each other [and] when advances of this kind [were] made to me on his part, they were rec[eived in a way] that showed at last I had no inclination [to embrace them because] I wished to stand rather upon a footing of m[ilitary protocol rather than of] personal attachment.[5]

Hamilton was even more confidential to James McHenry, another staff member of Scotch-Irish descent now serving under the Marquis de Lafayette, writing with biting sarcasm, "The Great Man and I have come to an open rupture" and denouncing Washington's well-known "ill-humor."[6] At long last, Lieutenant Colonel Hamilton had become his own man, having suddenly emerged from Washington's giant shadow by exerting his own sense of independence. To Washington's credit, he attempted to soothe over the spat within an hour by dispatching Tench Tilghman of his staff with an apology that revealed the depth of the commander-in-chief's feelings for the young man and showed he needed him to continue working at the head of his personal staff. However, Hamilton remained aloof and steadfast in his position of indignation, despite the urgings of the Marquis de Lafayette and General Schuyler. And to Hamilton's credit that revealed his maturity, he readily agreed to dutifully continue to serve on Washington's staff because there was a war to be won—faithful duty proceeded unabated by him for another ten weeks. However, as could be expected, the rift between the two men of widely divergent backgrounds ensured a chilly atmosphere at headquarters throughout the early months of 1781. But both men took the high road, doing what was best for the country and what was necessary under the circumstances.

Finally, it all came to an end, after Hamilton's last mission with Washington as interpreter with General Jean-Baptiste Donatien de Vimeur, Comte de Rochambeau, France's commander of its expeditionary force in North America, to confer on strategy in Newport, Rhode Island, in March 1781. After the mission's completion during the second crucial meeting between the two commanders, Washington returned to his New Windsor headquarters, while Hamilton rode more than one hundred miles north to the Schuyler mansion in Albany, New York, and to the arms of his new wife, Elizabeth, or Betsey, Schuyler. Without fanfare, this point was literally the symbolical fork in the road for Hamilton and Washington, because "one of the most brilliant productive partnerships" of the entire American Revolution on either side had come to a sudden and inglorious end, because of the egos and pride of two strong-willed men of ability.[7]

Hamilton continued to faithfully serve his country despite the break with Washington, because he could never for a moment, as he penned, "think of quitting the army during the war."[8] Hamilton had continued for two additional months after their feud to help "Washington prepare for the Virginia campaign, which ended in the surrender of Cornwallis."[9]

When only fourteen years old and consumed with the burning ambition to escape the confines of a dead-end job, Hamilton had confessed in a letter a distinct hatred for the daily "groveling and [lowly] condition of a clerk" like a lowly servant—a situation not unlike the one in which Hamilton had found himself at the low point of his distinguished service at Washington's headquarters.[10]

As Hamilton had written to friend Ned Stevens from Saint Croix, revealing the core of his complex personality that partly explained his February 16, 1781, rift with Washington, "to confess my weakness, Ned, my Ambition is prevalent [so] that I contemn the grov'ling . . . condition of a Clerk or the like, to which my [ill] Fortune" had early condemned him.[11]

Like other astute patriots, Hamilton correctly realized that the only chance for winning decisive success, given Washington's quite extensive limitations as a general compared to his professional and highly educated opponents, especially in overall tactical terms, lay in "succour [sic] from the French."[12] As early as late March 1777 and not long after Hamilton had joined Washington's staff, Tench Tilghman, Washington's personal secretary and Hamilton's good friend, penned to his father, a Maryland Loyalist, with confidence: "A War with France, which you may depend upon is inevitable, must unhorse the present Ministry [of King George III] and all their Connections. France had been wisely weighing the [sizeable] Value of that [American] Commence with Eng., has madly lost."[13]

Like the views of the sage Tilghman, Hamilton's insightful words about the crucial importance of French assistance were no exaggeration in the least, because America's fortunes had sunk to new lows and prospects for success never appeared bleaker by the summer of 1780 and early 1781, especially after the loss of Savannah and Georgia and then Charleston and most of South Carolina to the British war machine.[14] And now after six years of war, the Declaration of Independence that had been issued from Philadelphia in the summer of 1776 with such high hopes was nothing more than a meaningless proclamation, as the British came surprisingly close to winning the war.[15]

The Heaven-Sent French

Official French intervention and the recognition of the infant United States of America had only resulted because of General Horatio Gates's sparking victory that forced the surrender of "Gentleman Johnny" Burgoyne's entire British, Hessian, and Loyalist Army in the wilderness of Upper New York at Saratoga in October 1777. In fact before the decisive success at Saratoga, the increasingly common view and popular consensus across America that only massive French intervention could now ensure an infant nation's survival was no exaggeration. French intervention was very nearly a miraculous development based on happenstance. The first unofficial French agent had come to America, Chevalier Julien Alexandre Achard de Bonvouloir et Loyauté, who initiated the all-important connection between France and America in late 1775, wrote how he had learned from the Americans, without a navy, "that they won't be able to hold [the thirteen colonies against the might of England and her allies] without a nation that protects them by sea."[16] Insightful and intelligent, Tench Tilghman had written prophetically in 1778 of his belief that France would enter the war to rescue America in the end: "The uncommon preparations by France in the West Indies cannot be for nothing. She has at least 8,000 men in her islands" of the Caribbean.[17]

Young King Louis XVI, who was eager to regain all that had been lost by France, including Canada—then known as New France—and valuable sugar islands in the Caribbean, during the Seven Years' War (French and Indian War) and to destroy the robust British economy based on international trade, realized as much about the strategic situation and America's almost endless weaknesses. He was also partly inspired by young Marquis de Lafayette's early volunteer service under Washington and his republican zeal that had inspired the people of the French nation to support the Americans. The king summoned Comte de Rochambeau, who was France's best general and had won distinction during the Seven Years' War, to report immediately to his lavish palace at Versailles early in 1780. During the journey of around a dozen miles, Rochambeau knew that the urgency of the king's summons meant that an important mission lay in store for him, perhaps even the long-anticipated invasion of arch-enemy England.

At his luxurious palace, Louis XVI informed Rochambeau that he would be in charge of a secret mission of leading an expeditionary force to America. But Rochambeau was surprised to learn that he was ordered to place himself under the command of a foreigner and former Virginia militia officer, George Washington, who lacked both tactical ability and experience, although he had been learning on the job to become a better general and matured considerably since the early days of the war. The decision stunned the kings of Europe, especially King George III.

To his great credit and despite being an aristocrat from a wealthy, well-connected family who had been raised at the family's lavish chateau in the picturesque valley of the Loir River located southwest of Paris, Rochambeau was ideally suited to serve as Washington's top lieutenant—an intellectual and experienced general who was even-tempered and hard-working. Even more, he was tactically brilliant, blessed with a strong moral character, a self-effacing personality, and the wisdom of Solomon. The immensely talented Rochambeau traced his ancestry to courageous French knights who had served in the Crusades to the Middle East and aristocratic nobles who had fought with distinction under previous French kings, including as secretary. He was destined to bestow many of the key qualities that Washington lacked during the Yorktown Campaign, making the Virginian a better general when everything was at stake.

After preparing to enter the priesthood, he gained an education at France's finest military academy. While fighting the king's enemies in Europe for decades, he had learned the fatal consequences of bickering among military leaders and allies. During the most decisive campaign of the war, the two men from opposite sides of the Atlantic brought out the very best in each other.

King Louis XVI's secret expedition to America was destined to catch the British by surprise, especially the Royal Navy. Therefore, nothing would oppose the Atlantic crossing of the French expedition. Rochambeau's tireless reorganization efforts before the war resulted in greatly enhanced military capabilities of the French army and especially its now formidable navy that had recovered from its sharp setbacks during the Seven Years' War—which also caught the enemy by surprise. Even more than Washington, Rochambeau was the true architect of the victory at Yorktown because of what he accomplished both before and during the war.

Despite the threat of a British invasion of France and to his credit, King Louis XVI remained firmly committed to sending Rochambeau forth with a mighty expeditionary force and artillery to outmatch what the British possessed in the South, while promising to send a second division to reinforce Rochambeau after he arrived in America, which had been ravaged by half a dozen years of war and with the badly depleted American Army on its last legs. With a favorable tide and wind when there was no British fleet to stop him, Rochambeau finally set sail for America in early May 1780 with more than five thousand troops, including respected army chaplains of the Catholic faith. After the lengthy journey of more than two months across the rough waters of the Atlantic in an armada of more than forty vessels, including warships appropriately named *Neptune, Provence,* and *Amazone* and more than thirty troop transports—although with no clear disembarkation point in America having been established at the safest harbor—the French expeditionary force finally settled into position at Newport, Rhode Island. Here, Rochambeau was destined to stay for an extended period of nine months, including throughout the winter of 1780–81, without having delivered a decisive stroke and without a definite offensive plan. The cautious and careful Rochambeau had decided to wait for the promised second division to be sent to him from France before attempting to strike a decisive blow as desired by King Louis XVI.[18]

Quite simply, the king and his ministers envisioned a hard-hitting economic war against the vast British Empire that had been founded on a thriving global trade, crass exploitation of colonial resources, and the world's most powerful navy that ruled the seas as France had learned during the Seven Years' War. The French lusted for the opportunity to knock out its main economic rival, gain a new lucrative trading partner in America, and recapture some of the rich French sugar islands in the Caribbean.[19]

But French pride was also a key determinant of this timely intervention because of everything that France had lost in the Seven Years' War. Therefore, in the words of one of Rochambeau's nephews, a high-ranking officer, "France was looking to take revenge for the Peace of 1763."[20] Perhaps Lord Lyttleton said it best, emphasizing how America had now become "the dagger of France" and the sharp "instrument of the assassination of her parent!"[21]

Indeed, the French-American Alliance had been forged with high hopes and eternal optimism in 1778 in no small part from the intense French hatred—the old Catholic versus Protestant antagonism that had fueled European warfare for centuries—of England, coupled with the decisive defeat of General John Burgoyne by Major General Horatio Gates, in Saratoga, New York, in October 1777. However, with expectations sky-high, this alliance had failed to reap decisive results. General Philip Schuyler, Hamilton's father-in-law, had played roles that helped to secure the much-needed victory at Saratoga, which had caused King Louis XVI and the French to sign the crucial alliance with the New World revolutionaries, but pivotal results were not forthcoming.

With no illusions remaining about this war or the Continental Army's severely limited capabilities to wage a war of attrition, Washington had admitted that he could not achieve victory in any future campaign without adequate manpower and resources. In fact, no important victory by the Americans had been won since Saratoga, with this long war having stalemated in Washington's area of operations. Any decisive success could only be achieved if the Continental Army and French army worked closely together and as one, especially if they utilized the considerable assets of the French Navy.[22]

Even Rochambeau's men at Newport had become discouraged because of the overall lack of progress and the absence of revolutionary zeal among the weary Americans. In the words of the Vicomte de Noailles, one of Rochambeau's favorites and a member of one of France's most aristocratic families among the upper class elite, "The gallant Frenchmen had come to America to deliver America entirely from the yoke of her tyrants, but all they seemed to be doing was waste time and money in Newport."[23]

Like seemingly everyone else, General Washington was equally discouraged by the lack of results and America's ever-weakening war-waging capabilities, after the so-called Gallic saviors of the New World arrived in Newport. He wrote in bitter frustration about "the totally deranged situation of our affairs" and admitted the "utter impracticability of availing ourselves of the generous aid" from the French to make any dramatic impact in a decisive way.[24] A lingering distrust, historic anti-Catholicism, and ancient anti-French stereotypes by Americans—of course, Washington and some of his top officers had fought against the French during the French and Indian War—had caused serious divisions between these allies of convenience.

Having long realized that the Continental Army's survival in a lengthy war of attrition was as important as winning victory while wisely refusing to risk decisive defeat by a superior opponent, Washington described to the Marquis de Lafayette how "the French court have often complained to me of the inactivity of the American army [and] They have often told me, 'Your friends leave us now to fight their battles, and do no more risk themselves.'"[25] This common view was expressed by the disappointed French at Newport from what they had learned in America, to their shock and consternation. One surprised French officer concluded how the war-weary inhabitants "appeared to have little of that enthusiasm one would suppose to belong to a people fighting for its liberties."[26] Most important, the entire key for any successful campaign for the allies rested primarily upon French sea power, because the powerful British Navy had long ruled the seas. As the experienced Rochambeau informed Washington in no uncertain terms, "No major enterprise could be undertaken unless there was at least temporary command of the sea."[27]

But at long last, this strategic situation of stalemate began to change in February 1781 by a series of developments with a gradual drift toward a relatively untouched theater and new arena of operations in Virginia, when Sir Henry Clinton dispatched none other than Brigadier General Benedict Arnold to the Chesapeake, America's largest estuary of about two hundred miles in length, to launch raids into the Virginia interior. This was one factor that encouraged Cornwallis to invade North Carolina in the fall of 1780, because he envisioned conquering Virginia and uniting with British troops already stationed there. Washington was beginning to realize that the war was shifting south as he dispatched Major General Nathanael Greene south in fall 1780 to replace the disgraced General Gates following the destruction of the Southern Army at Camden, South Carolina. He, therefore, had sent Baron von Steuben, a gifted drillmaster who had considerably enhanced the war waging capabilities of Washington's Army with his training and drill program, with Greene. Greene then shortly ordered von Steuben north to meet the growing threat in Virginia.

But with the increase of British activities in Virginia, the inexperienced von Steuben shortly needed help of his own. From his headquarters at New Windsor in the late winter of 1781, Washington made a key decision, giving the Marquis de Lafayette, despite his youth and inexperience, an extremely important command of more than one thousand men: "The destination of this detachment is to act against the corps of the enemy now in Virginia [and] You will take command of this detachment."[28]

Virginia was now rapidly becoming the main stage of operations in the spring of 1781 after years of a tense quiet and general inactivity. From his headquarters in New York City, General Henry Clinton, who was Lord Cornwallis's superior and overall commander of the British forces in America, had decided to make the Chesapeake region a new area of operations, desiring to establish a naval base for future conquests on the mighty estuary that paralleled the Atlantic coast. The Chesapeake, which spanned north to south, was a broad estuary that had been created by the waters of some of the South's most famous rivers, including the Potomac, Susquehanna, York, James, and the Rappahannock.

General Arnold had been also sent by Clinton to Virginia with the mission of establishing this much-needed naval base at the most favorable location on the Chesapeake. The port of Portsmouth, Virginia, south of Yorktown, seemed like the most feasible candidate. He had captured Richmond, located on the James River, in January 1781 and caused panic across Virginia, after facing little patriot opposition. That's when Washington had sent the Marquis de Lafayette to Virginia to confront America's arch villain and traitor, Benedict Arnold, who had betrayed America by compromising West Point with the intent of allowing the British to easily capture the mighty fortress on the Hudson. The Marquis de Lafayette was instructed to drive Arnold out of Portsmouth, if the British attempted to establish a naval base there, and out of Virginia. However, that ambitious objective proved impossible when Arnold was reinforced by troops under General William Phillips, who then took overall command, with Arnold recalled by Clinton.

At this time, Washington most of all desired to capture New York City, which had consumed him for years, including throughout early 1781, despite fast-paced developments in Virginia. Unlike Washington, Lord Cornwallis believed that the war could be won in Virginia, which was the largest state and inadequately protected. But General Washington's burning ambition was destined to be thwarted by fate and circumstances, especially the growing threat of the new theater of operations in Virginia. Additionally, in a happenstance of history, the eventual uniting of Rochambeau's and Washington's forces for a push south to the Virginia Peninsula to exploit the sudden availability of the French fleet from the West Indies that would develop in the near future, after the failure of the British Navy to intercede, gained traction. This was the decisive development that would eventually result in Cornwallis's surrender at Yorktown.[29]

England's Best Fighting General, Lord Charles Cornwallis

What was the hard-hitting British commander, age forty-two, really like as a man and leader, beyond the popular stereotypes of the fumbling British aristocrat that have been long perpetuated by so many American nationalist historians? Oddly, in 1781 much of Hamilton's career and destiny had been long tied to the top British battlefield commander in America, whom he had thwarted with the accurate fire of the young man's New York cannon on the Raritan River near New Brunswick, New Jersey, in late 1776 during Washington's long retreat all the way from New York to eastern Pennsylvania.

Lord Charles Cornwallis, who hailed from England's upper-crust elite, was the antithesis to Hamilton, the illegitimate son of the Caribbean, in almost every way in regard to social status and privileged background. A distinguished major general and the best fighting British commander in America, Cornwallis had been born to British royalty, the first son of the first Earl Cornwallis. When his father died in 1762, he had inherited his father's title as a member of England's ruling elite. Fate had destined that they repeatedly squared off against each other during the course of the American Revolution, as if a personal grudge between the two men had developed, including when Hamilton's roaring cannon had stopped his lordship at the Raritan to earn him distinction as Washington's "Little Lion."

However, despite all of the considerable skills and abilities as a tactically astute commander, Lord Cornwallis was cursed with fatal flaws and possessed an Achilles' Heel: a penchant for gambling that led to recklessness, an over aggressiveness that was dangerous to both himself and his command, and an immense pride founded on sparkling tactical achievements on battlefields in both Europe and America. Unfortunately for England, these personal qualities, along with his equally egotistical superior, Sir Henry Clinton, led to an arrogant overconfidence that he and his troops could accomplish anything against the detested rebels, which bordered on fantasy. Such personal weaknesses of his lordship played a large role in sending Cornwallis and his army to their decisive defeat at Yorktown in October 1781.[30]

Before the climactic showdown at Yorktown in the fall of 1781, Cornwallis had become England's winningest general in multiple theaters of war both before and after his wife's tragic death. Tench Tilghman, a faithful member of Washington's staff on which he served as secretary despite the fact that he hailed from a Loyalist Maryland family, including his father while his brother served in the British Navy, described in a letter how Cornwallis was responsible for turning the tide of battle to thwart Washington's attack at Germantown, Pennsylvania, on October 4, 1777. He said the British "attribute their salvation to the Bravery of Lord Cornwallis, who rallied their Men and brought a Reinforcement" in the nick of time.[31]

By the time of the Yorktown Campaign, Cornwallis was a bitter man not only because of sagging British fortunes in America but also because he had recently lost the love of his life, Jemima Tullikens, age thirty-two. She was his beautiful, loving wife who succumbed to disease and a broken heart in the fall of 1778 because of her husband's longtime absence. Cornwallis never recovered from Jemima's tragic loss, writing to his brother how her death "effectively destroyed all my hopes of happiness in this world."[32]

Now Cornwallis was engaged in a brutal conflict that he was unable to win. The struggle for the heart and soul of America had become brutal by 1780, especially in the Southern theater. This increasingly vicious war had produced a good many hard men on both sides, and Lord Cornwallis was one. Less than three months before his defeat at Yorktown, the *New Jersey-Gazette*, Burlington, New Jersey, condemned the harsh actions of Cornwallis and his men by emphasizing how "most disgracefully has he [Cornwallis] finished a plundering excursion into the heart of Virginia."[33]

Unlike young Hamilton who remained idealistic and unjaded by the war's brutalities, the jaded Cornwallis had been corrupted by this war, sacrificing the moral high ground to his pursuit of glory and decisive victory at any cost. During the withdrawal across Virginia to the deathtrap on the York River at Yorktown, he would even stoop so low as to have "ordered his men to poison the inhabitants' wells with the corpses of the many escaped slaves who had died of smallpox."[34]

Quite simply, this savage war of attrition in the South had brought out the worst in Lord Cornwallis, especially after Jemima's death, for which he rightly felt considerable guilt. He had voluntarily decided to return to America to once again engage in the futile bid to win the war in an attempt to forget all about the sad passing of his beloved Jemima, but he could never forget the love of his life no matter how hard he tried. As fate would have it, there very likely would have been no Cornwallis at Yorktown to be trapped and forced to surrender his entire army to change the course of American and world history without his wife's death.

Eager for action, the duty-minded Cornwallis had returned to America to take command in the South with his usual devotion to duty and his desire to conquer. In his lordship's own words about the decision that sealed the fate of not only the most distinguished career of any British officer in America but also Great Britain's determined bid to return the thirteen colonies back into the fold by conquering the South, "I am now returning to America [because] I find this country [England] unsupportable to me. I must shift the scene; I have many friends in the [British] army [and] I love that army."[35]

The love of an army and a love lost—his beautiful, devoted wife—ultimately played a key role in the final downfall of the British "Hannibal" at Yorktown and the winning of American independence.[36]

Chapter II

The Long, Twisting Road and Strategic Situation that Led to Yorktown

Success in life, like in military campaigns, has often been first spawned from a series of setbacks and reversals until it appears that no hope for success possibly remains. The Yorktown Campaign is a classic example of this military truism, because a series of unprecedented American disasters across the South had the British extremely confident and complacent, when finally on the verge of winning the war by early 1781, or so it seemed. Consequently, what ultimately happened at Yorktown cannot be fully understood without examining the war in the South and the many humiliating fiascos and disastrous setbacks suffered by American forces. And the real story behind the Yorktown Campaign and the looming decisive victory for the allies was mostly about the power of the revitalized French Navy and its availability to serve in American waters.

Fate and the accidents of history eventually united in unpredictable and accidental fashion to transfer the sleepy port in Virginia, once the state's leading port on the Chesapeake before it lost its lofty status to other eastern towns with better harbors, into the most strategic and important point in America by the late summer of 1781. Only a few reminders of Yorktown's former prosperity from the once-booming tobacco trade remained at the little port on the York River, including fine brick buildings and a nice harbor and wharf for deep-water vessels. As fate would have it, American independence was about to be ensured for all time by what was destined to happen at this obscure port along the south bank of the York River, where Washington and Rochambeau delivered their masterstroke.

How could this decisive strategic development, unimaginable only a short time before, have possibly occurred? How had the obscure tobacco port of Yorktown become the most important place in America by the early fall of 1781, when everything was at stake? How and why had destiny so suddenly taken a strange and unpredictable course that ensured that two old foes, Washington and Cornwallis, met once again at Yorktown in the final climactic clash?

The long, twisting road to Yorktown was cluttered with sudden changes of priorities and a series of blunders, especially those of the British, in 1781. Yorktown's significance caught the British by surprise, especially Lord Cornwallis and the blundering Royal Navy.

The Revolution began in eastern Massachusetts in April 1775; British strategists initially believed the revolt was local, but it gradually moved further south. Because of vast global commitments in the worldwide struggle for dominance, between rival European empires and monarchies, British efforts to subjugate America had lacked the necessary manpower and vigor to deliver a decisive blow in both New England and in the middle states year after year.

With England bogged down in a stalemated war largely because Washington had wisely refused to risk decisive defeat by engaging in a major battle, the French took full advantage to strike at vulnerable British commitments in the Caribbean, India, and Africa after the signing of the French Alliance in 1778. To his credit, Washington eventually admitted the severe limitations of his own abilities, especially as a tactician, and remained smartly focused on ensuring that the Continental Army always survived to fight another day during what had become a lengthy war of attrition.

As they had learned the hard way, English forces in America remained too small for the impossible task of conquering an expansive continent that seemed to have no end and a new people inspired by a nascent sense of nationalism, republican spirit, and Age of Enlightenment ideology. Therefore, by early 1781, the British had been largely reduced to occupying the major seaports along the East Coast, including New York City; Charles Town (Charleston), South Carolina; and Savannah, Georgia.[1] However, a bullheaded King George III, whose arrogance and pride knew no limit when it came to the thirteen colonies, was determined to fight to the bitter end, because he was under the delusion that America would be just the first domino of the vast colonial empire to fall. It was widely believed, in the words of Prime Minister Frederick North (a.k.a. Lord North), that "should America succeed [the] the West Indies must follow them [and then] Ireland would soon follow."[2]

To break the frustrating stalemate in the northern and middle states, the British embarked upon a new strategy in 1780 to conquer the South. Based upon the long-existing hope in a massive uprising of Loyalists, many more of whom existed in the South than in Puritan-based New England, this new British strategy was overly ambitious because it rested on this shakiest of foundations. The long road that led to Yorktown began with the British capture of Savannah, Georgia, in late December 1778. Then, Sir Henry Clinton, commander of British forces in North America, targeted the strategic port of Charleston, South Carolina, thanks to the initiative and strategic benefits gained with Savannah's capture, because the port served as the strategic springboard for invading farther north and all the way to Virginia.

Ascertaining fresh opportunities in the South, Clinton understood the supreme importance on taking the key port that rivaled New York City, the Queen City of the southern colonies and America's fourth largest city. Clinton had failed to capture Charleston in 1776, but with the change in strategy he attempted to once again. A mighty fleet and nearly nine thousand British, Loyalist, and Hessian troops sailed south toward the South's largest port on the Atlantic. With Lord Charles Cornwallis by his side, Clinton based his new southern strategy on capturing the strategic port city before the arrival of the hottest of the Deep South summer when the usual ravages of disease decimated invading European troops.[3]

The so-called southern strategy promised a great deal because the lightly populated South looked ideal for "a thrust at a more exposed and vulnerable point [and British leaders] proceeded on the assumption that, if the Southern provinces should first be subdued and recovered in fact, the Northern [states] could thereafter be reduced by isolation and exhaustion"—the ambitious British plan to "cut the rebellious Union in two."[4]

Located on a narrow, sandy peninsula situated between the Cooper and Ashley Rivers, Charleston, like New York City, was virtually indefensible because of the surrounding deep waterways by which British warships and transports maneuvered with impunity. Nevertheless, Major General Benjamin Lincoln, an old French and Indian War veteran and country farmer from Massachusetts not well versed in the axioms of conventional warfare (especially naval), not only attempted to defend Charleston with unreliable southern militia but also drew all available Continental troops into the Charleston trap—a fatal miscalculation of the first order.

Clinton wisely decided not to unleash costly frontal assaults against the defenses of Charleston in what would have been a bloodbath. Instead, he wisely settled down to methodically reduce the city by siege, as if systematically reducing an old stone French fortress in Europe during the Hundred Years' War. On the sandy neck of the Charleston Peninsula north of the city, British siege operations pushed forward parallels ever closer to the American defenses from where they could be pounded with artillery manned by skilled gunners. Finally, the city was surrounded after the British belatedly gained complete control of the Cooper River and won a key victory just to the northwest at Monck's Corner, South Carolina, to cut off the thin flow of supplies and reinforcements to the besieged defenders.

More than five thousand Americans, including nearly thirty-five hundred Virginia and North and South Carolina Continentals, attempted in vain to hold Charleston's hastily strengthened defenses, thanks to the labor of large numbers of impressed slaves, as long as possible. Just before mid-May 1780, however, Major General Lincoln was forced to surrender the strategic city and an entire American Army—America's largest disaster of the war that opened the door for the subjugation of not only South Carolina but also perhaps North Carolina and beyond, especially strategic Virginia. With the primary American Army in the South eliminated when Charleston fell, the way was now open for Cornwallis to reap greater gains in the South as originally envisioned by optimistic London strategists. With Clinton planning to return to New York City, he now wanted to lead his forces into South Carolina's interior to subjugate the relatively few pockets of resistance and gain control of the rural countryside, after the Charleston fiasco shattered patriot morale and prospects for winning this war.[5]

Instead of growing disheartened, Lieutenant Colonel Hamilton was not discouraged. He hoped that Charleston's loss and the new British focus on subjugating the South would open up fresh opportunities for American arms in the middle states and elsewhere to strike a blow, including in faraway Virginia that shortly developed into a new theater of war of extreme strategic importance.

In this undying faith in America and its republicanism, Hamilton possessed the optimistic view of the necessity of persevering and fighting to the bitter end. As the ever-optimistic Hamilton wrote to the Marquis de Barbe-Marbois, the secretary to the French legation to the United States, "If it is a blessing, 'tis a blessing in a very strange disguise."[6] Indeed, in the end, Hamilton was proven entirely correct because Cornwallis's southern campaign proved to be a desperate and risky gamble, since it was much too ambitious in light of limited British resources.[7]

Meanwhile, the French Army and fleet of more than forty ships under Rochambeau had learned about the disaster at Charleston en route to America, thanks to the capture of a British cutter. General Lincoln's surrender of the South's most important city had eliminated the strategic port as a place of entry for the weary French expeditionary force that was in bad shape after the lengthy Atlantic crossing. Therefore, the French fleet had then headed north for Newport, Rhode Island, instead, arriving on July 11, 1780, and remaining there throughout the winter of 1780–81. Perhaps it was just as well that the Comte de Rochambeau had remained inactive while awaiting the king's promise to send a second division of troops because 1780 was perhaps the most disastrous year for American fortunes during the war.[8]

The British Army, with the talented Cornwallis at its head, embarked upon the conquest of the South with renewed vigor to win it all, after having been encouraged by the fall of Georgia, especially the easy capture of the strategic port of Savannah, in late 1778 and Charleston's capture in May 1780. The final blow to sagging American fortunes in South Carolina came on August 16, 1780, in the dreary pine forests located just north of Camden, South Carolina. Major General Horatio Gates, Hamilton's old enemy who had wanted to replace Washington as commander-in-chief of the Continental Army, had been easily vanquished by the far more capable Cornwallis, after the overconfident general had advanced on the key outpost of Camden without any knowledge that Cornwallis and his entire army had pushed north from Charleston. The fumbling Gates had fully expected his lordship to retreat into Charleston's fortifications upon his approach instead of boldly advancing to meet the threat.

This unprecedented fiasco at Camden confirmed Hamilton's and Washington's low estimation of Gates's generalship that had been so overblown by Congress and his political and army cronies since his victory in faraway New York at Saratoga. Because of Gates's tactical blundering in South Carolina when he no longer had the capable Benedict Arnold—who led the tactical offensive at Saratoga without orders from Gates—to play a leading role in winning the day, or the Virginia frontiersmen Daniel Morgan to do the hard fighting and tactical maneuvering, the last remaining American Army in the Carolinas was destroyed in short order. To Hamilton's vindication, America's much-celebrated hero of Saratoga was thoroughly disgraced, especially after abandoning his army to its dismal fate during the panic. Here, on a hot August morning at Camden, Lord Cornwallis had inflicted what seemed like "a possible death knell of the revolution."[9]

The Camden defeat had been thoroughly caused by Gates. With his own staff making no objections because he had just taken command of the Southern Army, Gates had committed a series of fatal strategic and tactical blunders, in part because he lacked a highly capable chief-of-staff like Hamilton, who had long made Washington a better general.[10] A supremely confident Sir Henry Clinton, who was already prematurely celebrating what he believed was the war's end, boasted that "the spirit of rebellion [was now seeing its] almost dying embers," after so many British victories in the South, especially at Camden.[11]

Washington's most able top lieutenant, Major General Nathanael Greene, had been then sent south by the Virginian to rescue the southern theater, where the resistance effort had completely collapsed, after the Continental Congress belatedly accepted Washington's initial advice. General Greene, a gifted strategist, then deliberately embarked on an unorthodox policy of a wide distribution of forces, which caused Cornwallis to adhere to an unwise lack of concentration of forces, making him more vulnerable to the fast-moving bands of partisans when deep in hostile territory. For ample good reason, the prudent General Greene respected Cornwallis's abilities and acted accordingly. For instance, he was not guilty of exaggeration when he wisely cautioned the Marquis de Lafayette, when he led an independent command after Washington's orders assigned him to the Virginia Tidewater, to demonstrate great care in confronting Cornwallis when he eventually advanced north from South Carolina and then from North Carolina, because "you have a modern Hannibal to deal with in the person of Lord Cornwallis."[12]

By any measure, Lord Cornwallis was a brilliant tactician and an aggressive commander who inspired his disciplined and well-trained men to do the impossible, but his superior tactical skills were not matched by his narrow strategic insights. Impatient to win the decisive victories in the South that would win the war, Cornwallis lacked proper prudence and caution when operating with an independent command because of his unbridled aggressiveness and soaring ambitions when no superior was nearby to rein him in.

And after having been given full responsibility for winning the war in the South, beginning in South Carolina after Sir Henry Clinton's return to New York City on June 6, 1780, that marked the apogee of British fortunes in the Southern Theater of operations, Cornwallis was ordered by Clinton to consolidate control of South Carolina before moving north to embark on his much-anticipated future conquests in North Carolina and then beyond. But in communicating directly to high-ranking officials in London instead of Clinton in New York City, which revealed the strength of his excellent political connections, Cornwallis reasoned quite differently from his more cautious superior.

By this time, his lordship had been stricken with a case of what he called Virginia fever. Although lacking sufficient manpower, Cornwallis emphasized the urgent necessity of waging a much wider war to achieve decisive results by eventually marching from South Carolina and into North Carolina and then all the way to Virginia in pursuit of remaining American forces and in the hope of rallying Loyalists to the Crown. His fatal ambition resulted in a long list of mistakes that eventually set the stage for the final showdown at Yorktown. He was convinced that the war in the South could be won in Virginia or even farther north, especially if Clinton advanced south from New York City and he pushed north to catch Washington and his Continental Army in between the two pincers.

Subjugating the South's extensive territory—many times the size of England—required an unprecedented degree of patience, care, and prudence that his aristocratic lordship lacked in his haste to win decisive victories and glory. Nevertheless, King George III and his ministers had long faithfully backed this proven winner (no British general had been more successful in North America than Cornwallis had been since nearly the war's beginning) without appreciating the wide discrepancy between Cornwallis's sound tactical skills and much less sound broad strategic vision that left him a victim to his ambitions in the end.[13]

Worst of all, London strategists and miliary thinkers, including King George III himself, had placed their faith in the fatally flawed strategy that offered the overly optimistic promise of victory in a stalemated war: that the South could be easily conquered by a mighty Loyalist counterrevolution based upon the mistaken assumption that most Americans in the South were still loyal to King George III.[14]

Cornwallis operated independently of Sir Henry Clinton, which ensured that they too often worked at cross purposes, especially when communications between the two were slow or nonexistent. He made his own decisions instead of his superior in far-away New York City, conducting an aggressive campaign that took him into North Carolina and then eventually into Virginia. But the earl's premature bold move north left South Carolina vulnerable, as Clinton realized, because it was not yet pacified as he had hoped and emphasized to his lordship in the past.

Setting the stage for decisive defeat in the days ahead, neither the British generals in America, from Cornwallis to Clinton, nor civilian leadership, nor the king in Windsor Castle possessed the required experience levels and keen insights necessary to prevail in a guerrilla war in faraway America, as opposed to the old conventional warfighting in Europe. While Cornwallis proved that he was a master of winning on the battlefield with superior tactics, this reality meant relatively little for what was actually needed to reap decisive victory in this lengthy war of attrition: a successful pacification effort that called for winning hearts and minds of the people, especially when guerrilla warfare was on the rise.

Lord Cornwallis, consequently, refused to relinquish the initiative and return to the safety of Charleston where he could have solved his supply and logistical problems or advance north up the coast instead of inland as he did. After Charleston's fall, meanwhile, South Carolina partisans, like Thomas Sumter, Andrew Pickens, and Francis Marion (the legendary "Swamp Fox"), and other small patriot bands rose up against the interlopers. In the South Carolina backcountry, Sumter and Pickens lashed out at the invaders, while Marion struck targets in the eastern lowlands. Emerging like ghosts from the dark cypress swamps and pine forests when least expected by the British, the partisans waged a highly effective brand of guerrilla warfare. The patriots, under daring commanders like Isaac Shelby, won victories at such obscure places like Musgrove's Mill, Blue Savannah, and other sharp 1780 clashes across South Carolina, where the overly ambitious British pacification effort had been prematurely thought to have already succeeded.

Violating key principles of concentration in force when deep in enemy country, Cornwallis's advance north in the early fall of 1780—to benefit from the recent harvest and the diminishing of the summer's intense heat—over a wide area and into piney lands of North Carolina left him extremely vulnerable to the roving bands of partisans, especially because he had pushed north through the piedmont and not to the east along the coast. For logistical reasons, a move up the East Coast would have been more prudent and smarter because of the availability of the British Navy for resupply and safety, but Cornwallis wanted to avoid the spread of coastal diseases among his relatively small force.

To protect his vulnerable left, or western flank, while he secured Charlotte, in south central North Carolina, he ordered Scotland-born Major Patrick Ferguson and his Loyalist command to advance too far west and away from the main army at Charlotte, North Carolina, and all the way to the foothills of the Blue Ridge Mountains at Gilbert Town, North Carolina. Then, like a phoenix rising, the backcountry men and the citizen-soldiers, who were mostly Scotch-Irish, of the Overmountain region west of the Blue Ridge in today's east Tennessee and the backcountry east of the mountains, rose up as one and launched an aggressive pursuit of Cornwallis's Loyalist task force, which consisted of his left flank guardians and promoters of the Loyalist counterrevolution in the West.

The resurgent patriots, unofficially led by Colonel Isaac Shelby, who commanded the Sullivan County militia of today's east Tennessee (then it was North Carolina), caught up with Major Ferguson, who commanded nearly one thousand men, at Kings Mountain in northwestern South Carolina, situated just south of the North Carolina border, on October 7, 1780. In barely an hour's time, this ad hoc force of hardy North Carolina, Tennessee, Virginia, and Georgia frontiers-men, including large numbers armed with deadly long rifles, from both sides of the mountains won the most surprising and unexpected victory of the war. This key victory reaped in early fall was won by volunteer citizen-soldiers of the local western militias led by experienced fighting men, like Shelby who was of Welsh heritage. In record time to meet the threat posed by Ferguson who had made the mistake of sending a direct threat to raze the lands and homes west of the Blue Ridge, they had formed a ghost army from remote frontier regions, especially the Overmountain area west of the mountains that the British knew little about, including even the names of settlements.

Then, another surprise patriot victory deep in the South Carolina backcountry was reaped over the famed light command (the British Legion of Loyalists) under Lieutenant Colonel Banastre Tarleton on January 17, 1781, at the Battle of Cowpens, South Carolina, west of Kings Mountain on Cornwallis's west flank. Tarleton's isolated detachment of light troops was vulnerable, like Ferguson's ill-fated command at Kings Mountain. Cornwallis's two forces of light troops, under Ferguson and Tarleton, were destroyed in short order, which boded ill for the northward invasion and Cornwallis's ambitions. Therefore, the Palmetto State was never subjugated largely because Cornwallis had turned his sights northward too early.

However, under the circumstances, Cornwallis had little choice but to gamble because conventional victories in the past had achieved nothing to solve the ever-escalating partisan problem or to win hearts and minds during a guerrilla war, especially because the Southern Loyalists had failed to rise up en masse as expected by British leadership on both sides of the Atlantic. Ruthless patriot reprisals (repayment for what they and their families had suffered) for Crown loyalty minimized Loyalist support and activities, especially after Ferguson's Loyalist command was wiped out at Kings Mountain.

Therefore, the British continued to primarily control only the South's large cities, Charleston and Savannah, while the rural countryside was dominated by roving bands of partisans eager for revenge—the usual situation in a guerrilla conflict in which a foreign invader had lost the crucial war for the hearts and minds of the civilian populace. Searching for a solution to his vexing strategic dilemma through his education in conventional warfare, Cornwallis continued to look longingly north toward Virginia, the heart of America's Southern operations and logistical base for South Carolina's partisan and patriot forces, as the sole remaining possibility for reaping a decisive success. Contrary to Clinton's wishes, Cornwallis still planned to abandon the Carolinas to link with Arnold's forces in the Chesapeake region of Virginia.

Lord Cornwallis applied his successful tactical concepts—ever the offensive—to the strategic situation, which was where he crossed the line as a prudent commander and made himself increasingly vulnerable the farther that he moved north. If Virginia could be secured, then Cornwallis reasoned that he could return later to South Carolina to restore the situation.

After reaping a costly victory during a bloody slugfest at Guilford Courthouse, North Carolina, over General Nathanael Greene, who commanded the Southern Department after having replaced General Gates, Cornwallis was not deterred in the least. His fatal obsession would shortly lead him even farther north through the piedmont into Virginia. Without serious consideration, he had elected not to withdraw back to the safety of South Carolina to consolidate gains.[15]

General Alexander Leslie was ordered south by Clinton from Portsmouth, Virginia, to Charleston to bolster Cornwallis's ranks in January 1781 for the spring offensive.[16]

Seemingly deemed by fate and circumstances, everything was now at stake in Virginia at a time (early 1781) when prospects for Great Britain winning decisive victory seemed closer than ever before. Indeed, the "success of the entire Southern scheme [of the conquest of America] hinged upon this move to Virginia," which was the decisive first phase winning the war in Cornwallis's agile mind.[17] He now believed that if he gained control of Virginia, then this "would be followed by the control of all America."[18] On April 10 Cornwallis wrote to Clinton about his strategic formula: "We must abandon New York [City], and bring our whole force into Virginia."[19]

However, Lord Cornwallis failed to fully realize the extent that his invading army already had been severely "crippled by the loss of two important detachments [Loyalists under Major Patrick Ferguson and then Tarleton's British Legion of Loyalists] at King's Mountain and Cowpens" to rob him of badly needed war-waging capabilities and crucial manpower needed for future conquests farther north.[20]

As the largest and most populated state in the Union and an important supplier of resources to southern patriots, Virginia was indeed a most worthy target in overall strategic terms. Fulfilling his own ambitions, Clinton's strategy that had opened up a new theater of operation in Virginia had begun with the ordering of expeditions, including under Generals Benedict Arnold, Alexander Leslie, and then William Phillips, who had surrendered with Burgoyne at Saratoga, into the Chesapeake Bay region. The sudden increase of activity had early alerted Washington and other leaders that the main British effort for controlling all America and the prospect of winning the war was about to be centered in Virginia.

Clinton desired a deepwater base in Virginia for the British Navy to support future operations for the South's complete subjugation and for future operations in the Caribbean, where the French were always eager to capture the rich British sugar islands, especially the great prize of Jamaica, and the economic stakes were exceptionally high. Even more, Clinton was adhering to the strategic advice of Lord George Germain, British secretary of state for America, who had emphasized the importance of the Chesapeake Bay region and the need to rely more on the British Navy and avoid the dangerous backcountry to no longer risk sharp setbacks like Kings Mountain and Cowpens. Like Cornwallis and Clinton, however, Germain lacked experience about how to counter effective irregular warfare, setting the stage for an even greater disaster in the South in the early fall of 1781 at Yorktown.

On April 25, after his exhausted troops were rested, Lord Cornwallis departed the key port of Wilmington, North Carolina, with only around fourteen hundred men and without oral permission or written orders from Clinton to embark upon his own campaign north into Virginia. Cornwallis's decision to avoid the coast created a logistical nightmare. Clearly, Cornwallis and Clinton were in far greater disagreement than ever existed between Washington and Hamilton. Unlike Clinton and as noted, Cornwallis was naively convinced that the conquest of Virginia would then lead to the complete subjugation of North and South Carolina and then complete pacification even farther north—a fatal delusion that drew him steadily north like a siren's song. However, here was a chance to break the strategic stalemate and win it all in his mind, because, as previously mentioned, if Cornwallis proved successful in the South and he continued to advance north beyond Virginia, then Clinton could move south from New York City to catch Washington's army and trap it between the two British armies.

The ever-impatient Cornwallis had simply refused to wait for orders from Clinton, who was indecisive out of concern about New York City's safety. For such reasons, his superior preferred to just stay in New York City in a defensive mode, while Cornwallis had acted boldly because there was a war to be won and the possibility of achieving decisive success lay in Virginia, which was the key to the overall conquest of the South. Therefore, Cornwallis did what no one expected, after the failure of North Carolina Loyalists to rise up as hoped and after the South Carolina, Provincial Regulars, and North Carolina Loyalists had been wiped out at Kings Mountain and the British Legion had been destroyed at Cowpens by suddenly abandoning North Carolina and moving north to take the war into Virginia with a badly-misplaced confidence.[21]

Indeed, it was entirely "doubtful if he ever surprised an American commander more completely (with the possible exception of Horatio Gates at Camden) than he did his own commander" Clinton, when Cornwallis boldly pushed into Virginia without orders.[22] Cornwallis was thoroughly convinced that, in his own words, "Until Virginia is in a manner subdued, our hold of the Carolinians must be difficult, if not precarious."[23]

The Franco-American Alliance and ever-intensifying global war had played a part in shifting the war to Virginia because of the economic importance of the rich sugar islands in the West Indies. Clinton needed a Chesapeake naval base from where a fleet of British warships could be dispatched to capture the lucrative French Caribbean islands, which was a more important theater of operations than North America to European strategists, both in England and France. To England, nothing was more important than the sugar islands, like Barbados, because of the fabulous wealth that they represented.

From Washington's headquarters at Valley Forge, Pennsylvania, the ever-insightful Tench Tilghman early understood how the Caribbean dynamic, the riches reaped from sugarcane cultivation, and the global war's demands were becoming more dominant in British strategic thinking. He also knew that France desired to restore revenues from the losses in the Caribbean stemming from defeat in the Seven Years' War. King Louis XVI desired to capture British sugar islands and to win the global economic war. Writing an insightful letter at the end of May 1778 in regard to the British evacuation of Philadelphia, Tilghman explained, "The British Army goes first [from Philadelphia] to New York [and] Ten regiments go to Jamaica . . . I shall not be surprised if all the Troops leave the Continent to save the Islands" in the Caribbean, because "France has ten Thousand Men there ready to strike."[24]

Hamilton's Continued Frustration and Disillusionment

As mentioned long before the final campaign opened in Virginia, a thoroughly disillusioned Hamilton still desired to leave the "family" of Washington's close-knit staff in a permanent break, after his clash with Washington at New Windsor in mid-February 1781. However, he was duty-bound and determined to continue his service in the army of his adopted nation that he loved. Knowing that his days as

Washington's chief-of-staff were over because he had decided that he could no longer work with the aristocratic Virginian, Hamilton decided to return to the vicinity of Washington's New Windsor headquarters. He then moved with wife Elizabeth Schuyler-Hamilton into a small Dutch house of brick and stone at DePeyster's Point on the Hudson River by mid-April 1781. This rented residence of the new husband and wife was located just across the river from Washington's New Windsor headquarters.

Hamilton then wrote letters to friends in search of a new position for which his immense talents were best suited. In an April 19, 1781, letter to General Greene, who headed the patriot resistance effort in the South as the overall commander of operations, Hamilton admitted how he just wanted to permanently escape from Washington's tight grip on his future to embark upon a new military career:

> I am about leaving him to be anything that fortune may cast
> up. I mean in the military line. This, my dear, General, is not
> an affair of calculation but of feeling. You may divine the rest,
> and I am sure you will keep your divisions to yourself. . . .
> Adieu, My Dear General. Let me beg you will believe that
> whatever change there may be in my situation there never will
> be any in my respect, esteem, and affection for you.[25]

Then, almost cleverly as if to disguise his eagerness, if not desperation, to begin a new career in a new theater, Hamilton then revealed his real purpose of his letter to Greene, who was Washington's top lieutenant in the South: "PS. Let me know if I could find any thing worth my while to do in the Southern army. You know I shall hate to be nominally a soldier."[26]

Meanwhile, Lieutenant Colonel Hamilton continued to press Washington by letters and perhaps even in person in his desperate effort to secure an appointment to a field command position. In late April 1781, with the spring campaign drawing nearer with the arrival of warmer weather, Hamilton was suddenly presented a new opportunity to his delight, when the Continental Congress in Philadelphia—ironically the largely incompetent body that he had long criticized because of its ineptness in seemingly all matters, especially military and political—made the decision to convert his lieutenant colonel rank as aide-de-camp to the same rank in the field with full seniority since his official March 1, 1777 appointment to Washington's staff.

Consequently, Hamilton now prepared to make another well-calculated move. Despite enjoying a blissful married life with Betsey, Hamilton was now even more eager to see action.

He bombarded Washington (only a few weeks after their mid-February breach at headquarters) with another request for active service far from headquarters. Never guilty of a lack of nerve, he took the initiative of even suggesting in what command he should be placed. In the past, Hamilton had only served as the captain of a New York artillery unit during the New York Campaign of 1776 and then when Washington's Army had crossed the Delaware for the attack on Trenton. However, he now most of all desired infantry service in the Marquis de Lafayette's Light Corps: "Unconnected as I am with any regiment, I can have no other command than in the light corps."[27] While he had even briefly entertained a "project of re-entering into the artillery," he simply had to have above all else, in his own words, "a handsome command for the campaign in the light infantry."[28]

This was no ordinary request from the ambitious lieutenant colonel, who craved combat in some important action. Light troops, who carried less gear for maximum mobility and were more effective in fighting in the rugged terrain and forests of North America since the days of the French and Indian War, were a regular feature of both armies by this time. The first light troops of the Continental Army had been the rifle units, including frontier Virginians under Daniel Morgan, who later emerged as the victor at Cowpens armed with long rifles, that had been established in the war's beginning. Later, a corps of light infantry evolved in Washington's Army from men picked from regular Continental Line regiments—a case of the best of the best.

The Light Infantry Corps, a division of two brigades, was created in mid-July 1780 for the 1780 Campaign, and Lafayette commanded the corps from August to November 1780. However, a new Light Infantry Corps had been created on February 1, 1781, for the upcoming campaign in Virginia and the Marquis de Lafayette, on Washington's orders, and Hamilton's future destiny would be tied to this crack unit of light troops in the Yorktown Campaign.

By desiring to command a unit of light troops and as planned, Hamilton wanted to go where the action would be heaviest, because these chosen troops usually led the advance, including in the attack, and guarded the rear during the army's withdrawals. From friends at headquarters, Hamilton already knew that the Light Corps would play an active role in the upcoming 1781 Campaign, and he most of all desired to be part of the new opportunities that would be presented in the South. As he wrote from DePeyster's Point (now known as Denning's Point) on the Hudson's east side to Washington on April 27, 1781, knowing that his only hope depended on the commander-in-chief's goodwill since Washington possessed the sole responsibility of appointing officers to the Light Corps, "Unconnected as I am with any regiment, I can have no other command than in a light corps, and I flatter myself my pretensions to this are good."[29]

Throughout his life, Hamilton "was a great risk-taker [but a carefully calculated one], given to gambits that sometimes paid off and sometimes made him his own worst enemy. Although he had his moody, even brooding moments, Hamilton was never indecisive"—a reality perhaps best seen in his relentless and aggressive quest to secure his much-desired appointment from Washington to command light troops in the upcoming campaign.[30]

Hamilton relied on words and the force of well-conceived arguments in a bid to be assigned to the Light Infantry Corps under his good friend the Marquis de Lafayette. With typical Hamilton brashness, he bluntly asked the key question of Washington, "How will you be able to employ me in the ensuing campaign" in the South, while knowing that Washington still wanted him to still serve as the head of his staff because of his outsized capabilities and talents?

A man of refined manners from the Virginia Tidewater planter elite who had been modeled on the aristocratic values of the British ruling class, Washington was caught off guard by Hamilton's extremely direct, if not audacious, maneuver to gain command of light troops. Appointing officers to the Light Corps was complex due to issues of seniority.

In consequence, Washington felt "not a little embarrassed" by the overall situation, both personally and professionally, because of the recent winter clash at the New Windsor headquarters and the fact that Washington, as the young man fully realized by this time, was guilty of having promoted less qualified junior officers above him while not promoting Hamilton in the past, because he did not want to lose him. However, the situation was additionally complicated for Washington because of the unrest in the army that had resulted in recent mutinies, including against unpopular Continental officers who had not trained their own light troops and then suddenly took command of them. This situation, of course, would have been Hamilton's case if suddenly appointed by Washington to command men who he did not know or had not trained.

Concerned about appearances because of the recent unflattering (for both men involved) personal incident at New Windsor, Washington was worried that any refusal of Hamilton's requests might automatically link him to a charge of personal animosity, if not vengeance—certainly ungentlemanly behavior according to the day's values of the upper class elite—stemming from the February 16 clash of personalities. That was part of Hamilton's strategic plan to force a favorable result from the protocol-focused and stubborn commander-in-chief.

General Washington quickly responded to Hamilton's latest request on the same day, April 27. He stated in detail the reasons why this convoluted situation caused a vexing personal dilemma for

Washington; he would have liked to have given the native West Indian an appointment, but his hands were tied for a number of reasons. Washington offered no possibilities for an independent command in Lafayette's Light Corps in part because the Virginian refused to be pressured into a hasty decision that he might regret if other officers rightfully protested the appointment.[31]

Complimenting Hamilton, which the young man must have seen as the bitterest irony, Washington admitted an undeniable truth: "No officer can with justice dispute your merit and abilities," which only complicated Washington's dilemma and overall situation. Worst of all to Hamilton, because the commander-in-chief was always worried about outward appearances and his exalted image, Washington emphasized issues of seniority in having made his decision. He correctly stated how deserving officers of higher rank and with lengthy records would object if he suddenly handed the native West Indian a coveted position in Lafayette's Light Corps, which must have driven Hamilton half-crazy.

Even more frustrating for Hamilton, he was certainly aware that Washington was in the process of obtaining higher rank and seniority for his friend Tench Tilghman, who had become a revered member of Washington's "family" before Hamilton (since August 1776). Why should he not choose Hamilton, who had accomplished far more for Washington than even secretary Tilghman? Had Washington's old Virginia-based and provincial dislike of New Englanders and New Yorkers (Hamilton was considered a New Yorker) resurfaced? Had Washington not forgiven him for what had happened on February 16 at headquarters when tempers had erupted? Hamilton was racked by such perplexing questions and doubts, leaving him still feeling victimized and frustrated.

Not deterred in the least, Hamilton made still another attempt to gain a field command, despite the most recent setback. The irrepressible Lieutenant Colonel Hamilton now employed even more logic and rational argument to Washington as additional leverage. In his latest tactical move, he now candidly emphasized to Washington with his usual straightforward honesty how if not for "my early entrance into the service [during] the campaign of 1776 [Trenton and Princeton], the most disagreeable of the war," then he would have advanced higher in rank as a line officer in the artillery arm. Hamilton should have been promoted at least to a full colonel's rank long ago. Once again, however, Hamilton encountered additional frustration with his latest tactical maneuver, because Washington once again failed to offer any openings.[32]

Hamilton hardly looked the part of deserving higher rank because of his youth and diminutive size that perhaps played a role for Washington, who was one of the tallest men in the Continental Army. During the Princeton Campaign and after reaping fame as the New York artillery captain who had stopped Cornwallis's aggressive pursuit on the Raritan River, one American officer had been shocked when he "noticed a youth, a mere stripling, small, slender, almost delicate in frame, marching . . . with a cocked hat pulled down over his eyes."[33] And another soldier had been equally stunned by the sight of Captain Hamilton, after his heroics at the Raritan when he had first come to Washington's attention, writing how his New York artillery unit "was a model of discipline [and] at their head was a boy, and I wondered at his youth [but] he was pointed out to me as that Hamilton of whom we had already heard so much."[34]

Lieutenant Colonel Hamilton now had no time to think about his glory days on past battlefields, however. But as with the series of setbacks during the ill-fated New York Campaign before Washington's surprise victories at Trenton and Princeton during the challenging winter campaign of 1776–77, Hamilton refused to be discouraged by Washington's refusals, because he continued to pester Washington with persistent requests to secure a field command for the upcoming spring and summer campaigns of 1781. After all, he correctly viewed this forthcoming campaign as his last opportunity to win recognition on the battlefield.

Repeated refusals by Washington only fueled his bulldog tenacity to never quit until he succeeded. In his carefully written May 2 letter, he suddenly renounced his desire for a field command "to obviate the appearance of having desired a thing inconsistent with the good of the service." Hamilton was as concerned about correct appearances and proper protocol as a true republican gentleman but seemed to have now relied on a bit of reverse psychology only five days after the commander-in-chief's refusal. In that letter to Washington in which he continued to play his high card, Hamilton penned a typically astute argument for obtaining a field command in new light corps if created for the upcoming campaign by making points that seemed to have been generated by a seasoned Philadelphia lawyer of a mature age:

> I am extremely sorry to have embarrassed you by my late application and that you should think these there are insuperable obstacles to a compliance with it. . . . I know less of the motives of dissatisfaction in the cases of Col. [Jean Joseph] Gimat and Major [William] Galvan; but I have understood, that it is founded on their being appointed in the light Corps for two successive campaigns [in the past]. I cannot forbear repeating, that my case is peculiar and dissimilar to all the former—it is distinguished by circumstances. I have before intimated—my early entrance into the service—my having made the campaign of 76, the most disagreeable of the war at the head of a company of [New York] artillery and having been intitled in that corps to a rank, equal in degree, more ancient in date than I now possess—my having made all the subsequent campaigns in the family of the Commander in Chief, in a constant course of important and laborious service: these are my pretensions, at this advanced period of the war, to being in the only way, which my situation admits; and I imagine they would have their weight in the minds of the officers in general. I only urge them a second time as reasons, which will not suffer me to view the matter in the same light with Your Excellency, or to regard as impracticable my

appointment in a light Corps, should there be one formed. I entreat they may be understood in this sense only.[35]

In addition, to retain the moral high ground and proper appearances just in case any doubts existed, Hamilton informed Washington that he was "incapable of wishing to obtain any object by importunity."[36]

Clearly, Hamilton agreed with the Virginian on only one point by having emphasized that his case was indeed "peculiar and dissimilar" from any other Continental officers.[37] Ignoring the technicalities of army protocol in the hope of cutting through the usual tangles of red tape and omnipresent seniority issues, Hamilton then relied on his best argument in attempting to convince Washington to give him a command in the Light Corps by reminding him of his "constant course of important and laborious service" for him at headquarters year after year—from early 1777 to the early months of 1781—of which the commander-in-chief was only too well aware and could not possibly deny.[38]

Indeed, as Washington's invaluable chief-of-staff and in the opinion of one historian,

> Hamilton [had] proved a prodigy [but] That was hardly the path to glory that Hamilton sought. Yet so long as the middle states [had] remained a central theater of action, he could subordinate his desire for a combat command [because] he was doing essential service and would still be at the general's side whenever battle offered.[39]

Since he naturally could not counter Hamilton's May 2 argument about his immense value as the head of his personal staff that was indisputable to one and all, Washington was unable to reply as quickly as he had on April 27. Therefore, Hamilton waited in vain for a response that never came from Washington. Hamilton's frustration and anxiety now reached a new high, fearing the worst and feeling that he has missed his last opportunity to fulfill his ambitions.[40] For ample good reason, because Washington had long thwarted his career, this feeling of deep resentment, if not anger, had been slowly building-up inside Hamilton for some time. In disgust, he had earlier written to his good friend Lieutenant Colonel John Laurens about his early failed attempts to break free of Washington's staff and escape the commander-in-chief's giant shadow that fostered an early sense of disillusionment toward Washington and the machinery of army politics: "I have strongly solicited leave to go to the Southward" to a new theater, but the excuses of denial were so spurious, in his opinion, that they "gave law to my feelings. . . . I am disgusted with every thing in this world but yourself and very few more honest fellows." That was before he had met the enticing Elizabeth Schuyler, who had changed his life forever.[41]

Putting aside his strong feelings, Hamilton had continued to faithfully serve Washington, which should have made the commander-in-chief more obliging toward him. He had even continued to play his longtime key liaison, translator, and advisor role with the French allies for the commander-in-chief. This work had included composing detailed letters in French that Washington signed or had Hamilton sign for him like so often in the past. As mentioned in March 1781 and like during the first meeting between the commander-in-chief and Rochambeau at Hartford, Connecticut, in September 1780 where Hamilton had served as interpreter and drafted the conference's results in a memorandum—endorsed by Tench Tilghman—entitled "Conference at Hartford," Washington and Hamilton had continued to work together. They had journeyed to Newport, Rhode Island, in a bid to convince Rochambeau to commit the French fleet to offensive operations in conjunction with Lafayette, now in Virginia, to eliminate the new British threat—the second meeting between Washington and Rochambeau, the Newport Conference.

The Hartford Conference had proved crucially important because of General Rochambeau's actions that followed what he had derived by conferring with Washington. He had sent his son, who served as his aide-de-camp, on a crucial mission to the king to secure not only vital funds but also additional troops, which all would be desperately needed for the upcoming Yorktown Campaign.

During this meeting at Newport, the top two allied commanders in America had focused with ever-growing concern on Arnold's aggressive actions in the Chesapeake region of Virginia, because he was entirely unchecked and doing considerable damage, including the freeing of large numbers of slaves—economic warfare that targeted the planter economy. As one of Virginia's largest slave-owners, Washington worried about the fate of his native state, especially when it came to the well-being of the institution of slavery. After all, he had recently lost more than a dozen slaves when a British warship had sailed up the wide Potomac and anchored near Mount Vernon, which stood on the bluffs overlooking the river. Hamilton had faithfully continued to work by Washington's side whenever he met Rochambeau, contributing all that he could to make the Franco-American Alliance work more smoothly for the upcoming most important and decisive campaign of the American Revolution.

Meanwhile, special envoy Colonel John Laurens, who was Hamilton's best friend, had been dispatched by Congress in January 1781 to France and the king's court at Versailles to secure greater French support (especially the sending of a mighty fleet to America because the war could not be won without ample French naval power) and additional loans, before it was too late. Of French Huguenot descent from a leading family of Charleston, Laurens was fluent in French like Hamilton, who had early learned to speak French from having grown up in the French Caribbean.

General Washington knew that such timely assistance, especially from the French fleet, was necessary to make his dream of capturing New York City a reality and, in his mind, to strike the decisive blow to win the war. In a letter to Laurens, Washington emphasized that America would certainly have little hope for success without the supreme advantages provided by the arrival of a French fleet, while Hamilton warned the young South Carolinian, in his first diplomatic mission overseas, that the French Ministry would severely test him, which was sage advice. The no-nonsense South Carolinian was not a diplomat by nature like the sophisticated and cosmopolitan Hamilton. Consequently, Laurens quickly ruffled aristocratic French feathers, as Hamilton had feared, of the political elite by his aggressive, direct approach—typically American to the much more subtle and diplomatic French. Even toward King Louis XVI, he violated traditional customs and proper protocol that the South Carolinian knew nothing about. Nevertheless, young Laurens, who hailed from one of the richest and most influential families in the coastal lowland, reaped excellent results by securing the desperately needed increased aid, especially financial, returning to America in triumph in August 1781 after a mission extremely well done.

Washington and Lafayette, without Lieutenant Colonel Hamilton, then journeyed from New Windsor in the middle of May to confer with General Rochambeau in their third meeting between the two allied commanders about strategy for the upcoming 1781 Campaign, especially for the need for a stronger French fleet for joint operations. While Washington still stubbornly desired a combined allied effort to attack Clinton at New York City, Rochambeau wanted to reinforce Lafayette in Virginia, knowing that this was the most strategically important theater where far greater advantages could be exploited than in New York. These meetings between Washington and Rochambeau laid a central foundation for the upcoming unified effort to march south and trap Cornwallis in Virginia, when the French aristocrat finally agreed to move his forces south to link with Washington outside of New York City in the first phase of the campaign that was destined to end at Yorktown. However, Rochambeau made no definite commitment about attacking New York City and maintained strategic flexibility by waiting to make a final decision based on future developments as they occurred, especially in faraway Virginia. However, the genesis of the Yorktown Campaign was formulated between Washington and Rochambeau at Wethersfield in general principle.

The open breach between Washington and Hamilton had become complete by the time of the Wethersfield conference. How deep was this breach? During their last diplomatic mission together with the French at Newport in March, for instance, Hamilton had lodged alone in a tavern for the night by himself. Messages had been passed between Washington and Hamilton by courier. By this time, General Washington might have felt guilty to some degree for having refused Hamilton what he wanted after more than four years of faithful service.

After the mission ended, Hamilton had abruptly departed in a hurry without paying a bill to a hairdresser to maintain the look of a proper gentleman and for his wife's upper-class tastes, evidently because he lacked funds because of the low lieutenant colonel's salary and his refusal to take any money from his wealthy father-in-law. As noted, he had then ridden to Albany and the Schuyler family instead of returning with Washington to the army. Hamilton had almost certainly requested permission to visit his new home in Albany instead of departing on his own. Once he reached Albany, Hamilton had found solace in a wise personal advisor in the form of his sympathetic father-in-law General Schuyler, with whom he discussed his unfortunate situation in detail.[42]

Exciting New Possibilities in Virginia Theater

Hamilton continued to realize that America's future now largely lay in the hands of America's powerful European allies. In his own prophetic words from an April 30 letter to Robert Morris, Hamilton emphasized that only by the increasing amount of military and financial aid from France could America and the Continental Army finally have within their power "stopping the progress of their conquests, and reducing them to an unmeaning and disgraceful defensive," like at Yorktown.[43] Most of all, Lieutenant Colonel Hamilton felt confident because all the parts for success seemed to be gradually falling into place like the pieces of a puzzle, because, in his words, "the game we play is a sure game, if we play it with skill" in the days ahead.[44]

And Hamilton knew that invaluable French resources must now be concentrated for a final effort in the South. Meanwhile, developments were progressing at a rapid pace in Virginia, after his lordship had made his latest move north. Cornwallis had crossed from North Carolina into Virginia, where he believed that the war in the South could be won to fulfill King George III's greatest desire and ambition. As he expressed in a letter to General William Phillips, who was in the Portsmouth, Virginia, area with his troops, Cornwallis emphasized his strategic view that the Carolinas could not be successfully held without first subjugating Virginia.

On May 20 Cornwallis's army reached the town of Petersburg, Virginia, on the muddy Appomattox River and just around thirty miles south of Richmond, Virginia. Here, he united with existing troops formerly under the command of Phillips, who had just died of disease, to bestow Arnold overall command in the Virginia theater. With Arnold's departure and return to New York City on Clinton's orders, Lord Cornwallis suddenly gained command of the largest number of men—more than seven thousand—that he had ever led in a campaign or battle.

Audaciously acting on his own, Cornwallis only revealed to Clinton that he had taken the war into Virginia after he occupied Petersburg located around a hundred miles into Virginia, north of the North Carolina border. Cornwallis's move so far north and into Virginia thoroughly exposed the differences in the strategic thinking and ambitions of Clinton and his top subordinate. While Cornwallis believed that Virginia was the key to winning the war in the South, Clinton thought quite differently, planning to mount an offensive against Philadelphia and opposing major operations in Virginia. Even more, Clinton's defensive-mindedness had kept the aggressive Cornwallis in check before Cornwallis had been saddled with the new responsibilities of Phillips and Arnold of securing a permanent base on the Chesapeake for the British Navy to support any future operations inland and in the Caribbean.

To counter the ever-growing threat to his home state, Washington counted on the combination of the forces of Baron von Steuben and Lafayette, which had been bolstered by Virginia militia. This was the gradual escalation of forces by both sides that was destined to make Virginia the most decisive theater of operations in the months ahead. Continuing a short distance north, Cornwallis then forced Lafayette to withdraw from Richmond on the James River. However, in overall strategic terms, these were all meaningless developments and actions of a nondecisive nature.[45] But most important, Lafayette smartly kept his force intact and in position for future action by staying safely out of harm's way to eventually play a key role in bottling-up the British Army before the arrival of the allies under Washington and Rochambeau, after Cornwallis had already boasted with an arrogant confidence how "the boy cannot escape me."[46]

But the prospects of the new British campaign in Virginia possessed a great deal of potential as envisioned by both Clinton and Cornwallis, as revealed in his superior's longtime desire for the establishment of a naval base on the Chesapeake. In overall strategic terms, the distinct possibility existed that Cornwallis could act in conjunction with Clinton's forces from New York City based on the establishment of a good deepwater port on the Chesapeake Bay in Virginia, especially if Germain dispatched reinforcements that were much needed because England was now fighting an expansive global war. Then, Washington's Army could be entrapped in a pincer movement with Clinton moving south and Cornwallis moving north to finally catch the wily fox, if there was no offensive launched against Philadelphia as Clinton was contemplating. Capturing America's capital meant little in the war.[47]

Meanwhile, Lord Cornwallis was still saddled with Clinton's original orders to Arnold to establish a base on the Chesapeake, which he was now bound to obey to ensure an increase of future operations in Virginia. However, Arnold had rejected Clinton's suggestion of Portsmouth, Virginia, which had been emphasized to Clinton. Then, during the early summer, Clinton would order Cornwallis to take a good defensive position, either at Williamsburg or Yorktown, and then dispatch six of his regiments to New York City, which he believed was vulnerable to a strike from the allies. British plans and commanders continued to be at odds, while Rochambeau and Washington were already working closely together with a single goal of vanquishing the British and kicking them out of North America.[48]

Meanwhile, Hamilton continued to remain in limbo with the weather growing warmer. Consequently, he feared that he was about to miss the most important campaign of the war. As mentioned, Hamilton had disconnected himself permanently from Washington's staff by this time, ruled out resuming a career in the artillery, and had failed in his repeated efforts to secure from Washington a field command in the Light Corps. However, during this dark period of a rainy April, the Marquis de Lafayette offered some hope. From the "Head of Elk" at today's town of Elkton, Maryland and located at the northern head of Chesapeake Bay, Lafayette had written to Hamilton about how he would be most helpful to the cause if he remained on Washington's staff. However, Lafayette then wrote, "If you don't stay there you know what you promised to me" and then explained the plan for the creation of "a new corps of light infantry" for the upcoming expedition south.[49]

Hamilton remained close to headquarters to be privy, through friends on Washington's staff, to any new developments for the upcoming campaigns, while staying in a rented house or room.[50] Clearly, this was especially an important time for him to remain close to the army. After the central foundation of the Yorktown Campaign had been laid out at the Wethersfield Conference in May, a new mood of bright expectations was in the air at Washington's headquarters and in the army in general.

On May 17 Tench Tilghman wrote to Robert Morris of recent developments of extreme importance: "Mr. [John] Laurens is in France and has been favorably heard [in his key mission of securing additional troops and money from King Louis XVI] which is a favorable circumstance. . . . With a little foreign assistance and your good Management they will mend here. We are full of supplies and the present prospect of a Harvest is glorious."[51] The optimistic mood of Washington's headquarters continued into June, while the weather grew hotter and expectations continued to rise. In a June 12 letter to his brother William, a Loyalist like their father James, Tilghman emphasized with confidence that "Great Britain must by this time see that she cannot affect the conquest of this Country and that all the maritime powers in Europe [France, Spain, and Holland] are determined she shall not."[52]

Chapter III

Outfoxing the Fox by a Skillful, but Desperate, Maneuver

The series of the most recent personal setbacks to the advancement of his military career only made Hamilton more determined to succeed. Seemingly, the most effective way to motivate Hamilton was to throw formidable obstacles in his path.

Then, at long last, the relentless Hamilton finally devised a brilliant winning strategy out of desperation. He now made his most determined attempt to force Washington's hand and change his mind by outmaneuvering the Virginian's persistent intransigence.

Quite simply, it was now or never for Hamilton to fulfill his greatest ambition at America's most crucial moment with what might be the last campaign on the horizon, if complex and intricate plans worked out between Washington and Rochambeau, who were just waiting for the chance to pounce if the right opportunity was suddenly presented in Virginia. Therefore, Hamilton was about to make his final calculated move and last gamble because the moment was right and it was a case of "now or never."

Lieutenant Colonel Hamilton was not even deterred from his objective by the rise of another possibility. Out of necessity, he was also weighing an entirely new career, and one which was sure to garner him proper recognition. He had received a May 30 letter from father-in-law General Schuyler, who was about to depart Albany for Philadelphia to serve as the New York delegate in the Continental Congress. The general's letter brought exciting news that might rescue the young man from an inglorious end to his military career and certain oblivion. Schuyler explained that with his considerable political influence, Hamilton would have little trouble in winning election to Congress and joining the esteemed New Yorker as a delegate from the same state: a rather remarkable development for someone who had only recently migrated to America without prospects, much money, or friends. But Hamilton most of all wanted a field command with Lafayette's Light Corps and not another desk job with additional piles of paperwork and more long hours with egotistical and feuding politicians.

However, this possible high-level position in government—a stepping stone to greater things in the future in the political arena—was nevertheless tantalizing. Prudently, Hamilton kept all options open, but it was clear that his father-in-law was thinking was in terms of the overall good of his daughter and the family's welfare. In private, General Schuyler, the revered patriarch of one of New York's leading families, might have been delighted to learn that Washington had not given Hamilton a field command for the upcoming campaign because he certainly did not desire for Elizabeth to become a widow not long after their marriage.

In a final bid to force Washington's hand, Hamilton departed New Windsor in June with his wife, now three months pregnant (though not yet known), to Albany more than one hundred miles to the north. He left the Continental Army behind on an extended leave on the eve of a new campaign. The sudden departure was a direct message to Washington to instill a greater degree of guilt, especially so shortly after his most recent refusal to assign a field command to the young man.

As on that ill-fated February 16 when the tempers of Washington and Hamilton had flared, Tilghman was dispatched by Washington to try to convince Hamilton to reconsider. But Hamilton failed to budge an inch, still embracing his determined stance.

But in the end, it was simply impossible for Hamilton, overflowing with energy and ambition, to idly waste time in upper New York at Albany on the Hudson River, while awaiting the long-anticipated appointment to a New York delegate's seat in Congress. Well aware of the presence of his many enemies in Congress, Hamilton feared that General Schuyler, who wasn't fully aware of the extent of anti-Hamilton feeling in the august body because he was still nothing more than an immigrant upstart in the politicians' eyes, would not be able to gain a position for him, similar to when Hamilton was unable to obtain approval from the Continental Congress for the envoy position to France for fundamentally the same reason. While Schuyler implored Hamilton to be patient in Albany, he was not a patient man, especially when America's destiny called and with an important campaign on the horizon.

While in Albany, Hamilton had first learned that the Marquis de Lafayette, who commanded the Light Corps, had been ordered by Washington to the Virginia Tidewater to reinforce Baron von Steuben, who was in a tight strategic situation beyond his limited tactical capabilities. This was the same Light Corps that Hamilton had wanted to lead. Fearing that he had been forgotten in Washington's mind and with the Light Corps under Lafayette destined to play an important role in the upcoming campaign in Virginia, Hamilton instinctively knew that only action could now secure his long-sought goal, and correspondence had provided an opening. In May from Richmond, Virginia, the Marquis de Lafayette had written to Hamilton, requesting him to serve as his artillery commander in Virginia in this new theater of war. Dressed in his finest uniform of blue and determined to force the issue, Hamilton mounted his favorite horse. He then rode away from the Schuyler family mansion and a loving wife.

In early July, Hamilton proceeded south to Fishkill, New York, without telling anyone about his new plan of mounting still another attempt—his most aggressive one to date—to force Washington's hand. Here, he rented a room near Washington's headquarters during the first week of July. With his mind focused beyond the immediate demands of the busy routine of working on Washington's staff, he then wrote detailed articles for a national audience about what was needed to remedy America's ills—financial, political, and military—which seemed to have no end. Revealing his profound views as a political and economic thinker under the pen name of "The Continentalist," these well-conceived essays were published in the July and August issues of the *New York Packet*, which had relocated to Fishkill. With gusto, Hamilton attacked the considerable weaknesses and failings of the Articles of Confederation, which had proved incredibly inadequate for meeting the war's stern demands. Hamilton, with his usual uncanny insight, emphasized that a strong centralized government, ironically one like that of the British Empire, was now urgently necessary to wage a successful war.

Like a cunning poker player (and with peace of mind knowing that Elizabeth was safe and comfortable at her father's stately mansion in Albany), Hamilton now carefully weighed his options in a complex game with the commander-in-chief, while keeping a close eye on recent military developments to the south, which would dictate his future course of action. He sent word to Washington, perhaps by his friend Tilghman, that he still desired a field command. But Washington made no reply, and the icy silence made Hamilton fear that the Virginian had already concluded the matter, and not in his favor. Therefore, on Sunday, July 8, while devout Continental Army chaplains gave spiritual guidance to the ragged soldiers of faith in camp, Hamilton decided to return to the army's encampment just before his "Continentalist" articles were published.

Suddenly, Hamilton, an excellent horseman, rode to Washington's headquarters while his army was encamped at Dobbs Ferry, Westchester County, New York. There, on the east bank of the Hudson River and west of White Plains, New York, Hamilton made his unexpected appearance because he prophetically knew that, as he had written to Robert Morris from the General Philip Schuyler mansion, "events may turn up in the course of the summer [of 1781] to make even the present campaign decisive." Therefore, Hamilton handed one of Washington's aide-de-camps, evidently good friend

Tench Tilghman, still another letter to the commander-in-chief that once again requested an active assignment.

Most important, inside his direct letter to Washington was his staff officer's commission in an official resignation. If Washington once again refused his last request, diplomatically written with his usual skill, he was done with the Continental Army forever. The highly polished and tactful threat made Washington realize that the young man meant business and every word of his ultimatum. Though shocked by Hamilton's drastic action, Washington took no offense primarily because he respected the West Indian's sheer persistence and abundant talents both on and off the battlefield. Quite simply, he could now no longer refuse his longtime faithful chief-of-staff, because of the strength of their former relationship and the fact that the impetuous young man could still significantly contribute to the war effort well beyond the traditional staff officer role.

By this time, Washington had grown considerably wiser in regard to his personal and professional dealings with Hamilton. Thankfully for both men, the sage Virginian saw that here was a good chance—the final one in fact—to restore their severed friendship that had been shattered so unnecessarily in mid-February. The fact that Hamilton had so boldly stood up for himself like no other officer in the Continental Army had instilled Washington with more respect for the young man, whose determination and will were as strong as his own.

However, after handing in his letter to Washington, Hamilton heard nothing that day or the following day, July 9. But on the steamy morning of July 10, Washington sent the self-effacing and ever-faithful Tilghman to implore Hamilton to retain his commission, and that Washington would see what he could do to find a field command for him. Of course, the increasingly cynical Hamilton had feared that only silence would continue to be forthcoming from Washington's headquarters. Consequently, Tilghman's words caught him by surprise. Washington's message to Hamilton revealed that the commander-in-chief would "endeavor by all means to give me a command."[1]

Hamilton described his most hard-hitting strategic maneuver to out-flank the considerable obstacle of Washington's intransigence to his wife: "I wrote the General a letter and enclosed him my commission," which was an unthinkable act only a short time before.[2] Tilghman's unexpected appearance revealed that he had already won the game against the cunning fox, who proved as evasive off the battlefield as on it, at long last. In a July 10 letter to Betsey, Hamilton described this remarkable development after so much relentless effort and bulldog persistence, when Washington came through with his long-awaited promise:

> This morning [on July 10] Tilghman came to me in his name, pressed me to retain my commission, and with assurance that he would endeavor by all means to give me a command nearly such as I could have desired in the present circumstances of the army [and] Though I know my Betsey would be happy to hear I had rejected this proposal, it is a pleasure my reputation would not permit me to afford her.[3]

Unfortunately, Hamilton's letter of resignation was evidently destroyed, because it has never been found to this day.[4]

Unknown to him at the time, the twenty-six-year-old Hamilton had succeeded by the use of Washington's own earlier strategy in getting his way against the odds, beating him at his own clever game. During the French and Indian War, Washington had resigned his commission *seven* times in order to get his way. Clearly, a young Washington and a young Hamilton were much alike in matters of pride and smart tactics to obtain their personal goals, which had ensured that the clash of strong personalities and will had been inevitable.

Hamilton most of all still hoped to gain command of an infantry battalion of the Light Corps in the Virginia Tidewater. The Light Corps was officially known as Lafayette's Division of two brigades. The Light Corps now consisted of three battalions that Washington had organized in early 1781. The old nagging wound—which caused

Washington some personal anguish and almost certainly some guilt—from the friendship severed on February 16 now began to heal, especially if he finally found that ideal field command (a battalion of the Light Corps) for Hamilton, as Washington had promised.[5]

During this period, Betsey was kept closely informed of developments by Hamilton. Here's more from his July 10 letter:

> Finding when I came here that nothing was said on the subject of a command, I wrote the General a letter and enclosed him my commission [but then Washington revealed that he] would endeavor by all means to give me a command nearly such as I could have desired in the present circumstances of the army [and] I consented to retain my commission and accept my command. I hope my beloved Betsy will dismiss all apprehensions for my safety; unhappily for public affairs, there seems to be little prospect of activity, and if there should be Heaven will certainly be propitious to any attachment so tender, so genuine as ours. . . . My good, my tender, my fond, my excellent Betsy, Adieu. You know not how much it must ever cost me to pronounce this word. God bless and preserve you.[6]

With the commander-in-chief's promise, General Washington's feisty "Little Lion" was about to roar once again on the battlefield in the near future, when Washington found the right field command in the much-touted Light Corps for him. Meanwhile, Hamilton remained with the army, quartering at the headquarters of General Benjamin Lincoln, Washington's second in command who had surrendered Charleston in May 1780. Hoping for the best, meanwhile, Hamilton prepared for once again engaging in active duty with a field command for the all-important 1781 Campaign in Virginia. From Philadelphia, General Philip Schuyler was kind enough to send Hamilton two fresh horses, one for riding and the other "a portmanteau horse," from his Saratoga stable, for the many challenges that lay ahead. Hamilton's "Old Gray Horse," which had fallen atop its lightweight rider at the battle of Monmouth, had died of either age, disease, or the effects of its wounds by that time. Hamilton had developed into "a splendid rider," and he needed fresh horses for his upcoming new role.[7]

Near the end of July, Hamilton still anxiously awaited final orders from Washington's headquarters, while he passed the time by serving on the court-martial of a New Hampshire officer who had physically fought with his superior. All the while, he continued to bask in his personal triumph that had once seemed impossible. Then, General Washington finally penned general orders to the army, which revealed that Hamilton had won the game:

> The Light Companies of the first and second regiments of New York (upon their arrival in camp) with the two companies of [New] York Levies . . . will form a Battalion under command of Lieutenant Colonel Hamilton and [Major] [Nicholas] Fish. After the formation of the Battalion, Lieutenant Colonel Hamilton will join the Advanced Corps under the Orders of Colonel [Alexander] Scammell.[8]

Of course, Hamilton could not have been more delighted with the new orders, including the addition of Major Nicholas Fish, who was as dedicated as he was capable. He especially cherished having Fish by his side, because the major, in Hamilton's words, was special "both as a friend and an officer."[9] The last day of July was the day for which Hamilton had long waited. It is not known how Hamilton celebrated the good news, but he might well have enjoyed a toast with his good friends on Washington's staff, especially Tilghman. At long last, Hamilton had won a coveted field command commission.

Lieutenant Colonel Hamilton received his long-awaited lieutenant colonel's commission in the Continental Line in late April, after Congress had officially converted his aide-de-camp's position. Because Hamilton was a New Yorker, and due to issues of seniority, Washington could not place him in a position as a commander of New Englanders, which would mean that highly qualified and experienced

New England officers, who had earned that right by years of faithful service, would have been bypassed. Most of all, Hamilton desired to be sent south to the Virginia Tidewater to join Lafayette, but Washington naturally wanted to keep him with his main army.

To Hamilton's benefit, the situation in regard to securing a coveted position had changed when a new light battalion was organized on the last day of July from the light companies of the First New York Regiment and the Second New York Regiment, and with the addition of two other companies of New York militia in preparation for the new campaign in the South, which allowed Hamilton to gain the command of the new light infantry from New York. Hamilton also secured a company of veterans of the largely black First Rhode Island Regiment of Continentals, which was embedded in the command of New York light troops. Later, on August 19 and fortunately for the overall quality of the battalion, the inexperienced men of the two New York militia companies were joined by two companies of the Connecticut Line—the final creation of the seven-company light battalion of Hamilton's command (two New York light companies, one Rhode Island company, two Connecticut provisional light companies, and two New York companies) of around two hundred men, Brigadier General Moses Hazen's Second Brigade, Lafayette's Light Division.[10]

Besides being thrilled over having Nicholas Fish as the new battalion's major, Hamilton rejoiced that he was under the immediate command of the ever-popular Colonel Alexander Scammell, the former adjutant general who was revered in Washington's eyes and greatly admired by the army. Scammell now commanded the army's light infantry while Lafayette was serving in Virginia. Hamilton's battalion joined the three other light infantry battalions, under Lieutenant Colonels John Laurens, Ebenezer Huntington, and Edward Antill.[11]

Twenty-six-year-old Hamilton must have repeatedly read Washington's words from his general orders of July 31 that made his fondest dreams finally come true, because the designated Continental troops now "will form a battalion under command of Lieutenant

Colonel Hamilton" to serve in the crack Light Corps, which was widely considered to be the best combat unit in Washington's Army.[12] In his own words, a greatly relieved Hamilton rejoiced in the fact that he was finally "no longer a member of the General's family."[13]

Hamilton's hard-won field command was much more than a case of the fulfillment of a blind ambition to reap glory, as it possibly seemed at first glance. Hamilton's motivations were virtuous, befitting the honesty of a true republican warrior engaged in a holy war and a righteous crusade. He sincerely believed that he was serving in the noblest of causes, because he was not only battling for a republican cause and freedom for the common people of America but also fighting for the future betterment of all people. In a July 13, 1781, letter to his wife, Hamilton emphasized how he was fighting for "the cause of country humanity" and an infant republic's life.[14] As Hamilton later summarized in regard to what truly was at stake in this war, "It seems to be reserved to the people of this country, by their conduct and example, to decide the important question, whether societies of men are really capable" of winning this people's revolution and governing themselves as they wished.[15]

The war's most decisive campaign was hurriedly taking shape far to the south in the new Virginia theater of operations. After having inherited Generals Arnold's and Phillip's old mission of securing a naval base on the Chesapeake, Cornwallis wrote an ill-fated missive from his advanced position on the north side of the James River outside Richmond—where Lafayette's small force had attempted in vain to defend the town, on May 26, 1781—to his superior Sir Henry Clinton in New York City: "I hope I shall then have an opportunity to receive better information than has hitherto been in my power to procure, relative to a proper harbour and place of arms [but] At present I am inclined to think well of York[town]," which was located on the south side of the York River.[16]

A strange destiny and confusion in the British high command and its experienced aristocratic leaders were proceeding unabated to shortly make the little village of Yorktown the most important strategic spot on the North American continent. Indeed, the possibility of Cornwallis now occupying and fortifying Yorktown had been revealed in Clinton's July 11 order to Major General William Phillips, who had died by the time Cornwallis reached Virginia, which meant Cornwallis inherited his directives from Clinton:

> If the Admiral, disapproving of Portsmouth and requiring a fortified station for large ships in the Chesapeak [*sic*], should propose York Town or Old Point Comfort, if possession of either can be acquired and maintained without great risk or loss, you are at liberty to take possession thereof.[17]

While at Richmond, the earl had considered establishing a base at Portsmouth, Virginia, on the Chesapeake and then dispatched a sizeable number of troops as requested by Clinton to New York City, which called for withdrawing southeast down toward the end of the narrow Virginia Peninsula nestled between the York and James Rivers. But Cornwallis and his engineers had discovered that Portsmouth was entirely unsuitable, ensuring that he eventually made the most fateful decision of his life and career and a rendezvous with destiny at Yorktown instead of Portsmouth.[18]

However, Cornwallis's actions and decisions would be in keeping with those of Lord George Germain, who was in charge of overall British strategy for the winning of the war, rather than Clinton. Clinton had received Germain's May 2 dispatch in mid-July, in which he had emphasized the strategic necessity that "the Prosecution of the War [should be] from South to North" in the desperate pursuit of decisive victory, because Germain was under heavy political and domestic pressure, including from King George III, to win the seemingly endless and ever-expensive conflict in America. And, once again, Germain still adhered to the central belief upon which the Southern campaign was entirely based, despite little evidence: the massive rising of Loyalists.[19]

Indeed, as Hamilton had surmised with his usual on-target insight, a golden opportunity now existed for America's fortunes if properly and wisely exploited. On July 14, 1781, the editor of the *American Packet*, in Philadelphia, Pennsylvania, emphasized in no uncertain terms the following:

> The United States of America have at this moment a fair prospect of establishing their peace and independence, which may be soon realized, if the Americans be not wanting in themselves. The Britons, by turning their arms to the Southern States, have experienced what the wise and sagacious predicted from this measure; they have greatly exhausted and dissipated their army, and found it easier with a collected force, covered by a superior navy, to penetrate into a thin settled country, than to spread themselves over it, and maintain their conquests. The climate, and the brave persevering efforts of the patriots in that quarter, have almost ruined the army of Cornwallis. . . . The present, then, is the critical day for America [because] Union and vigor through the present campaign, may lay a foundation of liberty and happiness to these States. Having expended already so much blood and treasure in their glorious cause, it should be a first principle in the mind of every free citizen, that the only way to reap the fruits of all, and to make a safe and honorable peace, is to conduct the remainder of the war with vigor.[20]

And, fortunately for America, this was exactly the thinking of Washington and Rochambeau, who continued to see that a great opportunity lay to the south in Virginia with the opening of a new theater of operations, especially if French naval support was forthcoming.[21] Already, a sense of anticipation was running high among many Americans in the know, such as Governor Richard Howley, of Georgia, a congressman by 1781, who wrote with eager anticipation, "Everything conspires to compete the destruction of British hopes in our Southern world."[22] Benjamin Rush, a signer of the Declaration of Independence, wrote to General Gates of the fast-paced developments in Virginia: "Before this reaches you the fate of Great Britain and the repose of Europe will probably be determined in the Chesapeake Bay."[23]

Remarkable Resurgence of a Failed Alliance

Very good reason existed for the marked degree of excitement not seen in the Continental Army in years. Washington's Army was in a positive mood, buoying confidence and spirits among the men in the ranks, while fueling expectations for future success. The summer of 1781 had witnessed a magnificent resurgence of the allied effort at long last. Fortunately, for Hamilton, the rise of the French war effort coincided with his own personal rise, because of his own efforts to strengthen the vital allied relationship. After all, the American-French alliance, which was about to reach its high point in the summer of 1781, had gotten off to the shakiest of starts at Newport during the previous summer, when no American had greeted the Gallic newcomers from so far away, to the astonishment of the French.

What has been often overlooked about the Yorktown Campaign was how extremely low the Franco-American effort had sunk before it suddenly rose like a phoenix in 1781. In fact, considerable fear had existed among Americans about their French allies. Even the war-weary residents of Newport, which had been occupied by the British for years, had initially believed that the French were invaders who were not supporting the American cause. Therefore, Rochambeau and his idealistic Old World liberators had been early shocked by the considerable lack of enthusiasm among Americans when the mightiest French force ever sent to America arrived at Newport, partly because the old animosities from the French and Indian War still lingered.

Adhering to his old agenda, Washington had continued to seriously contemplate an attack on New York City, which became an obsession that had been bolstered by Rochambeau's arrival. However, the sudden appearance of British warships off Newport to negate the

French presence changed the strategic picture. This disadvantageous situation forced Rochambeau to rethink the overall strategic situation because of the formidable threat posed by Clinton and the British Navy under Rear Admiral Sir Thomas Graves.

Because of British sea superiority, the French expeditionary force had been trapped at Newport. Washington feinted toward New York City, causing Clinton's forces to fall back to protect America's most important city. Nevertheless, the French had been effectively bottled up at Newport, resulting in a frustrating stalemate by August 1780. As in the past, the expectations of an allied masterstroke had been early thwarted. After these frustrating setbacks among the allies in 1780, expectations for 1781 only slightly improved because it was believed that the allies' future endeavors could only improve.[24]

As feared by the Marquis de Lafayette, the inactivity of a seemingly impotent French expeditionary force had been a political and public relations disaster that fueled the pervasive American fear that the French were not enthusiastic about waging war far from home. In desperation, Lafayette, consequently, had implored Rochambeau to march upon New York City and strike a decisive blow. But to his credit, the veteran French commander had correctly felt that he was too weak for such an ambitious undertaking against the strongly fortified city on the Hudson. Therefore, the French had remained inactive at Newport, awaiting the arrival of a reinforcing second division from France as promised by King Louis XVI. No one had been more than discouraged than Washington about the overall strategic situation. Because of the failures of 1780, he lamented how the "flattering prospect which seemed to be opening to our view in May is vanishing like the Morning Dew."[25]

Allied unity and cooperation had continued to be tentative in early 1781 partly because of the recent Newport debacle and damaged relations between the new allies, boding ill for the outcome of the 1781 Campaign. Even Washington had proved slow in warming up to the French, who he had fought against as a younger man and had been a prisoner of twice. Anti-Catholic sentiment, especially in New England but also across America, was extremely high, which lingered from the long and bitter French and Indian War. In part because he did not speak French, Hamilton's translation ability notwithstanding, Washington had long put off his first meeting with Rochambeau until late September 1780—the Hartford Conference. Not only were the Americans still disillusioned with the alliance at this time, but also the French were equally disappointed by these New World revolutionaries, who were far more provincial and backward than they had previously imagined.

From the beginning, the disturbing sight of the glaring weaknesses of the American forces—rustic revolutionaries worn-down by the lengthy war—had been the most appalling sight of all to French eyes. The astonished French asked themselves: where was the American people's love for liberty? So few soldiers served in the ranks and enthusiasm for the war seemed nonexistent among the war-weary populace. Indeed, the French increasingly questioned the depth of America's commitment to its own struggle for liberty. It also seemed to French leaders that the Americans had no strategic plan for winning the war except for Washington's burning desire to capture New York City that was well-fortified with sizeable numbers of troops and artillery. For such reasons, true unity between allies had seemed on the verge of extinction and only slowly developed to reach maturity in 1781.

As mentioned, Lieutenant Colonel Hamilton was partly responsible for this timely resurrection. He had been a key player by Washington's side at Hartford and other key allied conferences, which has been often overlooked or minimized by historians. Washington had only belatedly agreed to meet Rochambeau at Hartford in September 1780 to improve a fractured relationship and devise a winning strategy. By this time and as noted, the French Alliance had been under severe strain on both sides of the Atlantic because of the lack of decisive results with the war having stalemated, almost as if the French Alliance had never been signed in 1778. After flooding America with supplies and money for years, the French saw the lack of strategic results and the string of humiliating loses, like the fall of strategic

Charleston in May 1780, causing aid to slow down by early 1780. King Louis XVI and the French court even began to have second thoughts about having decided to enter the conflict in support of the fledgling revolutionaries.

After all and as noted, the 1780 Campaign had been especially costly to France and without decisive results. Because he dreamed about the unleashing of an allied offensive on New York City, unlike the French, including Rochambeau, Washington had been long "wary of the [initial] meeting" at Hartford in September 1780. But such was not the case with the forward-thinking and ever-positive Hamilton, who had early seen endless possibilities if the allies could work harmoniously together: the key to decisive victory in this war. Because the Continental Army and the nation itself were in such bad shape and barely maintaining their existence, the Washington-Hamilton team had long requested additional French aid and funds to fuel one last attempt to secure a decisive success, which coincided with John Laurens's diplomatic effort in France. The ever-optimistic Hamilton had viewed this crucial meeting between Washington and Rochambeau as a golden opportunity that needed to be exploited to the fullest.[26]

Hamilton's brilliance, therefore, had once again risen to the fore in regard to the September Hartford meeting. By this time, Washington's Army had dwindled to only around 3,500 men, which was smaller than their allies' force of only a single division at Newport where the French had been idle for more than a year. For ample good reason, the French correctly doubted their allies' war-waging capabilities that had reached new lows. "Never one to take the defensive in military or political affairs," Hamilton had provided Washington with the correct model of how to play the diplomatic game at a critical time when the political, cultural, and psychological situation with the new ally was as complex as it was critical.[27]

Fully aware of the Continental Army's considerable weaknesses and basing his decision on his deep knowledge of French psychology, Hamilton had proposed to Washington that he should take the initiative during his Hartford meeting with Count Rochambeau. He had suggested for Washington to early shift the blame (which the alarmed French who had already placed on the Americans) squarely on the French for the lack of a united offensive campaign between allies. In the words of Hamilton that revealed the shrewd political and psychological thinking that lay behind his bold initiative, "It is of great importance to us that it would appear we are ready and in condition to act; our allies not."[28]

Thinking like an experienced diplomat, Hamilton had hit upon a magical formula to not only begin to mend the alliance when it was much needed but also resurrect a combined French-American effort before it was too late. General Washington had embraced Hamilton's strategy to the fullest during this key meeting. Hamilton had not only translated to ensure the smooth flow of communication between Washington and Rochambeau at Hartford but also made other timely contributions to the most crucial alliance in the annals of American history. With Generals Lafayette and Henry Knox also in attendance at the conference, Washington, following Hamilton's suggestion, had informed Rochambeau that had "the second division of French forces [only one division was now at Newport] arrived in time, or had the whole come in the 1st instance, the resources of the Country would have poured upon us."[29]

Thanks in no small part to Hamilton's masterful ploy and presence as translator and advisor, Rochambeau (who wisely never saw the merit in Washington's idea of the risky joint offensive to capture New York City because of the strength of the city's ring of earthen defenses and rows of cannon) and Washington had made considerable headway at the Hartford Conference. Most important, they had initially agreed that naval superiority was the key to future operations and that New York City should be the primary target in theory, but without Rochambeau making a definite commitment because of his reservations, as he was only placating Washington. Demonstrating stubbornness and inflexibility, Washington long continued to believe that the war could be won by capturing the most strategic city in North

America, a view not shared by the far more experienced Rochambeau because the costs would be too high and success highly questionable.

But General Washington was then stunned when Rochambeau had emphasized that thirty thousand men (a reasonable estimation with Clinton's garrison of around eleven thousand troops holding the city's network of defenses) were necessary to overwhelm the city's powerful defenses, and that success was only possible if half of the attacking force was American and the other half French. Washington knew he could not contribute such a large quota of fifteen thousand troops because of the apathy and war-weariness that dominated the country. He, therefore, had initially remained noncommittal. Instead and perhaps at Hamilton's suggestion, Washington then advanced his plan of dispatching French troops to the southern theater. However, Rochambeau had initially balked at this idea, because this would result in the division of French ground and water contingents to the enemy's advantage.

In the end and most important, Washington had agreed to the quota of fifteen thousand as estimated by Rochambeau, very likely on Hamilton's advice, despite knowing that the very best that he could produce was only ten thousand. He and Hamilton had hoped that Congress would act to make up the manpower difference by issuing urgent appeals to the state governors, but this was no guarantee for the much-needed results. In consequence, the conference at Hartford had concluded without any formal or official agreements having been reached between the two allied commanders for the upcoming campaign, because the overall situation was still in flux and indefinite.

Nevertheless, Hamilton's clever gamesmanship as successfully employed by Washington had played a role in mending the early wide divide that had long existed between the allies, while helping to set the stage for the upcoming campaign that decided America's fate. Significantly for the Campaign of 1781, Hamilton's initiative also played a part in securing additional French funds (a gift rather than another loan). But most important, Washington's and Hamilton's efforts had gained the promise that additional efforts would be made to have Admiral Comte de Grasse's powerful fleet dispatched from the West Indies and to America later in the year to cooperate in a joint American-French offensive effort in the summer. After all, decisive allied victory could only come with naval superiority and command of the seas. This dynamic team's initiatives to gain French sea superiority for combined offensive operations were thereafter continued by Hamilton's best friend Laurens, who was well versed in the French language, after he had departed on his key mission on the appropriately named frigate *Alliance* in February 1781. Washington had informed young Laurens, who was about Hamilton's age, to inform the French court of Versailles that "without a foreign loan our present force which is but the remnant of an army cannot be kept together for this campaign [of 1781], much less will it be increased and in readiness for another."[30] Rochambeau described the importance of Lauren's vital mission: "This officer [from South Carolina] received orders to represent to the Court of France, in the clearest light, the state of distress of his country" in no uncertain terms.[31]

Although still unenthusiastic about an attack on New York City because of its powerful defenses and sizeable garrison, Rochambeau fully cooperated in accordance with his government's wishes, especially by the king at Versailles. He had anxiously awaited news from his aide-de-camp son, after he had been dispatched to King Louis XVI to secure funds and additional troops. Rochambeau had requested another conference with Washington—the third one, held in the Wethersfield, Connecticut, on May 21—to discuss their strategic plan for the upcoming campaign. Once again, Washington advocated a joint offensive against New York City, while Rochambeau, who possessed considerable experience in European warfare in which he had distinguished himself, saw the greatest opportunity in Virginia to catch their opponent (Cornwallis) by surprise instead of New York City, where a major assault had been expected for years and thus defenses had been considerably strengthened. Hoping to redeem his summer 1776 loss of the city, however, the stubborn Washington continued to emphasize that the capture of New York City was the key to decisive victory. Under orders from the French government to allow Washington to dictate strategy because he was the overall commander of both armies, Rochambeau agreed to move his army from Newport and link with Washington's Army outside New York City.[32]

On May 23, Washington wrote a letter to the French minister to America, Chevalier De La Luzerne, with an official request to send the French West Indies fleet, under Admiral Comte de Grasse, to assist in the upcoming joint operations against New York City. At the conclusion of the Wethersfield Conference, Rochambeau had sent a copy of the proceedings to the much-decorated admiral in a secret communication that was unknown to Washington. It was a clever, if not brilliant, maneuver to undercut Washington's somewhat unreasonable ambition of capturing New York City, because Rochambeau emphasized to de Grasse that he believed that the greatest opportunity existed in Virginia and not in New York City.

Therefore, Rochambeau included his personal request for Admiral Comte de Grasse to sail from the West Indies with four to five thousand troops to the Chesapeake and not to New York City, emphasizing that their American ally lacked resources, especially manpower, and needed a great deal of help. Rochambeau now eagerly awaited de Grasse's reply.[33] Quite simply, Rochambeau had set the stage for "the matter [the Chesapeake or New York City to] be resolved if de Grasse would sail for the Chesapeake rather than" New York City.[34]

Rochambeau had correctly spied the best opportunity for decisive success in the South, especially after his son brought news from France on May 6 that additional funds, 6 million livres, and troops and a superior naval force under Admiral Francois-Joseph Paul de Grasse from the French West Indies would be forthcoming in late July or August. That was the crucial news that Rochambeau had been waiting to hear before committing himself. The king and his ministers had reconfirmed their earlier strategic decision that the war could be won in North America and not in western Europe by invading the British Isle. Ironically, this was the key to British victory in the Seven Years' War (French and Indian War), when England's leaders, especially

Prime Minister William Pitt, decided that France could be decisively defeated by focusing on North America. For this mighty all-out allied effort to win decisive victory and to avenge what had been lost in the Seven Years' War, funds totaling around 24 million livres, including a sizeable loan of 10 million livres from the Dutch and other sources, became available to the war in America.[35]

As mentioned, Hamilton had long desired to serve in the South with either Laurens (before he became the French envoy to the court of King Louis XVI and crossed the Atlantic) or the Marquis de Lafayette: his two closest friends. Symbolically, with his diplomatic skill, Hamilton's tireless efforts in ensuring greater harmony between the vastly dissimilar allies by soothing a wounded and highly sensitive "Gallic pride," after the anti-French Boston riot and the allies' fractured relationship, was now about to pay the highest dividends in the 1781 Campaign.[36]

This final strategic decision among allies took full advantage of British arrogance and hubris, especially in regard to the continued confidence in British naval superiority without consideration of Admiral de Grasse's expected arrival in the summer of 1781 that would dramatically tip the balance in favor of the Allies. As one American soldier who served under Lafayette in Virginia said in a July 11 letter, "England was so far gone in the conquest of America, as to announce to the different counts of Europe, that the four Southern states [Georgia, South Carolina, North Carolina, and Virginia] were wholly in her possession."[37]

Lord Cornwallis's overly ambitious campaign to subjugate Virginia had begun promisingly enough, which only added to the overconfidence and hubris that decisive success lingered on the horizon. When the British Army from North Carolina under Cornwallis had marched into Petersburg on May 20, 1781, only Lafayette's small force of ill-prepared militia had attempted in vain to defend the state. When Cornwallis pushed north from the Appomattox River country, Lafayette had been forced to abandon Richmond and prudently withdraw north, but he continued to perform his dual mission of monitoring his lordship's movements and keeping at arm's length from the master tactician. Richmond shortly fell to Cornwallis.

Because orders from Clinton were to remain stationary instead of unleashing a decisive blow by continuing to invade north, Cornwallis was only able to send out raiding parties as far north as Mount Vernon and as far west as Charlottesville, Virginia. Here, Governor Thomas Jefferson, who possessed no military experience and was more of a heady intellectual than a military man, had been unable to organize adequate resistance to defend his state and was forced into hasty flight to make a narrow escape.

After laying waste to the tobacco port of Richmond and failing to come to grips with the elusive Lafayette, Lord Cornwallis had suddenly switched strategy. Departing Richmond on June 13, he turned southeast down the Virginia Peninsula toward Williamsburg (around fifty miles southeast of Richmond) and closer to the sea to reestablish communications with Clinton in New York City, rest his weary troops, gain much-needed supplies, and fulfill Clinton's wish to establish a naval base to dominate the Chesapeake. Indeed, Cornwallis was only obeying Clinton's orders to secure a deepwater naval base for British warships; the ever-aggressive Briton only reluctantly complied with orders. The overall strategic plan to confine Cornwallis as much possible in the Chesapeake region was based on a viable fighting force under Lafayette to follow if he marched southeast down the Virginia Peninsula.

To comply with Clinton's orders to send three thousand troops (nearly half his army) by ship to New York City and with strategic options rapidly fading away, on July 4 Cornwallis began the march southeast to the port on the Elizabeth River that led to the harbor of Hampton Roads, Portsmouth, Virginia. Turning to pursue despite his weaknesses, Lafayette kept Washington apprised of the most recent developments, especially when Cornwallis abandoned Virginia's interior and pushed southeast toward the coast. The Marquis de Lafayette correctly saw this southeastward movement of Cornwallis as a British retreat from him out of weakness—a strategic reality that emboldened

Washington and offered greater possibilities of perhaps striking a decisive blow.

As mentioned, this ever-increasing opportunity for the allies had
gradually manifested itself in Virginia because Cornwallis, to his disgust since he knew that this was no way to win a war, was belatedly
complying with Clinton's orders to establish a new fortified point on
the Chesapeake for British naval operations at the place of his own
choosing. Against his best instincts and relying on the advice of
naval and engineering officers in deciding that Old Point Comfort,
Virginia, which was located at the extreme southern tip of the Virginia
Peninsula southeast of Yorktown, was unsuitable, Cornwallis belatedly
decided upon Yorktown as the site of the future British naval base. He
chose Yorktown because of its deepwater harbor and good anchorage,
although no British warships or supply ships were now located at the
little tobacco port on the York River, which entered the Chesapeake at
Yorktown—a late fulfillment of his original desire, per Clinton's insis-
tence, to establish a base at Yorktown in May.

Of course, Clinton's orders to secure a naval base faraway from
New York City, where Clinton was completely out-of-touch with fast-
paced developments in Virginia, were guaranteed to fix Cornwallis in
a stationary position and make him even more vulnerable. Therefore,
this ever-aggressive "modern Hannibal" in a resplendent scarlet uniform was destined to lose his trademark flexibility and initiative—the
key to his prior successes—when far from support and on his own, he
decided to fortify Yorktown during the intense heat of summer. Quite
simply, Yorktown was a trap from the moment that Cornwallis finally
decided that this place would be the naval base that his superior had
long desired.[38]

However, Lord Cornwallis had become wary now that he had lost
his mobility, writing prophetically how Yorktown and the Chesapeake
region were "ever liable to become a prey to a foreign Enemy, with a
temporary superiority at Sea."[39] Meanwhile, far to the north, the first
phase of the overly ambitious plan to capture New York City began
when four thousand French soldiers under Rochambeau departed

Newport on June 11, after more than a year of inactivity in Rhode Island. In the exquisite white uniforms of the Bourbon monarchy, the French marched south toward America's most strategic city on the Hudson, embarking on a 220-mile journey through the heat and humidity of late spring.

Advancing in multiple columns with Rochambeau at the head, the French Army of four divisions, with only light artillery in tow because heavy artillery had been left behind in favor of swifter movement, pushed southwest with the goal of linking with Washington's Army at Philipsburg near Dobbs Ferry, New York. Physician James Thacher wrote in his journal on July 1, 1781,

> A division of our French allies are on their march from Rhode
> Island, to unite with us in the service of the campaign [and
> therefore] Great preparations are continually making for some
> important operation, and it is in general conjectured that the
> object of the campaign is to besiege New York.[40]

Spirits among the Americans soared with their first sight of the finely uniformed French troops marching into Washington's encampment in early July with splendid discipline and confident step—a reinforcement of nearly eight thousand troops, after they had moved more than two hundred miles in eighteen days from Newport. Lieutenant Colonel Hamilton, who led his new battalion of the Light Corps, now might have contemplated the strange destiny that three of these veteran regiments—the pride of France—had been recently transferred to America from his native West Indies.

In a July 13 letter from Norwich, Connecticut, one American soldier wrote how the "French troops have safely arrived in camp, and every preparation is making for a speedy and important movement."[41] Clearly, moving light and fast would be the key to victory for the allies, if Cornwallis was to be cornered and defeated in record time. Consequently, Washington had already issued orders for Hamilton's battalion and other light troops of Lafayette's Light Corps to "always [be ready and] fit for action and free from every incumbrance."[42]

Few men in either army realized that the early original concept of the urgent necessity of the two vastly different allies operating as a united, integrated force working in close conjunction in a single campaign had been the early brainchild of Hamilton, who understood both cultures and societies like few other Americans. Hamilton had first proposed to the Marquis de Lafayette, his trustworthy friend, his innovative integration plan "some considerable time" before the arrival of the French, in the words of Major Nicholas Fish.

The Marquis de Lafayette had then passed the novel concept of a joint command, an entire French expeditionary force sent to a foreign country to be under the command of a foreign general (Washington), to his influential family connections at Versailles, where King Louis XVI reigned supreme. The highest military and civilian authorities approved Hamilton's idea, which became a beautiful reality in 1781.[43]

Thanks to the uniting of allies in an integrated army (unlike the segregated effort at Newport that had led to a dismal failure and dissention among allies), the most well-coordinated effort between allies was about to be conducted. Without exaggeration, a British soldier in Clinton's command in New York City explained the strategic situation that shortly unfolded, in which,

> the arrival of a French fleet [an eight-squadron from Newport and under the command Admiral Jacques-Melchior Saint Laurent de Barras, who carried the French siege artillery, from the end of July] A very formidable squadron of the British line, commanded by admiral [Admiral Sir Thomas] Graves, is . . . supposed to be in the vicinity of our combined enemies, we may conclude the present to be the most interesting and critical era since the commencement of the American rebellion; for an expected action at sea, is likely to become decisive of the inadmissible idol, independence [of America].[44]

Learning more about the enemy's movements in Virginia, Hamilton wrote to Colonel Hugh Hughes on July 25, 1781, "Cornwallis ha[s] recrossed [the] James River and was supposed to be proceeding to Portsmounth [Virginia]—thence perhaps in whole or in part to N[ew] York and South Carolina."[45] Of course, Portsmouth had been rejected in favor of Yorktown.[46] At this time, many American fighting men felt a sense of outrage upon learning this summer that England's officials had boasted to other European leaders how the entire South had already been conquered.[47]

During this period, meanwhile, Lieutenant Colonel Hamilton was doing all that he could to prepare his light troops for the many challenges that lay ahead, especially in leading the army's advance south to a new theater of operations faraway. On August 7, 1781, he wrote directly to Washington in the hope of gaining support from him on a matter of importance for the overall welfare of his light troops to improve their upcoming performance in a new campaign:

> I applied . . . for Shoes for the Two Companies of Levies [and] I have reason to believe a distinction was made last campaign in favour of the advanced Corps. . . . Your Excellency is sensible that the service of an advanced Corps must be in general more active than of the [Continental] line, and that in a country like this, the article of shoes is indispensable. If the man cannot perform the duty required of them, [then this situation will hamper their overall effectiveness and the safety of the Continental Army's advance.][48]

Decisive August 14

Meanwhile, Washington's and Rochambeau's troops maneuvered, easing into positions in what appeared to be an effort to reduce the great prize of New York City by siege or so it seemed and as Clinton long had feared. However, the turning point in strategy came on August 14, when the news of Admiral Comte de Grasse's response to

Rochambeau arrived at Washington's headquarters by way of a communication from Admiral Jacques-Melchior Saint-Laurent, Comte de Barras at Rhode Island. From Newport, Admiral Barras revealed to Washington that the French fleet under de Grasse would sail from St. Domingue (today's Haiti) on August 13, after having prevailed in campaigning against the English in the West Indies. Today's forgotten forgotten French naval successes, including the capture of the island of Tobago on June 2, 1781, the southernmost island in the Caribbean, allowed him to turn his sights to North America with confidence and the luxury of time.

Most important, Admiral de Grasse's letter to Rochambeau, who had earlier emphasized to de Grasse in a secret message unknown to Washington that the Chesapeake offered the greatest opportunity for decisive success, informed him that he was indeed sailing from the West Indies for the Chesapeake and not New York City. The overall strength of the admiral's expeditionary force consisted of more than three thousand troops and nearly thirty warships, which were accompanied by smaller vessels. This timely reinforcement of French naval power would decisively tip the balance in Washington's and Rochambeau's favor to usher forth the next and final phase of the belated fulfillment of the Franco-American Alliance of 1778, challenging the British naval superiority and altering the strategic situation on land in an unprecedented manner. However, only a narrow window of opportunity existed, because de Grasse informed the general that he could stay in American waters only until October 13, before returning to the Caribbean to protect the valuable sugar islands, engage in future operations with the Spanish Navy, and avoid the dangers posed by the hurricane season.

An overjoyed Washington—who had no choice but to finally forsake his unrealistic New York City obsession because of the exciting news of Admiral de Grasse's promise—and Rochambeau now envisioned a bold pincer movement: the allied army advancing on the isolated Cornwallis at Yorktown by land and the French fleet sailing from the other direction to trap his isolated British and Hessian garrison at the small port town, if the British Navy could somehow be negated.

Of course, this crucial allied decision to immediately march south was timely and the correct strategic move, while making good tactical sense because New York City was too heavily fortified, brimming with cannon and more than ten thousand veteran troops. Most important, de Grasse took the risk of deciding to bring his entire fleet with him to the Chesapeake at a time when British naval leaders had assumed that he would divide the fleet by sending half to America and half to France—a most serious miscalculation in strategic thought with broad repercussions.

In a most ambitious plan, Washington and Rochambeau agreed to march their combined force the more than four hundred miles south from the New York area to capture the increasingly vulnerable Cornwallis now stationary on the Virginia Peninsula, before he departed or was reinforced. Most important, on August 14 when they learned that the French West Indies fleet was headed northwest toward the Chesapeake, Washington immediately saw with clarity the immense strategic possibilities that were first revealed by the promising words of the Marquis de Lafayette from Portsmouth: "Should a French fleet now come to Hampton Roads [at the Chesapeake Bay's entrance], the British army [of Cornwallis] would be ours, I think."[49]

With Admiral Comte de Grasse's French fleet now sailing in the stiff breeze from the French West Indies toward the Chesapeake, Washington informed the Marquis de Lafayette, "By the time this reaches you, the Count de Grasse will either be in the Chesapeake [and] you will immediately take such a position" to prevent Cornwallis from slipping out of the potential trap on the lower end of the Virginia Peninsula.[50]

Allied prospects for success were improved by yet another key development of which Washington and Rochambeau were not aware. Instructions from none other than Louis XVI had been captured in early June and placed in Sir Henry Clinton's hands at his New York City headquarters. Because of the lack of allied success since the establishment of the French-American Alliance in 1778 and the great expenses in supporting the nonproductive American war effort, Louis XVI emphasized that Admiral de Grasse's expedition to America from the French West Indies represented nothing less than the *final* effort to support what certainly seemed like a failed American war effort and to win decisive victory in North America.

Consequently, with this timely warning, the cautious Clinton embraced an even more firm defensive mode and remained primarily concerned about protecting New York City, allowing developments to play out in Virginia at an ever-increasing pace without his input, to the detriment of Cornwallis far away on the Chesapeake—a too hasty surrender of the strategic initiative in a development of great importance that was entirely unknown to Cornwallis in Virginia.[51] By early August, a prophetic Lord Cornwallis, who had become resigned to his fate of dutifully obeying Clinton's orders by having established a fortified point for a naval base at Yorktown and with no illusions remaining, gloomily reported to his superior in New York City, "It will be a work of great time and labor, and after all, I fear, not very strong."[52]

Chapter IV

Special Destiny Calls, Moving South at Last!

Washington's perplexed men of the Continental Army attempted to make some sense of the twisting currents of grand strategy. To his credit, Washington kept his secret about his ultimate destination even from his staff officers, to ensure that the crucial information never leaked out to the enemy from deserters or Loyalists. In his journal on August 15, surgeon James Thacher penned the following:

> General orders are now issued for the army to prepare for a movement at a moment's notice [and] The real object of the allied armies the present campaign has become a subject of much speculation. Ostensibly an investment of the city of New York is in contemplation [since] The capture of this place would be a decisive stroke. . . . But New York is well fortified both by land and water, and garrisoned by the best troops of Great Britain. . . . General Washington possesses a capacious mind, full of resources, and he resolves and matures his plans and designs under an impenetrable veil of secrecy, and while we repose the fullest confidence in our chief, our own opinions must be founded only on doubtful conjectures.[1]

Indeed, after realizing that the Virginia theater in the Chesapeake was the key to achieving decisive victory, Washington continued to wisely keep his strategic secret to himself even as late as mid-August. Washington's personal secretary on his staff, Jonathan Trumbull,

guessed after mid-August about where they were headed and what
grand strategy had developed at allied headquarters:

> By these maneuvers and the correspondent march of the
> troops, our own army no less than the enemy are completely
> deceived. No movement perhaps was ever attended with more
> conjectures, or such were more curious than this. . . . Not one,
> I believe, penetrated the real design.[2]

In preparation of the many stern challenges that lay ahead far
to the south, Washington's staff had undergone change before the
new campaign. Twenty-nine-year-old Lieutenant Colonel David
Humphreys, a Yale graduate, was one of Washington's aides by this
time, having joined in June 1780. It has been thought by some historians that Jonathan Trumbull Jr. had become Washington's military secretary at this time, after replacing Colonel Robert Hanson Harrison,
the senior—both in age and period of service—member of the "family." In his midthirties, Harrison resigned in March 1781, after serving under Washington since November 1775. He then returned to
southern Maryland, because of his father's declining health and then
recent death. Washington's inner circle had now shrunk to only the
hard-working Tilghman and David Humphreys. Washington tried to
fill the void left by Hamilton's departure by taking on suitable "family"
members, but no one was to come close to matching Hamilton.

The talented Trumbull became an aide-de-camp of the commander-in-chief in June 1781, serving as Washington's secretary with
Tilghman. The death of Harrison's father left Harrison's two young
daughters, Sarah and Dorothy, on their own (their mother had
died before the war) at Walnut Landing, Charles County, southern
Maryland, not far from Washington's Mount Vernon. Harrison also
departed from Washington's staff to take care of legal business in the
Potomac River port of Alexandria, situated around fifteen miles north
of Mount Vernon and up the Potomac River, after having faithfully
served Washington for six years.[3] Harrison's service had "left him

with serious physical problems"—just another high price paid by the widower for his longtime faithful service to his Washington.[4] In an April 19, 1781 letter, Hamilton wrote with regret to General Greene that "Harrison has left the General to be a Chief Justice of Maryland."[5]

Jonathan Trumbull Jr. has been often confused with John Trumbull, who had only served less than a year on Washington's staff (from the summer of 1775 to June 1776), before retiring in February 1777. Jonathan Trumbull was the youngest privileged son of New Jersey's colonial governor (1765–1784), Jonathan Trumbull Sr. and Faith Robinson-Trumbull. The youngest graduate of the Harvard class of 1773, he was destined to be America's first college graduate to become a professional artist. Trumbull united art with an unprecedented degree of historical accuracy like no other American artist of his day, becoming famous for his art work that focused on key moments of the struggle for liberty. Trumbull's fine artwork earned him the title of the "Patriot Artist of the American Revolution." Trumbull had first served in a Connecticut regiment of the Continental Army from the early days of 1775, before retiring out of frustration in a situation well-understood by Hamilton: Trumbull's expected colonel's commission was not forthcoming.

Schooled by the Anglo-American artist Benjamin West in London before the Revolutionary War ended, Jonathan became the first American artist to produce art works of high quality devoted to contemporary wartime events from Bunker Hill to Yorktown.[6]

Jonathan's older brother Joseph Trumbull died from "exhaustion from overwork," while serving as the Continental Army's first commissary-general.

During this crucial campaign for America, Washington's staff officers included Laurens, Humphreys, Tilghman, David Cobb, and William S. Smith. They were all lieutenant colonels and aide-de-camps for "His Excellency," while Trumbull and Tilghman served as Washington's official secretaries. These talented and hard-working officers were destined to serve Washington extremely well during the Yorktown Campaign.[7]

For roughly a month outside New York City, the allies became better acquainted after having united as one. The Americans and the French had been bitter enemies during the course of the French and Indian War, and their hostility had been based on a good many ancient prejudices. Earlier at Newport, one French officer had complained of the extent of anti-French prejudice among the Americans, writing how the British, when they had occupied the town, had "made the French seem so odious to the Americans . . . saying that we were dwarfs, pale, ugly specimens who lived exclusively on frogs and snails."[8]

Even British propaganda was doing its insidious work in a psychological war, with a New York newspaper printing intercepted letters written by aristocratic French officers, who maintained that the Americans were "ignorant, superstitious, without education, without taste, without delicacy or honor," which was closer to the truth than generally admitted by American historians to this day.[9]

French officers, especially the refined epicureans of the upper class elite that made up the Gallic officer corps, also complained about America's weak coffee, salad dressing saturated with vinegar, and the truly unthinkable—dinners of meat and potatoes served on the same pewter plate! This was all entirely uncouth and unbearable to the pampered French elite who had embraced the cause of liberty with a passion but not the same cultural proclivities and nuances, especially when it came to cuisine.

The combined operations fostered collaboration. The French troops from the West Indies of Major General Marquis de St. Simon's division, the Gatinois, Touraine, and Agenois (officially designated as the Fourteenth Regiment) regiments, made a magnificent impression upon Hamilton, stimulating a measure of pride in his native Caribbean. On August 19, believing Clinton would remain in his defensive position, Washington and Rochambeau turned their troops (four thousand Frenchmen and twenty-five hundred Americans) south toward Virginia and Yorktown, 450 miles distant. Departing Dobbs Ferry on the warm evening of August 20 and confident for success in the Virginia Tidewater, the allies embarked upon their most grueling march in their boldest maneuver to date to catch the British by surprise.

Lieutenant Colonel Hamilton's disciplined light troops of his battalion, under the command of Colonel Alexander Scammell, led the way as part of the army's advanced guard through upper New Jersey. This trek south through the landscape of fertile fields and hardwood forests of the rural countryside was "epic [and] One of the longest in the entire war, it was an act of astonishing boldness, comparable to Washington's crossing of the Delaware in 1776 but on a much larger scale."[10] All the while, the motivation of the men in the ranks of the Continental Army could not have been higher, including in Hamilton's light battalion, because, in the words of one American, "General Washington and the army are gone to take Lord Cornwallis in his mouse-trap."[11]

Before departing Dobb's Ferry, Hamilton's battalion had taken final shape. He rejoiced in the fact that "two companies each [composed] of a Captain, two Subs [subalterns or lieutenants], four Sergeants and Fifty Rank and File" were "immediately formed from the Continental Line [and] it is expected that the companies will be composed of good men engaged either for the [rest of the] War or three years."[12]

Seemingly having thought of everything in his typical meticulous fashion, Hamilton already had his troops in good shape for the long march south and ready to travel light in accordance to Washington's specific orders for the light troops. Fortunately, Hamilton's appeal to Washington for new shoes for his ill-shod men was successful. Once again, Hamilton proved that he knew how to get things done in a hurry and when most needed.[13]

Most important, Hamilton had stripped his men of all unnecessary baggage and gear to facilitate moving as swiftly as possible during the lengthy trek. By this time, he benefited from the fact that wife Elizabeth had secured for her husband all the necessary "camp equipage" for the grueling campaign that lay ahead.[14] Equally significant,

Hamilton had his men uniformed as well as possible. In his own words, "Nothing is more necessary than to stimulate the vanity of soldiers [and] To this end a smart dress is essential [because] When not attended to, the soldier is exposed to ridicule and humiliation."[15]

Hamilton was elated to lead a battalion south. On August 22, not long after marching three days to Haverstraw, New Jersey, Hamilton finally found spare time to write to his wife, evidently in his canvas tent at night by candlelight. With his wife back at the family's mansion that overlooked the Hudson River in Albany, Hamilton had initially hoped to remain within riding distance of the love of his life when he resumed active service, but this was now no longer possible. A courier was about to ride to General Schuyler's headquarters in Albany, presenting an opportunity to send belated word to Betsey along with his meager savings from a lieutenant colonel's salary so that she would not have to rely upon her wealthy father's money.

Feeling guilty that he had been unable to say good-bye before embarking on this risky campaign, Hamilton finally broke the news to Elizabeth, which she certainly feared by this time, with assurance that he would not be in harm's way—a revelation that, no doubt, came as a shock to his pregnant wife. His letter indicated his sheer joy in once again leading troops in an active campaign:

> A part of the army My Dear girl is going to Virginia [which he reminded her not to disclose to anyone], and I must of necessity be separated at a much greater distance from my beloved wife. . . . I cannot ask permission to visit you. It might be thought improper to leave my [light] corps [under Scammell] at such a time and upon such an occasion. I cannot persuade myself to ask a favour at Head Quarters, I must go without seeing you. I must go without embracing you. Alas I must go.[16]

He also informed Elizabeth to write him in the future in care of Richard Peters, who was the secretary of the Board of War, of

Philadelphia. Hamilton also told his wife to expect for him to return home to Albany in October or November, which he hoped would keep up her spirits and ease her fears.[17]

Like his men in the ranks, Hamilton was jubilant about the prospects of nabbing the infamous Lord Cornwallis. In the joyous words of one American officer from the North, "We shall soon look in upon Cornwallis as stern as the grave."[18] In this same August 22 letter, Lieutenant Colonel Hamilton informed his wife that he was safe and sound. He even presented the most benign strategic scenario that would ensure the prospect of engaging in no heavy fighting to ensure no unease for his wife: "It is ten to one that our views will be disappointed by Cornwallis retiring [south from Virginia] to South Carolina by land."[19]

Perhaps this letter most fully revealed the true heart and soul of the "Little Lion," because of course he was hoping that Cornwallis would not retire into South Carolina. Hamilton was not guilty of hyperbole in his words to his new wife in faraway Albany. Destiny itself seemingly was about to carry Hamilton forward on its wings. His statement that he would return by autumn revealed his optimism, as he knew that Admiral Comte de Grasse's fleet would be sailing back to the West Indies by this time.

Partly because of the lack of cavalry, the march south was not detected by the British, while Clinton continued to only worry about New York City's safety. Keeping his opponents firmly in place, Washington had feinted cleverly, as if planning to assault New York City from the south, before pushing southwest through New Jersey during the next phase of the march to Virginia. Washington had also created a number of well-conceived ruses, including the appearance of a permanent encampment on New Jersey soil opposite Staten Island and leaking misleading intelligence communications to fool the British.

Washington thus guaranteed that the increasingly anxious Clinton would not send any warnings or reinforcements to Cornwallis until it was too late. After pushing southwest toward Philadelphia, Washington crossed the Delaware (a river of destiny in late December 1776 when

Washington won his miraculous victory at Trenton) by way of Trenton Ferry, with horses and oxen, which pulled the artillery pieces, swimming across the swirling waters of the wide river.[20]

On the second to last day of August, a mystified surgeon James Thacher, who knew much less about the fast-paced strategic developments than Hamilton, wrote in his journal,

> Our destination has been for some time [a] matter of perplexing doubt and uncertainty; bets have run high on one side that we were to occupy the ground marked out on the Jersey shore, to aid in the siege of New York, and on the other, that we are stealing a march on the enemy, and are actually destined to Virginia, in pursuit of the army under Lord Cornwallis [and Washington's troops] are pursuing our route with increased rapidity towards Philadelphia.[21]

On the long march south to the infant nation's capital of Philadelphia, Thacher wrote about the startling realization that lifted spirits throughout Washington's ranks and boded well for future developments in Virginia:

> Our destination can no longer be a secret. The British army, under Lord Cornwallis, is unquestionably the object of our present expedition. It is now rumored that a French fleet may soon be expected to arrive in Chesapeake bay, to cooperate with the allied army in that quarter. The great secret respected our late preparations and movements can now be explained. It was a judiciously concerted stratagem, calculated to menace and alarm Sir Henry Clinton, who was already in a defensive mode because he knew that de Grasse and his warships were on the way to America, for the safety of the garrison of New York [City], and induce him to recall a part of his troops from Virginia, for his own defence; or, perhaps, keeping an eye on the city, to attempt its captured, provided that by the arrival of a French

fleet, favorable circumstances should present. The deception has proved completely successful [and] His Excellency General Washington, having succeeded in a masterly piece of *generalship*, has now the satisfaction of leaving his adversary to ruminate on his own mortifying situation, and to anticipate the perilous fate which awaits his friend, Lord Cornwallis, in a different quarter.[22]

Meanwhile, Hamilton continued to lead his light battalion with the army's advanced guard of around twenty-five hundred men during the arduous march south toward Philadelphia and the steamy lowlands of the Virginia Tidewater. Hamilton was confident that his well-trained Continental battalion of seasoned troops of Lafayette's Light Corps could successfully meet any challenge. Indeed, he felt increasing confidence, knowing that he could rely upon a capable and trusty right arm in Major Nicholas Fish, his second in command and former King's College classmate. Most important, Hamilton had made sure that the two companies of New York militia had been replaced by battle-hardened veterans of two Connecticut companies of Continentals to increase his light battalion's capabilities and combat prowess.[23]

Despite the hot weather and choking clouds of rising dust, the march was swift partly because Hamilton's men had shed all extra gear. After all, Washington had emphasized how the "success of our enterprise depends upon the celerity of our Movements, delay therefore, may be ruinous to it."[24] Indeed, Washington and Rochambeau needed to join forces with the Marquis de Lafayette, who was keeping Cornwallis bottled up on the Virginia Peninsula, as soon as possible for the crucial union of all three forces, before his lordship at Yorktown decided to attack Lafayette in an attempt to break out of the trap on the narrow peninsula.[25]

Philadelphia, the Infant Republic's Capital

The arrival of the French at the capital of Philadelphia resulted in a joyous celebration among the populace. Washington and his troops had prudently bypassed the capital in September, leaving the French to reap the laurels and wild applause to lift the spirits of a war-weary people. Philadelphians marveled at the fancy white uniforms of Bourbon France and the precision drill of the French regulars, especially the grenadiers in high fur caps to present a more fearsome appearance on the battlefield. But the overall experience in America's capital was initially less than gratifying to some French troops, because the capital city's streets "were extremely dirty, and the weather warm and dry, we raised a dust like a smothering snow-storm, blinding our eyes and covering our bodies with it."[26] In an August 30 letter, one Philadelphia citizen never forgot how during "the evening the city was illuminated, and his excellency [Washington] walked through some of the principal streets, attended by a numerous concourse of people, eagerly pressing to see their beloved general."[27]

More from the letter was reported in the pages of the *New York Gazette and Weekly Mercury* newspaper:

> Yesterday, at one o'clock in the afternoon [of September 2], his Excellency the Commander-in-Chief of the American armies, accompanied by the Generals Rochambeau and [Marquis de] Chastellux [second in command of the French forces], with their respective suites, arrived in Philadelphia. The general was received by the militia light horse in the suburbs, and escorted into the town. He stopped at the city tavern, and received the visits of several gentlemen [and then] About three o'clock he went up to the State House, and paid his respects to Congress. He then returned to the superintendent's, where his Excellency the President of Congress, and the generals . . . and several other gentlemen, had the pleasure of dining with him. After dinner, some vessels belonging to the port, and then lying in the stream, fired salutes to the different toasts which were drank.[28]

For two full days, the French troops lingered in Philadelphia and soaked up the applause from an excited populace in the kind of festive reception that they had expected on their initial arrival in America.[29] Like Washington's soldiers, the people of America's capital were awed by the disciplined bearing of the French troops, because they were Western Europe's finest. Physician James Thacher, the capable surgeon of a New England regiment of light troops in Colonel Scammell's command who had risen from humble roots on his own abilities, wrote,

> French army exhibit their martial array to the greatest advantage [and the officer's] military dress and side-arms are elegant; the troops are under the strictest discipline, and are amply provided with arms and accoutrements, which are kept in the neatest order; they are in complete uniform, coats of white broadcloth, trimmed with green, and white under-dress, and on their heads they wear a singular kind of hat or chapeau [which] is unlike our cocked hats, [worn by confident young officers like Hamilton].[30]

Of course, the homespun Americans, including many soldiers wearing tattered civilian clothing, presented a much less distinguished appearance. One shocked French officer wrote that among Washington's men there "were some fine looking men; also many who were small and thin, and even some children twelve or thirteen years old. They have no uniforms and in general are badly clad."[31]

General Washington's Forgotten Black Soldiers

But the most surprising sight of all to the French was the large number of African American fighting men in the ranks of Washington's Continental Army. In the words of Baron Ludwig von Closen, an experienced captain of the German Royal Deux-Ponts Regiment,

I had a chance to see the American army, man for man. It was really painful to see these brave men, almost naked with only some trousers and little linen jackets, most of them without stockings, but, would you believe it? Very cheerful and healthy in appearance. A quarter of them were negroes, merry, confident, and sturdy. . . . Three quarters of the [First] Rhode Island regiment consists of negroes, and that regiment is the most neatly dressed [in white uniforms like the French], and best under arms, and the most precise in maneuvers.[32]

Another amazed French officer described the American army by writing that "the men were without uniforms but covered in rags most of them were barefoot. They were of all sizes, down to children, who could not have been over fourteen [and] There were many negroes, mulattoes, etc."[33]

The forgotten story of the significant contributions of black fighting men in the ranks of Washington's Army when its numbers were at low ebb during the Yorktown Campaign is a glaring omission in American military historiography—the most forgotten American contribution during the final showdown at Yorktown. In fact, African American fighting men, slaves but mostly free men of dignity and pride, served faithfully and with distinction from the beginning to the end of the war, including in the Continental Line regiments of every single state. An estimated seven thousand black fighting men, both on land and sea, including a good many Africa-born soldiers, served the cause of America during the revolutionary struggle.

Hamilton respected and admired the black fighting man, considering them equal to white soldiers. Blacks of an experienced company of the veteran First Rhode Island served in Hamilton's light battalion of Lafayette's Light Corps. Blacks were numerous in New England Continental and militia commands, especially those from New York and also Connecticut, which included one musically talented black soldier who carried his prized fiddle atop his knapsack for the playing of music at night.[34]

Ironically and unknown to his black fighting men, Washington had recently lost seventeen slaves at Mount Vernon, when a prowling British warship had anchored nearby in the Potomac to provide a beacon of freedom, while a good many other blacks fought for freedom in the ranks of the Continental Army at exactly the same time.[35]

A Special Destiny Continues to Call to Hamilton

During the long march south over the rolling countryside, Hamilton hoped for the best in this campaign. Ever the realist, he fully realized that the complexity of the allies' bold strategy was risky. But he informed Betsey with an exaggerated emphasis that he would return safe and sound: "Cornwallis [almost certainly will be shortly] retiring to South Carolina [and specifically to Charleston, which would have been his wisest and most prudent move on his part] by land."[36]

However, Lieutenant Colonel Hamilton seemed not to fully realize that Cornwallis, the ever-aggressive former Guards officer, was the most ambitious British commander in North America. In truth, consequently, there was no possibility of Cornwallis returning back into the Carolinas, because he had long ago settled on his own personal strategy of boldly forging ahead regardless of the cost.[37]

All the while, Hamilton's hopes for seeing action reached a new high during the balmy days of early September. Not long after departing Philadelphia, when situated just south of the capital at Chester, Pennsylvania, Washington received the most uplifting news that Admiral Comte de Grasse's fleet, thirty-six ships of the line, had reached the entrance of the Chesapeake at Cape Henry, located at the southern end of the entryway into the Chesapeake Bay on the Virginia mainland, with Yorktown located on the York River to the northwest, on August 29. De Grasse landed much-needed French reinforcements to bolster Lafayette's command to ensure that they kept Cornwallis bottled up on the thin Virginia Peninsula. This vital information that now guaranteed the allies' sea and land superiority sent the elated commander-in-chief into a rare display of emotion that astounded nearby French officers. Washington personally brought Rochambeau the news and then hugged the much-surprised smaller Gallic general, who was exquisite in his refined and polished Gallic manners, in delight.

More than a dozen British ships under Sir Samuel Hood, which had been dispatched by Admiral Sir George Rodney, who commanded in the Leeward Islands of the Caribbean, were in pursuit of Admiral Comte de Grasse after he had departed the West Indies. They had reached the warm tidal waters of the Chesapeake first. But then Hood made a fatal mistake. Assuming incorrectly that de Grasse had sailed north to threaten Clinton at New York City, Hood then left Cornwallis's Army on its own, when he sailed north to protect England's most strategic city in North America and join the fleet under Graves.

Then, Graves led nineteen warships south from New York City for the Chesapeake. Graves had learned that Admiral Jacques-Melchior St. Laurent de Barras, who commanded only a squadron of eight ships that now sought to link with Admiral de Grasse's fleet, had departed Newport with his warships and transports with siege equipment and heavy artillery, which had been left behind by Rochambeau to ensure a more swift march to Virginia. That was a most ominous development for the stationary Cornwallis at Yorktown, because the French plan had long envisioned the unleashing of the greatest of all surprises on Cornwallis by a timely uniting of Admiral de Grasse fleet with Barras's squadron with the crucial siege guns.[38]

In his journal after Washington presented Rochambeau the good news about the key location of de Grasse's fleet, surgeon Thacher wrote about the relaying of the vital information that sent the army's spirits soaring: "An express has now arrived from Virginia, with the pleasing intelligence that Admiral Count de Grasse has actually arrived at the mouth of the Chesapeake bay, with a fleet of thirty-six ships of the line, and three thousand land forces, which are landed, and have joined our troops under the Marquis de la Fayette, in Virginia," while the "royal army, under Lord Cornwallis, has taken post in Yorktown."[39]

Meanwhile, Cornwallis continued to busily fortify Yorktown. He had originally envisioned having to face an attack by water and not from the land side of Yorktown, which helped to hasten his undoing. For once, after so many successful campaigns in this war, the proud Lord Cornwallis had finally met his match in the combined allied effort, which was calculated to take full advantage of Cornwallis's mistakes and those of his bumbling superior, Sir Henry Clinton, the two of whom had become the most inept of leadership teams.[40]

Hamilton could hardly wait to get back into action. He had finally revealed the great secret upon which the entire campaign and America's future was now based to Betsey on September 6: "Tomorrow we embark for Yorktown."[41] With unbridled confidence, he also added the encouraging words that were well founded: "Our success [is] certain."[42]

Young Lieutenant Colonel Hamilton could be forgiven for his neglect of proper matrimonial duties because he was now part of the most determined allied bid in the history of the alliance to take full advantage of "the most decisive opportunity of the whole war," in the words of Francisco Saavedra de Sangronis, a key Spanish official and officer in Havana, Cuba.[43]

Surprisingly, this most important strategic decision of the war— the descent of the allies on Cornwallis because of British naval inferiority in American waters and the extensive requirements of a global war, including in far-away India—had not been originally formulated in America or France. The sending of Admiral de Grasse's fleet to America had only been possible because of the large donations of funds from Havana's wealthy Spanish citizens, including aristocratic ladies who had selflessly donated their diamonds and other precious jewels. Forgotten by Americans today, Spain had become one of America's allies, and the Cuban people had supplied the crucial financial support to Admiral de Grasse in mid-August 1781 that made success possible.

Indeed, the French-speaking and Spain-born Saavedra, who was headquartered at Havana, Cuba, had been assigned by the Spanish king, Carlos III, to coordinate the military activities of France and Spain. Bourbon Spain was a belated ally to America but now made its most vital contribution. Saavedra had developed the bold plan with Admiral de Grasse for the Gallic fleet to deliver a blow to British forces in America and then to quickly return to the Caribbean for the Franco-Spanish offensive to capture the greatest British prize in the Caribbean, Jamaica. Few historians have realized that the "most important strategic decision of the war, to attack the isolated British on the Yorktown Peninsula, was made by French and Spanish military men in a Haitian harbor" of Cap Francois on the north coast at the French colony of St. Domingue.[44] Indeed, "the bottom dollars upon which the edifice of American independence was raised" in Havana by the lavish donations of the Cuban people.[45]

After "having completed a march of two hundred miles in fifteen days," Washington's troops began to embark on vessels down the Elk River in northern Maryland to gain the head of the Chesapeake Bay around twenty miles distant and then on south to Virginia.[46] Hamilton's light battalion and other light troops—around eight hundred crack fighting men in total—were ordered to first embark upon transports for the trip to the Chesapeake Bay port of Annapolis, Maryland, which was the state capital. The long trip south would involve a full week's journey, partly with the light troops leading Washington's advance, which was the customary role of the highly mobile light troops.[47]

Here, at the head of Elk River before the departure all the way to Virginia, a confident Hamilton had written to Betsey about the exhilarating news of the most strategic development—the French West Indies fleet under Admiral de Grasse in the Chesapeake without a British fleet in sight—that was so extremely favorable to America's fortunes: "Circumstances that have just come to my knowledge assure me that our operations will be expeditious, as well as our success certain."[48]

After the first elements of Washington's Army linked with the Marquis de Lafayette's forces in the Virginia Tidewater and after Admiral Comte de Grasse unloaded more than three thousand French troops on Virginia soil to reinforce Lafayette in early September after having sailed up the wide waters of the James River, the allies then turned their sights on their primary target, Cornwallis's Army of British, Hessian, and Loyalist troops. Without having encountered any Royal Naval opposition, de Grasse had remarkably won the race to ensure the crucial timely unity of force.

Now reinforced by thousands of French troops, the young Marquis de Lafayette had played a masterful role in having faithfully kept watch on British forces in the Chesapeake and keeping the British bottled up on the narrow Virginia Peninsula. Sergeant Joseph Plumb Martin, born in the picturesque hills of western Massachusetts and a devoted minister's son, said, "We prepared to move down and pay our old acquaintances, the British at Yorktown, a visit [but] I doubt not but their wish was, not to have so many of us come at once. . . . We had come a long way to see them."[49]

On September 7, a correspondent for the *Pennsylvania Packet* in Lafayette's encampment revealed the rising spirits among the allies during the descent upon Yorktown:

You have seen the British troops and the troops of other nations, but you have not seen troops so universally well-made, so robust, or of such an appearance, as those General [Marquis de] St. Simon [who commanded the three well-trained French regiments of the West Indies garrison] has brought to our assistance. These are all under the command of our general [and I see] a general impatience in the French army to complete the Gordian knot in which our second Fabius [La]Fayette has been entangling his lordship; some of its cords already press him, and, I believe, if there were hopes of succeeding, he would attempt to cut it. But notwithstanding his lordship is, perhaps, the first officer in the

British service, yet he may not be in possession of the sword of Aleides. . . . We have a brave army to contend against [and] with all the necessities for a gallant resistance; and in number fully sufficient for the defense of their post; but we shall do very well, for to the common motives of our profession will be joined an emulation arising from fighting by the side of our allies. The British are entrenching at York[town] with great industry. Every thing is landed from their shipping, and dispositions made for their destruction.[50]

Indeed, thanks to the multiple failures and lack of unity of the British command structure, especially the army and navy that had not worked in conjunction, Cornwallis's fate was sealed in early August, when "Cornwallis tied himself irrevocably to the defense of the Yorktown post."[51]

While tried veterans like Sergeant Martin were eager to meet the famous British earl and his men who had long terrorized the South and vanquished one American army after another, Cornwallis was unaware that he was becoming a victim of the fast-approaching Allied pincer movement by land and water. Most of all, Cornwallis still counted upon British sea superiority, but this was no longer automatic like in the past. Unlike Clinton since June, he was unaware that Admiral Comte de Grasse's fleet had reinforced land and sea forces in Virginia. Therefore, Cornwallis remained stationary at Yorktown while hurriedly strengthening the defenses at a frantic pace, despite holding an increasingly vulnerable position with each passing day, while the formidable American and French forces drew ever-closer during the intense Virginia heat of late summer. Meanwhile, in New York City with around eleven thousand troops, Clinton continued to do nothing to reinforce Cornwallis by land or to pursue Washington and Rochambeau, who continued their steady southward advance without meeting any obstacle.[52]

The depth of Cornwallis's hubris and folly was revealed when he remained unflustered even by the arrival of the entire West Indies fleet under de Grasse and the landing of large numbers of French troops, because he had placed his faith on the power and prestige of the British Navy, which he was sure would rescue him in a timely manner. However, he was not aware that Washington had forsaken the idea of attacking New York City and was now headed south at a rapid pace. After all, Washington was never known to have previously embarked on such a fast-moving march of such vast strategic importance, which was Cornwallis's trademark style.

Fortunately, the strength of French arms, both naval and infantry, had been fully restored after the defeats of the Seven Years' War (America's French and Indian War), including the loss of New France (Canada), thanks in no small part to Rochambeau's tireless efforts. With the French Alliance now working smoothly like never before, Washington and his men could rely upon a most formidable ally.[53]

With high hopes, Hamilton and his troops, sailed down the broad Chesapeake Bay from the Head of Elk (the bay's northern tip located north of the port of Baltimore), Maryland, and safely reached the Chesapeake harbor of Annapolis, Maryland. Here, only about halfway to Yorktown, the Americans waited for the French warships to score the all-important victory over the English fleet from New York City out in the Atlantic's waters after Hood had linked with Graves on August 28 to shockingly discover that the entire French fleet was in the Chesapeake on September 5. Success at sea was vital because it had to be won before the French vessels could return to the Chesapeake to screen, ferry, and land troops on the Virginia Peninsula.[54]

While waiting at Annapolis, Hamilton became more reflective and philosophical, knowing that the fate of America and the lives of so many young men and boys had been arbitrarily dictated by a swirl of events well beyond their control. He might have felt guilty in having embarked upon a dangerous new campaign with a wife waiting for him at home or might even have had a dark premonition about his fate in this campaign.[55]

Decisive Naval Battle of the Virginia Capes

The superior French fleet then departed the Chesapeake with colorful banners waving in the wind to engage the British fleet. Under the bright September sunshine and with the late summer heat at its height, the naval forces of Graves and Comte de Grasse finally met off the Virginia Capes at the mouth of the Chesapeake Bay just off the Virginia coast.

Initially shocked at the sight of the anchored French fleet awaiting him at the entrance of the Chesapeake, Rear Admiral Thomas Graves was handicapped by the knowledge that he could not risk losing the British fleet, which would compromise the entire British position in North America, including vital New York City. This development further imperiled Cornwallis because his naval guardians were already under a severe disadvantage before the first shot had been fired.

This relatively brief encounter at the mouth of the Chesapeake was the most decisive naval battle of the Yorktown Campaign that could have been won by Graves if the naval action was not so mismanaged and if he had not been hampered by the aforementioned strategic concerns.

Proving he was not up to the challenge, Graves's badly managed attack proved ineffective, resulting in a relatively short (four hours) battle, especially as a decisive one. It took less time than a total sea battle in the traditional sense because the French were more focused on achieving a land success rather than one on water, while the British were focused on preserving the fleet needed elsewhere, especially at New York City. Nevertheless, Rear Admiral Graves squandered a very good opportunity to reap a victory over the French fleet on September 5.

Thereafter, the two fleets only maneuvered and shadowed each other because each had other more pressing priorities. Licking his relatively slight wounds (but personnel losses among the British seamen were high) from such an important battle at sea without sinking a single ship to the Atlantic's bottom, Graves refused to wholeheartedly engage the British fleet, which ensured that he would not move his fleet into the Chesapeake Bay to save Cornwallis. The French fleet sailed back to the bay's entrance to replace the cork in the bottle. All the while, Cornwallis continued to confidently believe that he would be saved by the British Navy.

The lengthy list of errors, poor judgements, and miscalculations committed by Graves, Clinton, and Cornwallis were unprecedented and, of course, all worked immensely in the allies' favor, while the team of Rochambeau, Washington, and the French Navy continued to work together in flawless fashion like a well-oiled machine making all the right decisions at the right time. Most important, the small French fleet, with its siege equipment and artillery under de Barras had departed Newport and escaped detection. De Grasse then sailed north and returned to the Chesapeake to reunite with de Barras. With the concentration of nearly forty warships, the French had gained an absolute superiority at sea to not only deter Graves but also everyone else. Cornwallis had no way of knowing that Rear Admiral Graves had decided to return to New York City instead of obeying his superior's orders to enter the bay and assist Cornwallis, who could not escape by sea and was left on his own.[56]

This crucial naval clash (although tactically indecisive but strategically crucial) of the Virginia Capes was not only the true turning point of the Yorktown Campaign but also the most important naval battle of the American Revolution. And, of course, Admiral de Grasse's bold decision to transport his entire fleet and large numbers of troops from the West Indies to the Chesapeake to catch British leadership by surprise had made it all possible. In his journal, surgeon Thacher described the importance of the high stakes naval battle and what it meant in overall strategic terms: "Should the British have obtained the victory, and should they get possession of the Chesapeake bay, we shall be unable to proceed on our voyage [down the Elk River to enter the head of Chesapeake Bay], and our expedition will be entirely defeated."[57]

Thacher shortly learned of the decisive French success just off the Virginia coast on September 15:

The gratifying intelligence is announced that the naval engagement between the two fleets has resulted in the defeat of the British with considerable loss, and the French have now the sole command of the Chesapeake bay [and] This event is of infinite importance, and fills our hearts of joy, as we can now proceed on our expedition.[58]

Indeed, the surprising French victory at the Battle of the Virginia Capes not only doomed Cornwallis and the overly ambitious plan of the conquest of the South, but also "cost them in war in America" in the end.[59]

But in fact, the relatively brief Battle of the Virginia Capes was only the last chapter of a monumental failure of British leadership at the highest levels, especially in regard to the Royal Navy that was thought to have been all but invincible. Indeed, Admiral de Grasse had benefitted from a good deal of luck because back in July,

Graves, commanding British navy units in New York, had gotten word that a big convoy of goods and supplies for the Patriots had sailed from Europe and that it was vital that it be intercepted. This caused Graves to put to sea with a sizeable fleet, confident that if the French struck north from the West Indies, Rodney and Hood would take care of them. In truth, Rodney and Hood tried [but not hard enough for fear of losing the fleet that would endanger British control, including New York City, of North America]. Rodney was ill and had turned over his command to Hood, urging him to intercept De Grasse [but] By a quirk of fate, Hood had sailed into the Chesapeake ahead of De Grasse and finding no enemy there had gone on to New York [and, therefore] Nobody [at all] took care of De Grasse—an error fatal to the fortunes of Lord Cornwallis.[60]

Indeed, "the Royal Navy had sailed away [and now] Cornwallis was left without a Union Jack in sight."[61] In the end to guarantee the safe arrival of Admiral de Barras and the heavy French siege guns, the Battle of the Capes proved to be "one of the most decisive military confrontations in the world's history [and] it may have decided the fate of the whole North American continent because it eliminated the possibility of either reinforcement or evacuation of Cornwallis's troops."[62]

But Washington's difficulties were still not over. Eager to capture the great prize of Jamaica in conjunction with his Spanish allies, Admiral de Grasse notified Washington on September 18 that he needed to depart the Chesapeake no later than October 15 and return to the West Indies because of strategic priorities. Worried that this timetable would allow Lord Cornwallis to escape, therefore, Washington boldly took the initiative. With Tench Tilghman and other trustworthy favorites, he personally visited the admiral's massive flagship *Ville de Paris* to engage in an impromptu conference, without Rochambeau's knowledge, to try to change de Grasse's mind. Washington's plan succeeded, with de Grasse agreeing to stay until the end of October before heading back to the Caribbean.[63]

As early as July 28, de Grasse had informed Rochambeau in no uncertain terms, "I shall not be able to use the soldiers long; they are under the orders of the Spanish who will need them" for the united offensive to capture Jamaica.[64]

Hamilton Keeping the Home Fires Alive

Still at the head of his troops, Lieutenant Colonel Hamilton was likewise jubilant with the good news of French naval superiority. On the same day as the French success, September 15, while at the Chesapeake port of Annapolis, Hamilton wrote a long letter to Betsey, but it was not a glowing one. It is not known but perhaps Hamilton, who was known for his mood swings, possessed a gloomy foreboding about his own fate in this campaign and experienced guilt from having chosen dangerous active service, while his young wife in Albany was worried to death about her new husband's fate. Or he might have just witnessed the deaths from disease of some of his battalion members, and then had attended their hasty burials in shallow graves at obscure places in the middle of nowhere far from homes and families. Had Hamilton made a tragic mistake in embarking upon one last campaign and risking his life once again in fighting what might be his country's last battle? During this period of uncertainty, Betsey continued to suffer from a good deal of stress over the situation. Perhaps at some point, she might even have wondered if marrying Hamilton had been a mistake now that she was pregnant with his child. After all, why was he not now with her when she needed him the most? What if he was killed in some reckless charge for no gain in a vain pursuit of glory? Betsey naturally worried that she might never see her husband again and become a widow at a young age.

In a long letter on September 6, Hamilton had attempted to ease his wife's anxiety and to bolster her faith for his safe return when an important success lingered on the horizon: "Cheer yourself with this idea, and with the assurance of never more being separated [because] Every day confirms me [of shortly] devoting myself wholly to you." But Betsey was not encouraged by Hamilton's somewhat cynical letter that reflected one of his periodic dark moods with Hamilton's trademark philosophical overtones:

> How chequered [checkered] is human life! How precarious is happiness! How easily do we often part with it for a shadow! These are the reflections that frequently intrude themselves upon me, with a painful application. I am going to do my duty. Our operations will be so conducted as to economize the lives of the men. Exert your fortitude and rely upon heaven.[65]

Betsey was indeed going through a more difficult time than Hamilton imagined. Consequently, General Philip Schuyler became increasingly concerned about his young daughter's overall condition and physical and mental welfare. About this same time, the well-respected New York general wrote a letter to Hamilton in which he lamented Betsey's disturbed emotional condition, because she "was so sensibly affected by your removal to the southward that I apprehended consequences." Fortunately, Betsey recovered in time, but slowly under severe physical and mental strain. General Schuyler then informed Hamilton that "she is now at ease" to calm the mind of his wayward son-in-law.[66]

Hamilton had only gradually broken the news that he was about to engage in a new campaign, employing considerable tact and care and disguising what he knew to be true.[67] Tench Tilghman, a handsome young man from a leading Maryland family of Talbot County on the Eastern Shore, had been enchanted by Betsey Schuyler before Hamilton had swept her off her feet. In light of the difficulties now experienced by her because of her husband's devotion to duty, Tilghman had been prophetic about the Hamilton-Betsey match when writing about their fast-paced and passionate relationship that led to marriage: "Alas poor Polly! Hamilton is a gone man, and I am too old [in his mid-thirties] for his substitute—She had better look out for herself and not put her trust in Man. She need not be jealous of the little Saint."[68]

In his journal, Tilghman had described an initial meeting with Hamilton's wife in August 1775:

I found none of them at home but Miss Betsey Schuyler the Generals 2nd daughter. . . . I was prepossessed in favor of this young Lady the moment I saw her. A Brunette with the most good natured lively dark eyes that I ever saw, which threw a beam of good temper and benevolence over her whole Countenance. Mr. [Robert] Livingston informed me . . . that she was the finest tempered Girl in the World.[69]

Bound for the Chesapeake and a Meeting with Lord Cornwallis!

After a week of anxiously waiting at Annapolis, Hamilton and his light battalion (the second battalion of General Moses Hazen's Brigade, Lafayette's Division, Light Corps), as the advanced guard, boarded one of de Grasse's ships—thankfully no longer the slow, clumsy transports that had brought them to the Maryland state capital on the Chesapeake, but sleek, fast-moving vessels by comparison—and headed for the Virginia Peninsula. After delays and mishaps and in keeping with their role of leading the way for the army as light troops, Hamilton and his men were among the first of Washington's troops that landed at Archer's Point or Archer's Hope (known today as College Landing) on a tributary of the James River only about a mile from Williamsburg. Here, on September 20, Hamilton and his men, with flintlock muskets on shoulders, went ashore on the low-lying grounds of the Virginia Peninsula and pushed toward Williamsburg, the location of William and Mary College, which was located just northwest of Yorktown. On September 10 Lieutenant Colonel Hamilton and his troops were encamped just outside the small village at College Landing, located not far from Williamsburg and northeast of Jamestown, on College Creek that flowed south into the James River. Hamilton was now reunited with his two best friends, the Marquis de Lafayette and John Laurens, and all three conversed in fluent rapid-fire French that Washington and the vast majority of Americans were entirely unable to understand. As a boy without expectations of any kind, Hamilton had first learned French from his mother Rachel Faucette on the tropical island of Nevis. Faucette was the daughter of French planter and physician John Faucette.

John Laurens, the young South Carolinian and son of Henry Laurens, one of the past presidents of the Continental Congress, had just returned from his successful diplomatic mission in France, where he had secured the invaluable French assistance. Laurens now served on the staff of the commander-in-chief that Hamilton had long desired to escape and succeeded in finally breaking away. Like Hamilton and every inch a fighter, Laurens was determined not to miss the upcoming action to decide America's fate, and he would be by Hamilton's side during what they viewed as another glorious adventure in battling for the cause of liberty—the daring assault on strategic Redoubt Number Ten in mid-October 1781.[70]

The *Pennsylvania Packet* correspondent with Lafayette's command described the overall strategic scenario and the thorough preparations for the descent southeast upon Yorktown:

> The light infantry [including Hamilton's command] are advanced to Williamsburgh; the Pennsylvanians lay near us, and it is the talk of the camp that the French troops will take their position to-morrow in its vicinity. The French ships lay in James River, to prevent a retreat in York River, and at the [Virginia] capes.[71]

After General Washington's arrival at Williamsburg, Hamilton made his usual good impression. He stood straight and tall in front of his battalion of light troops when they were reviewed by the dignified commander-in-chief, who never felt more confident for success than at this time.

Significantly, these were the officers and men of the crack Light Corps who were the ones that Washington had specifically picked to lead the way to Yorktown at the army's head. He had chosen Hamilton's old friend and King's College schoolmate Nicholas Fish as his second in command of the light infantry battalion, and a better choice could not have been made. Here, Hamilton also rejoiced in once again meeting his old teacher from the academy at Elizabethtown, New Jersey, thirty-year-old Lieutenant Colonel Francis Barber, who had been born in Princeton. Barber had served with distinction, having been wounded at the Battle of Monmouth. Only five years older than Hamilton, Barber had commanded New Jersey light infantry. This made him a worthy addition.

Meanwhile, additional American and French units continued to arrive by water during the third and last weeks of September to build up the muscle to be shortly directed against Lord Cornwallis. Cornwallis did nothing to impede the landings of thousands of American and French troops.[72]

Closing the Trap

With beaming confidence for future success, Washington and Rochambeau watched when "about four thousand French troops, with a train of artillery, marched into this city [Williamsburg] a Tuesday last from the northward."[73] By September 26, American and French forces—around 16,500 troops—were all united as one around Williamsburg in the balmy weather of early autumn with a single purpose: the destruction of Cornwallis and his army. A journalist from the army's encampment wrote the following:

> The American army and their allies, near Williamsburg . . . formed the line of battle to-day. To-morrow morning they expect to march to a position near York, to commence a siege. They made a brilliant appearance as to numbers, and are fifteen thousand strong, not including the Virginia militia [and] We congratulate our friends upon the prospect of reducing his lordship, and restoring peace and liberty to our country.[74]

Washington and Rochambeau realized that fighting could begin at any moment because the aggressive and unpredictable Cornwallis might launch a desperate offensive effort to break out of the trap.

Washington established the official order of battle on September 27. During the upcoming advance slightly southeast from Williamsburg toward Yorktown situated on the south bank of the York River, Hamilton's light troops, like other men of the Light Corps, were assigned to leading the advance on Yorktown as the allied army's right wing of around fifty-five hundred Continental troops and around three thousand Virginia militiamen. These Virginia veterans from the backcountry, who fought the Battle of Kings Mountain in early October 1780, were deadly riflemen armed with the Long Rifle. Meanwhile, Rochambeau's left wing consisted of the French expeditionary force, which had journeyed around 650 miles across country, starting in Rhode Island, to play their dominant role at Yorktown. All in all, the allied army was most formidable at around 16,500 men, the largest force ever commanded by Washington, as Rochambeau continued to allow the Virginian to command, as specified by King Louis XVI.

On September 28 Washington's troops marched out of Williamsburg with flags flying and drums beating in the early fall sunshine in the Virginia Tidewater. The veteran Continentals headed slightly southeast along the sandy road, lined by thick woodlands of the peninsula covering the level ground on each side, leading toward Cornwallis and Yorktown. With flintlocks on shoulders, including excellent weapons made in France courtesy of shipments from King Louis XVI, Washington's seasoned men moved onward with a jaunty step through the late summer heat of the sweltering Virginia lowlands.

Now viewing unfamiliar Virginia Tidewater not previously seen by him, Lieutenant Colonel Hamilton detested the monotony of the dreary landscape, consisting of flatlands covered by tangled brush that had never been cleared. Despite the site of the first English settlement of Jamestown, this low-lying country was still very much a wilderness area. Here, the terrain was poorly drained and swampy, where giant cypress trees—with their broad bases that began to widen underwater—towered high. Only an occasional small clearing had been hacked out of the dense forests by slaves or poor white settlers to raise a meager crop of tobacco planted and harvested by black enslaved people.[75]

These conditions guaranteed the rise of sickness in the days ahead for the men of Hamilton's battalion and the army in general. Like the men in the ranks, physician James Thacker, born and raised in Massachusetts where plenty of fresh water springs abounded unlike the swampy lowlands on the Virginia Peninsula, complained how the "water in this vicinity is extremely brackish and disagreeable [and] This part of the state of Virginia is celebrated for their excellent tobacco which it produces."[76]

Meanwhile, Hamilton sometimes missed his old friends at Washington's headquarters. In Hamilton's absence, the commander-in-chief was most fortunate during the war's most critical campaign to have the following officers on his staff. He continued to benefit from the excellent services of some very good aide-de-camps for the chore of operating the army at a high rate of efficiency. South Carolina's John Laurens, whose recent efforts to secure additional French assistance, manpower, and financial had proved crucial for the war effort, had been partly fueled by his burning desire, like Hamilton, to return to active service as soon as possible. Maryland's hard-working Tilghman who was convinced by early 1779 that America had already advanced in pure republican virtues more than the "old musty [ancient] Republics of Greece and Rome." David Cobb was a bright, hard-working physician from Massachusetts. David Humphreys of Connecticut, had been serving in the "family" since June 1780. New York's William S. Smith was destined to marry a pretty daughter of John Adams, one of the leading founding fathers from Boston.[77]

Fated to be the longest serving staff officer for the austere Virginian, Tilghman was the only member of Washington's "family" who served there when Hamilton had joined it on March 1, 1777.[78]

Highly Motivated French Fighting Men

Now advancing from Williamsburg as the left column during the descent upon Yorktown, Rochambeau and his generals of the expeditionary force were likewise capably supported by invaluable staff officers. A trained military engineer with a talent for map-making and an abundance of other skills, Louis-Alexandre Berthier, who had joined Rochambeau's expedition force along with his brother, Charles-Louis, as soon as he had learned about the mission to save America, was among the best of these well-educated professionals of the French

Army. He now served on the quartermaster general's staff as the best cartographer in the army. Like Adjutant General Colonel Thomas Pickering, who was no longer a member of Washington's staff officers and who helped orchestrate the American Army's movements in advance to Virginia, Berthier had planned and mapped out the lengthy route of the French Army's march south to Virginia while also leading one of the three French columns. With advanced knowledge about the terrain and route and blessed with a topographer's eye, Berthier had guided one of the French divisions on the march south. He now possessed the main campaign map designating the route of the march. Berthier also preformed duties comparable to Hamilton when he had served as Washington's chief-of-staff. A personal friend of the Marquis de Lafayette, young Berthier became Napoleon Bonaparte's legendary model chief of staff second to none during the Napoleonic Wars. Like Hamilton had been for years to Washington, so the brilliant Berthier became Napoleon's invaluable right-hand man at headquarters during one campaign after another when he became the master of most of Western Europe.[79]

As usual, Napoleon said it best in regard to the incomparable Berthier, whose contributions had long made the ambitious native Corsican an even better general: "There was not in the world a better chief of staff, that is where his true talent lay, for he was not capable of commanding 500 men." In this last regard, Berthier was the antithesis of Hamilton, who had already proved himself to be a highly capable leader of troops—both infantry or artillery—during active campaigning and in key battlefield situations.[80]

What was the average French fighting man in the enlisted ranks of commands, as in the Bourbonnais Regiment (officially the Thirteenth Regiment) and the Agenois Regiment, really like? Who were the Frenchmen from the peasant class who fought and died for America? These French fighting men have too often remained anonymous in the books of American historians, almost as if they did not exist. Their outsized contributions should place them in the spotlight. Perhaps none, other than black soldiers who served in the ranks of

Washington's Continental Army and Hamilton's own light battalion, have been less acknowledged and understood than the average French soldier. Interestingly, far more American soldiers were married men, unlike the French fighting men, who were single in part because of their long terms of service.

Private Hans Stiegel, of German heritage, served in the Despenan Company of the Touraine Regiment, consisting of two battalions and under the command of Colonel Vicomte de Pondeux of Rochambeau's expeditionary force. He hailed from the little village of Kertzfeld. His native homeland was the fertile region located along the French-German border of the Alsace region situated on the banks of the majestic Rhine River—the historic boundary between the Gallic and Teutonic nations. Stiegel not only fought for America's liberty during Yorktown but also died of disease not long after the surrender of Cornwallis's Army, breathing his last in November 1781. To this day and like so many other French soldiers, the final resting place of Private Stiegel, who had changed his first name to Jean and served as a member of the St. Domingue (today's Haiti) contingent of three regiments, on American soil is only known to God.

Named after his father, Hans, when he was born in 1762, Stiegel was a Catholic, which reflected his German heritage and the region from which he hailed. The son of a humble shepherd of a small rural town and farming community, he was baptized and worshiped at Kertfeld's small Catholic Church amid a pastoral countryside of immense natural beauty. A member of the lower class, Stiegel's boyhood days were spent in the fields performing manual labor, mostly farm work like almost everyone else in the community. Receiving a nice bonus at age twenty, he signed enlistment papers in the fall of 1777 for a period of eight years, when a German-speaking recruiter of the French Army came to town in the hunt for young recruits. Like Stiegel, a large number of German-speaking men served in Rochambeau's expeditionary force. Here, during America's most climactic showdown, they fought against the German Hessians of

Cornwallis's Army in what was a mini-civil war among the Teutonic fighting men far from home.[81]

Like so many other Americans, one Pennsylvania soldier described the French soldiers in complimentary terms, observing a quality that made them some of France's best fighters: "The French Troops [are] in general young men but old in service."[82] Louis-Francois-Bertrand, the Count of Lauberdiere—schooled at a Paris military academy, a respected member of Rochambeau's personal staff, and the general's own nephew—hailed from a distinguished noble family, which traced its military heroics to distinguished ancestors who had fought in the Holy Land during the Crusades. He was only age twenty-one when he served during the Yorktown Campaign, battling for both France and America.[83]

Young Lauberdiere correctly viewed General Rochambeau's leading role as nothing less than America's savior. The young man explained that the French had saved the day for America in her hour of greatest need, because the rustic, ill-trained revolutionaries under Washington had already "suffered great losses [in part because they] believed the war would only last a short time [and had become] tired of it and faltered daily," until they were clearly losing the war by the beginning of 1781.[84] He was amazed at the republican nature and stoic bearing of Washington and his men: "There is no pomp of a marshal of France when orders are given but rather the grandeur, nobility and, as the same time, the simplicity due to a general of a poor republic."[85]

This overall impoverishment of Washington's soldiers and the army's severe manpower shortage were evident in what Lauberdiere saw during a review conducted by Washington. At that time, he was especially impressed by the sight of a new kind of fighting man who was motivated by selflessness and was inspired by the republican faith: "There are some very handsome men in all their regiments. We also see Negroes and mulattos" in the American Army.[86]

At this time, confidence and spirits had never been higher in Washington's Continental Army, because seemingly everyone, black and white, believed that decisive victory was on the horizon. Diehard

Continental soldiers like Tench Tilghman had kept the faith year after year, praying to God for the survival of the young republic. In the Marylander's words from a past letter that revealed his optimism and hopes for a bright future for the infant republic, "I am certain [that this war] will end in the Freedom of this Country which I hope to see a happy and settled one."[87]

Young Lieutenant Colonel Hamilton Reinvigorated

Hamilton's spirits remained high, despite the fact that he was now marching ever farther away from his beloved Elizabeth and Albany. He was determined to make the most of the opportunity just as he had taken advantage of the opportunity to lead his New York Battery with distinction and then to work for years by Washington's side at headquarters, which was the Continental Army's nerve center.[88]

Because Hamilton was imbued with the heady ideology of the Age of Enlightenment, his faith in America's sacred cause and the gospel of republicanism never wavered. Even during some of the revolution's darkest days when he labored on Washington's staff, Hamilton had earlier written to his friend John Jay of his personal philosophy about how, when facing severe adversity, it is necessary for one to always try harder: "We must not be discouraged at a misfortune [and] We must rather exert ourselves the more vigorously to remedy the ill consequences of it."[89]

Hamilton's undying faith was about to pay high dividends at long last.

"To break out of his coffin," Cornwallis had planned to charge up the Virginia Peninsula and hit Lafayette's command from the front and rear in keeping with his aggressive instincts. However, at the last minute, he had received new instructions from Clinton, who promised the arrival of British warships "any day." General Clinton's encouraging words had caused Cornwallis to cancel his ambitious plans of striking the Marquis de Lafayette—another tactical mistake.

The correspondent of the *Pennsylvania Packet*, a proud member of Washington's Army, described the final, unopposed descent upon Yorktown: "On Friday, September 28th, the whole army marched southeast from Williamsburg," with colorful flags flying and high hopes for nabbing Cornwallis and his entire army.[90]

On this same day, Hamilton and his well-trained troops of Lafayette's Light Corps drew ever closer to Yorktown.[91] By this time, this war had become a personal one between Cornwallis and Washington and his homespun Americans in part because they had for so long feared Cornwallis as a heartless British aristocrat. In the angry words of one patriot soldier, "The history of our transactions in Georgia and the Carolinas is a history of cruelty and injustice, unparalleled in the annals of civilized nations."[92]

This harsh view was no exaggeration because of the horrors stemming from the guerrilla warfare that had consumed the South with a vengeance. During the height of his futile attempt to harshly control South Carolina as partisans engaged in guerrilla warfare, Cornwallis wrote the following:

> I have given orders that all Inhabitants of this province who have subscribed and have taken part in this Revolt, should be punished with the greatest rigour, and also those who will not turn out [to sign the oath of allegiance] that they may be imprisoned, and their whole property taken from them or destroyed [and] I have ordered in the most Positive Manner that every [Loyalist] Militia Man who has borne arms with us and afterwards joined the enemy shall be immediately hanged.[93]

More complimentary and giving his lordship his just due, another American described Cornwallis as an "evil genius" because he was Great Britain's finest and most aggressive field commander and got results.[94] If Cornwallis was an evil genius, then Rochambeau represented America's guardian angel. However, King Louis XVI was destined to pay with his head, like his wife Marie Antoinette, during the French Revolution for his lavish spending and support for America—France was the first nation to officially recognize American independence with the Franco-American Alliance of 1778—that would hurl France into the dark depths of bankruptcy, instability, and turmoil.

The Gods of War seemed to be smiling on America and Rochambeau during this final campaign. For instance, in the words of one of Rochambeau's staff officers who was a member of one of France's noble families of the aristocracy, "We almost lost Mr. Rochambeau who, during the [early] reconnaissance [of Yorktown], took a map from his pocket. He was on foot on a small hill, his legs spread apart. A ball was fired which buried itself more than 2 feet in the ground between his legs."[95] Most of all, it was the supreme irony, and a most bitter one for Cornwallis, that "Britain's ablest and most aggressive field commander, was fated to spend the last months of his luckless campaign burrowing, mole-like, to resist the siege of Yorktown" against three times as many fighting men than he possessed, after the British Army had been steadily depleted, both army and navy, due to being severely overstretched by global commitments.[96]

Indeed, what had happened in only a few weeks of campaigning was astonishing: "The situation thus presented was the great surprise of the Revolution," because "Clinton is quietly left in the lurch at New York; Washington boldly marches four hundred miles away, and suddenly falls upon his famous lieutenant at a point where assistance cannot reach him."[97] Here, at the little port of Yorktown would be decided "the futures of a nation and an empire" in short order during the autumn of 1781.[98]

Located thirteen miles slightly southeast of Williamsburg and northeast of Jamestown on the south bank of the York River which served as the northern border of the Virginia Peninsula, Yorktown was a sleepy village on a thin point of mostly sandy land that stretched out in the waters of Chesapeake Bay. Safe from periodic flooding because of its elevation, this quaint town that had lost its former glory stood on river bluffs that overlooked the wide (barely less than a mile across at this point) tidal estuary of the York River that led to the Chesapeake Bay near its entry into the Atlantic's seemingly endless vastness that extended to the horizon.

Instead of attempting to escape the encroaching entrapment on the Virginia Peninsula in his mistaken belief that British superiority at sea was still unchallenged, Cornwallis had made his final decision of standing firm in a place entirely inappropriate and unsuitable for making a last stand. After taking up headquarters in governor of Virginia Thomas Nelson Jr.'s house of brick in Yorktown, Cornwallis still believed that he possessed ample time even though Washington and Rochambeau had closed in. However, with plenty of slave labor (around two thousand black people) collected from nearby tobacco and cotton plantations, he had possessed time since early August to prepare an extensive outer defensive line, based on a series of strong redoubts as outlined by talented British engineers, around the town.

With the Chesapeake blocked by French warships to eliminate his escape route by water, Cornwallis had no choice but to stand and fight, despite the fact that his long line of defenses was still unfinished. His final decision had been based on his faith that Admiral Graves would return from New York City and that Clinton, who had informed Cornwallis that relief by sea would reach Yorktown on October 5, would keep his promise.

But in truth, Lord Cornwallis had placed his faith in the wrong men at the wrong time. Cornwallis had been feuding with Clinton for so long that plenty of bad blood existed between the two men by this time. An unprecedented amount of British incompetence, so uncharacteristic of a well-honed war machine, guaranteed that no assistance would be forthcoming in time. But most of all, he had placed his faith in the wrong strategy from the beginning of his overly ambitious campaign to vanquish the South in his desperation to win it all—the shaky premise and ill-fated belief that decisive victory could be won in Virginia, which he considered the key to conquering the South and even farther north, if everything went according to the ambitious plan that had left no margin for error.

In the extensive defensive ring surrounding three-quarters of the old tobacco port, the strongest redoubts of Cornwallis's defensive network were situated along the York River located just southeast of town on his left, Redoubts Number Nine and Number Ten. Positioned in advance about two hundred to three hundred yards south of the inner defensive line to protect the left flank that connected to the York River, these two strong redoubts, or earthen bastions, stood close to each other (separated by 330 yards) to provide mutual support. At the farthest point on the left next to the river and situated just northeast of Redoubt Number Nine, the imposing Redoubt Number Ten, defended with four howitzers and three mortars, was the key to the entire sprawling defensive line nestled along the York River. However, because of its larger size (although less important than its sister redoubt to the northeast), Redoubt Number Nine possessed more than double the artillery of its neighboring redoubt near the river's south bank.

In total, Cornwallis, whose troops and thousands of slaves had been busily entrenching since August 2, had constructed ten redoubts along his outer defensive line. Meanwhile, on Lord Cornwallis's right, the Star (or Fusilier) Redoubt was situated on an open ridge that overlooked the river northwest of town. Located in the most strategic positions to protect Cornwallis's flanks, these three powerful redoubts guarded the coastal approaches to the town from two directions.[99]

Even from a distance, the British earthworks appeared formidable upon first sight to the Americans upon their arrival. Safely out of range of the rows of British cannon at this time, surgeon James Thacher described in his journal on September 27, "We arrived at Yorktown yesterday from Jamestown, and have encamped within one mile of the enemy's line of redoubts."[100] The *Pennsylvania Packet* correspondent wrote that the entire army reached a point "within one mile of the enemy's works at York[town], and formed the first line of circumvallation without any loss," which was taken as a good omen

Painting by Alonzo Chappel that depicts a pensive Alexander Hamilton standing in the trenches of Yorktown, Virginia, during the most eventful autumn of his life in October 1781. (*Wikimedia Commons*; Painting by Alonzo Chappel)

Sketch of a mature Alexander Hamilton. He served with distinction as the first secretary of the Treasury in United States history during the administration of President George Washington. Hamilton was the gifted right-hand man of President Washington at the nation's capital, like during the war years when he served as chief of staff. (*Wikimedia Commons*; From *The Century Book of Famous Americans: The Story of a Young People's Pilgrimage to Historic Homes* by Elbridge Streeter Brooks)

General George Washington in his prime. The Virginian from the Tidewater finally achieved his great goal of reaping decisive victory when the allies captured Yorktown in October 1781. (*Wikimedia Commons*; *George Washington Before the Battle of Trenton*, Courtesy of the Yale University Art Gallery)

Jean-Baptiste-Donatien de Vimeur, Comte de Rochambeau. He was the brilliant commander of the formidable French expeditionary force at Yorktown, while Washington commanded the American and French army. He was an experienced master in the art of siege warfare from decades of excellent service in Europe. (*Wikimedia Commons*; *Jean-Baptiste Donatien de Vimeur, Comte de Rochambeau, Marechal De France (1725-1807)*, Palace of Versailles)

Lord Charles Cornwallis was the finest British commander in North America. It, therefore, was a supreme irony that his army became trapped at Yorktown when Cornwallis followed the orders of his superior Sir Henry Clinton in faraway New York City. Cornwallis was promised reinforcements and relief from New York City that never arrived. (*Wikimedia Commons*; National Portrait Gallery)

Alexander Hamilton's closest friend, the irrepressible Lieutenant Colonel John Laurens, who served as a fellow staff officer with Hamilton under General Washington for years. Laurens possessed the key mission of striking the rear of Redoubt Number Ten on October 14. The South Carolina blueblood died heroically during an obscure skirmish in his native state on August 27, 1782, near the war's end. Charles Willson Peale's fine painting has revealed the best likeness of Laurens. (*Wikimedia Commons*; National Portrait Gallery)

Alexander Hamilton led the charge of his crack Continental troops on strategic Redoubt
Number Ten on the night of October 14, 1781. Hamilton's capture of it, located on the
British left flank next to the York River, was a key factor that caused Lord Cornwallis
to surrender the town and garrison in the most decisive allied victory of the American
Revolution to ensure the independence of the United States of America. (*Wikimedia
Commons*; U. S. Army Center of Military History, United States Army)

Today's reconstructed Redoubt Number Ten on the Yorktown battlefield.

(U.S. Army Heritage and Education Center)

The British defender's view looking south from the high parapet of Redoubt Number Ten.
(U.S. Army Heritage and Education Center)

The parapet of Redoubt Number Ten from the view of Hamilton and his attacking
Continental light troops on October 14. (U.S. Army Heritage and Education Center)

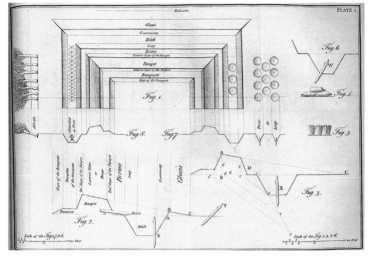

An engineer's plate of the outlines and dimensions of Redoubt Number Ten. (U.S. Army Heritage and Education Center)

Hand-constructed and portable defensive gabions employed by the British in the defense of Redoubt Number Ten. (U.S. Army Heritage and Education Center)

Side view of the daunting slope of Redoubt Number Ten as seen by Hamilton and his men when they overran the powerful defensive bastion. (U.S. Army Heritage and Education Center)

One of the British naval guns employed in the Yorktown defenses on Lord Cornwallis's orders. (U.S. Army Heritage and Education Center)

One of the French mortars that proved so deadly and effective during the siege of Yorktown. Washington's Continental Army possessed no such mortars. (U.S. Army Heritage and Education Center)

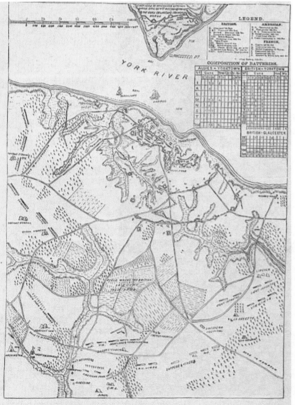

Map of the siege of Yorktown. (U.S. Army Heritage and Education Center)

The surrender of Lord Cornwallis's Army at Yorktown when "the world was turned upside down" in the famous painting by John Trumbull. (*Wikimedia Commons*; *Surrender of Lord Cornwallis*, Rotunda of the U.S. Capitol)

Detail from the John Trumbull painting of Cornwallis's surrender. Alexander Hamilton is depicted standing first in line among Washington's top lieutenants during the surrender ceremony at Yorktown. (*Wikimedia Commons*; Detail of the *Surrender of Lord Cornwallis*, Rotunda of the U.S. Capitol)

Beautiful Elizabeth Schuyler-Hamilton, the love of
Hamilton's life. She was at home pregnant with their
first child, Philip Hamilton, in Albany, New York, when
Hamilton was leading the charge on Redoubt Number Ten.
(*Wikimedia Commons*; *Portrait of Mrs. Eliza Schuyler Hamilton* by Ralph
Earl, Museum of the City of New York)

General Philip Schuyler, father of Elizabeth, who
loved Hamilton like a son. (*Wikimedia Commons*;
Painted by Jacob H. Lazarus (1822-91) from a miniature
painted by John Trumbull; Schuyler Mansion State Historic
Site, Albany)

by the men in the ranks for a successful reducing of the defenses and ending the career of Lord Cornwallis.[101]

With his lengthy eyeglass used by naval officers at sea, Washington surveyed the wide field of low-lying ground before the bluffs that rose along the south bank of York River, staring at the recently constructed earthen redoubts that dominated the level, barren landscape, which had been cleared for open fields of fire. General Washington was familiar with Yorktown from having visited the then-bustling tobacco town in his youth, so he knew the general lay of the land more intimately than most of his men, including his top lieutenants, and, of course, the French. As part of the first step of closing the trap, Washington aligned his troops to the right of the French in a lengthy line to cover a wide front about a mile from Cornwallis's defensive line now bristling with more than sixty artillery pieces. The Allies were divided into two wings: the French right faced Redoubt Number Three and all the way northwest to Redoubt Number One and beyond to Cornwallis's right, while the American sector spanned from Redoubt Number Four to Redoubt Number Ten that anchored the defensive line's left, southeast of Yorktown. More than sixteen thousand allied troops had been carefully placed in positions to begin a lengthy siege to eventually squeeze the life out of Yorktown.

Cornwallis was now entirely boxed in and completely surrounded on the land side, where he, ironically, had initially least expected an attack in the beginning. Meanwhile, "the flower of the French infantry," which contained many veterans of European siege warfare unlike the rookie Americans, including General Washington, effectively covered a longer area of the front than the Americans, while situated on the center and left, or west, of the crescent-shaped line of the allies. Three regiments—Touraine, Gatenois, Agenois—of around three thousand seasoned French troops from the St. Domingue garrison, who Admiral de Grasse had originally disembarked to reinforce Lafayette before the arrival of Washington and Rochambeau, were positioned on the far northwest, while Rochambeau's Army proper was situated between the West Indies regiments, under Vicomet de

Pondeux, and the Americans. The wisdom of General Rochambeau, a savvy veteran of more than a dozen sieges in Europe, rose to the fore from the beginning, ensuring that no American or French infantry assaults were launched before the arrival of the heavy French siege guns, including deadly mortars, that had been transported from Newport by Admiral Barras, while the first parallel line began to be dug by the book in a traditional siege operation.[102]

Indeed, the siege of Yorktown was orchestrated in masterful fashion by Rochambeau, age fifty-two, whose skills in the arts of siege warfare had been well-honed after decades (thirty-seven years of outstanding military service compared to Washington's barely five years) of serving France and the king since age sixteen, while Washington, who was seven years younger than the debonair and talented French commander, had been a Virginia planter, militia officer, and politician for more than thirty of those years. Young Lauberdiere, a privileged nobleman on the general's staff who was also Rochambeau's nephew, faithfully recorded the dramatic course of events at Yorktown. In almost disbelieving words, he revealed the undeniable true story behind the eventual success at Yorktown that has been often left out of the history books written by American nationalist historians, who had long minimized the French contribution, almost as if the victory at Yorktown was Washington's sole achievement: "General Washington had never conducted a siege and could not have any knowledge of this matter other than what he might acquire through careful thought [and] Rochambeau took direction of the siege" from the beginning.[103]

In his journal, surgeon Thacher wrote with delight about the entrapment of an entire British-Hessian-Loyalist Army on September 28:

> Yorktown is situated on the south bank of the [York] river, about fifteen miles from its entrance into Chesapeake bay [and Lord Cornwallis's] communication by water is entirely cut off by the French ships of war stationed at the mouth

of the river, preventing both his escape and receiving succor from Sir Henry Clinton at New York.[104]

Then, continuing a trend of poor decision-making among British leadership at the highest levels, Cornwallis made still another key miscalculation. On the night of September 29, instead of attempting to break out, or sortie, as was customary during traditional siege warfare to keep the Americans and French at bay, he abandoned his outworks (seven redoubts in total except Redoubts Number Nine and Ten that were situated on the left southeast of town and the Fusilier Redoubt on the right flank), which had been established in a broad semicircle about a mile before Yorktown—basically an outer defensive line. With this ill-advised decision of retiring into his inner defensive line that considerably shortened and constricted his front, Cornwallis drastically reduced the possibilities of holding out in time for the arrival of Clinton's anticipated reinforcements by several days at least and perhaps longer.

On the morning of September 30, consequently, the Americans could hardly believe their eyes with the realization that Cornwallis had abandoned his outer defensive line except Redoubts Number Nine and Ten and the Fusilier Redoubt, which continued to stand firm on the horizon in a threatening manner. However, according to his tactical reasoning, Cornwallis had only retired closer to the town to consolidate his defensive stance and make it stronger by shortening his defensive line based on the increasingly flimsy premise that Clinton's promised reinforcements (scheduled to arrive on October 5) from New York City would arrive in time to save the day.

However, Cornwallis had gambled once again. He had now left himself no margin for error in abandoning his outer defensive line, thinking too optimistically, if not naively. Cornwallis could never quite understand that it was a new day and now French naval superiority had already doomed him and his army. He had also retired to his inner line because of the overall weakness of his defending force, which had been decimated by disease and heavy losses like in the bloody clash at Guilford Courthouse, North Carolina. In truth, all prospects for survival were rapidly diminishing around his lordship with each passing day until nothing would remain except hopes and prayers that would never be answered. Unfortunately for him because of his increasingly desperate situation, Lord Cornwallis continued to believe in the abilities and honor-bound duties of Clinton and Admiral Graves, who were not worthy of such blind faith, and especially the legendary power of the British Navy.[105]

General Anthony Wayne quite correctly found a perfect historical analogy between Cornwallis's dire situation and that of the Swedish King Charles XII at Poltava, when he led the Swedish Army of Europe's most powerful empire of the day deep into modern-day Ukraine, where he had advanced too far from support and safety with the day's best fighting men, on July 8, 1709. In a most revealing letter to Joseph Reed, Wayne wrote with a cocky confidence how the

reduction of that [British] army will require time and some expense of blood, for we cannot expect that Lord Cornwallis will tacitly surrender 6000 combatants, without many a severe *sortie*—his political and military character are now at stake—he has led the British king and ministry into a deception by assuring them of the subjection of the Carolinas, and his manoeuvre into Virginia was a child of his own creation, which he will attempt to nourish at every risk and consequence—he is now in full as desperate a situation as his namesake Charles at Pultowa [*sic*]. I have for some time viewed him as a fiery meteor that displays a momentary lustre, then falls—to rise no more.[106]

With time of the essence because of Admiral de Grasse's planned November 1 departure, Lord Cornwallis, of course, should have been focused more on a lengthy defense of Yorktown rather than the overly optimistic expectations of the soon-to-arrive reinforcements. Most of all, he should have earlier attempted a desperate breakout.[107]

The correspondent of the *Pennsylvania Packet* described Cornwallis's most recent key tactical mistake with some astonishment and one for which he was about to pay dearly, writing, "On the 29th the Americans had a few skirmishes with the enemy, but little damage done on either side. In the night the British evacuated Pigeon Quarter, and three other redoubts, which are so high as to be able to command the town."[108]

But Cornwallis still attempted no breakout as fully anticipated by Washington and Rochambeau as a standard feature of siege warfare. However, he was not thinking long-term. Cornwallis was only concerned about the short-term at a time when he was outnumbered by more than two to one.

However, the relief that Clinton had optimistically informed Cornwallis would arrive on Friday October 5 departed New York City a week later than promised. Lord Cornwallis was now on his own to make the best out of an impossible situation, remaining passive day after day. During one of the war's most monumental examples of leadership dysfunctionality that was comparable to the Saratoga fiasco, when the comparable folly of Generals William Howe and John Burgoyne had led the way to disaster in upper New York during the decisive fall of 1777, Clinton and the Royal Navy had failed Cornwallis, who had likewise failed himself.[109]

Overly fearful about the considerable weakness of his garrison and especially his left flank, despite Redoubts Number Nine and Ten, Lord Cornwallis's folly of abandoning his outer works that hastened his dismal end only emboldened the around sixteen thousand American and French besiegers, who began to even more vividly envision an inglorious end for an entire British Army of around eight thousand men.[110]

On September 30, like his disbelieving comrades, surgeon Thacher was incredulous by the sudden and seemingly inexplicable tactical developments committed by Cornwallis that ultimately went against his best interests: "We are agreeably surprised this morning, to find that the enemy had, during the preceding night [and] retired within the town, leaving a considerable extent of commanding ground, which might have cost us much labor and many lives to obtain by force."[111] Sensing that Lord Cornwallis was now doomed, Massachusetts-born Sergeant Joseph Plumb Martin, a seasoned Continental since the 1776 battles around New York City, wrote, "Nothing remained but to dig him out [and] Accordingly, [we made] every precaution to prevent his escape" from the trap.[112]

The *Pennsylvania Packet* correspondent revealed the extent of Cornwallis's folly. These key defensive positions were

> taken possession of on Sunday morning at sunrise, under a heavy cannonade from Yorktown. The enemy next fled from a stockade, when the French grenadiers had advanced within fifteen yards of it, and retreated under cover of their shipping [and now] It was expected our troops would break ground [the first parallel] on the 1st instant. Cornwallis's forces in York[town] are supposed to be six thousand troops, including refugees, besides one thousand armed Negroes. He has possession of the river and Gloucester [on the York River's other side], strongly fortified and garrisoned by about one thousand men. . . . The easy capture of the outposts will greatly accelerate the future operations of our army.[113]

The Arrival of French Siege Guns

Finally, the eagerly awaited French siege guns, eighteen-pounders, mortars, and twenty-four-pounders, arrived to additionally seal Cornwallis's fate, after having departed Newport on August 25. They had been brought all the way by the warships of Admiral Comte de Barras, who had acted immediately upon receiving Rochambeau's orders to bring the siege guns that he had left behind in Rhode Island and to join him and Washington as soon as possible, after the French squadron had slipped past numerous British warships and vessels of two British admirals, Graves and Hood. The timely arrival of his light squadron of eight vessels in the Chesapeake just after the Battle of the Virginia Capes had been crucial for decisive success at Yorktown.

These heavy guns were about to severely pound the defenses and Cornwallis, who had no adequate answer to such a heavy arsenal.

The harrowing story of Admiral Barras's timely arrival was another remarkable development in a lengthy list of minor miracles with broad implications for the final showdown at Yorktown. Thanks to the French naval victory at the Virginia Capes having provided the golden opportunity for their safe arrival, these large-caliber and heavy siege guns had been unloaded with great effort at Trebell's Landing on the north shore of the turbid James River half a dozen miles to the south of Yorktown on Monday, October 1.

Now Cornwallis's lengthy line of defenses, hastily constructed around Yorktown from sandy soil (considerably less durable than heavier top soil farther inland) could shortly be systematically demolished. Some of the finest French artillery officers of Rochambeau's Army had been educated at the prestigious Metz artillery school, and they knew their long-arm business extremely well, benefiting from years of experience during European campaigns.

The Siege Progresses

Led by veteran French officers beginning on October 6 when French engineers supervised the digging of two trenches, the siege of Yorktown was conducted methodically with textbook precision by Rochambeau. As noted, Cornwallis and his men, who believed that the French had brought no siege artillery with them, which was true in regard to Rochambeau's forces, were in for a nasty surprise with Barras's timely arrival with the big guns, which dramatically changed the overall equation of the siege of Yorktown.[114]

Long overlooked by historians, the small, but effective, American "corps of sappers and miners" also played key roles throughout the siege, including during the upcoming assault on Redoubt Number Ten. Rochambeau's young nephew and aide-de-camp praised these forgotten Americans, who "seemed very fine [and are] not part of the artillery; it is under the command of the officers of the Corps of Engineers."[115]

Massachusetts Sergeant Joseph Plumb Martin, only age twenty and serving in the Continental Army's sappers and miners contingent, described the night of October 6:

> We this night completed laying out the works. The troops of the line were there ready with entrenching tools and began to entrench exactly where French engineers had designated, after George Washington had struck a few blows with a pickaxe, a mere symbolic ceremony, that it might be said "Gen. Washington with his own hands first broke ground at the siege of Yorktown."[116]

After much physical effort by around fifteen hundred American soldiers who worked rapidly in rotating shifts in the darkness, the first trench, or parallel, was nearly finished on the night of October 6–7. An inky darkness and rainy weather of early autumn in the Virginia Tidewater, driven by a light southeast breeze, provided a protective screen for the sweaty diggers. The first parallel significantly reduced the distance between the allies' first defensive line and Yorktown's inner defenses, tightening the noose around Cornwallis's Army. Completed in record time before dawn for safety's sake, this new trench extended for a distance of around two thousand yards, shocking British and Hessian defenders.[117]

Washington ordered his elite troops of Lafayette's Division (Light Corps) to occupy the new advanced position in an appropriate tribute of their prowess and capabilities as Washington's finest men.[118] After the long march south through scorching summer weather, some men of Lafayette's Light Corps looked in bad shape. Fortunately, however, looks were deceiving because these were Washington's best troops— experienced, tough, and hardy. In the words of one French officer, who was shocked by the amount of wear and tear that had been suffered by Washington's crack light troops, "It came out with little clothing, and their marches by the time they reached Virginia left the poor fellows almost naked."[119]

Lieutenant Colonel Hamilton's exact thoughts in regard to the overall bad shape of his light troops have not been recorded, but he had less reason for concern than the commanders of the nonlight troops. However, Hamilton knew that he needed to do something to raise the morale of his men, because of the extent of their weariness and overall jaded condition from the march of around 450 miles. Because Hamilton's troops were newly organized, they were better uniformed than the majority of the American troops, because the light troops were the elite of Washington's Army and were accordingly rewarded by the quartermaster corps. They had received the lion's share of supplies and equipment that was always in short supply, leaving them "the best equipped [troops] among the Americans."[120]

Hamilton was meticulous and highly detail-oriented, which translated into a thorough preparedness of his men. He was a disciplinarian but not to a fault because of his deep concern over his men's welfare and condition. Despite a heady intellectual with a philosophical bent, Hamilton still closely identified with his soldiers in the ranks, including those of lowly origins and immigrants like himself. He understood the importance of training and had created perhaps the best drilled battalion of the entire Light Corps just like when he had molded his New York artillerymen into disciplined cannoneers, who had thwarted Lord Cornwallis on more than on occasion, especially at the Raritan River to protect Washington's retreat. And now as a strange circumstance would have it, Hamilton was once again facing Cornwallis but in the most critical situation.

Chapter V

Hamilton's Special Touch on October 7, an Unforgettable Sunday

On the Sunday morning of October 7, Lieutenant Colonel Hamilton was shortly to take center stage in the drama that was about to be played out in the finest European tradition. And he would Americanize this forthcoming act in a special and unique way with his own Hamilton touch, because he adhered to the classical way of doing things to make the greatest impression and reap the highest psychological dividends to bolster the morale and esprit de corps of his men, when bestowed with the right opportunity at the right time.[1]

The Marquis de Lafayette's Light Corps had been given the honor by Washington to be the first American troops to enter the trenches to take permanent positions, after the first parallel was completed. The handsome young lieutenant colonel from the West Indies led his battalion of Continental light troops—around two hundred men primarily of the Second New York and the Second Connecticut but also a company of the First Rhode Island, which consisted mostly of black troops—forward in a neat formation across the open ground with confidence. In step and proper order that revealed their high level of discipline, thanks largely to Hamilton's efforts, they continued to march across the level plain situated before the first parallel. Wearing his best uniform of a full lieutenant colonel of the Continentals because he was always fastidious about his appearance, Hamilton confidently led the way before his light infantrymen toward the menacing Yorktown defenses. A worthy top lieutenant and trusty friend, New York's Major

Nicholas Fish, advanced near his former classmate before the lengthy formation, moving with crisp precision.

Exposed out in the open on level ground, Hamilton's New York, Rhode Island, and Connecticut veterans marched with firm steps before the eyes of both armies. Colorful battle flags of flowing silk flew above the ranks of Hamilton's advancing light battalion under the morning sunlight of October 7. Lieutenant Colonel Hamilton had ordered his young musicians, including teenagers and beardless boys, to play a martial tune with fifes and drums to brighten spirits and to add the proper atmosphere to the bold forward movement to occupy the most advanced position of the first parallel.

These veteran Continentals were now eager to show off their well-honed soldiery qualities on this sunny Sunday morning before the watching armies, which Hamilton meant to maximize to the fullest. He was determined to exploit the high level of confidence and esprit de corps by demonstrating his men's superior qualities to not only the army but also the enemy. In marching forward toward the new parallel that had been gouged across the sandy and level ground for hundreds of yards, Hamilton's advance at the head of his troops over the open ground with banners flying and music playing was little more than a routine maneuver to gain the new forward position.

However, Hamilton faced a personal dilemma because traditional sieges like Yorktown offered very few chances for men to demonstrate their prowess and courage like on an ordinary battlefield. Like other veteran officers, "Light Horse" Harry Lee, who had been nearly captured with Hamilton on September 18, 1777, just outside Philadelphia, now watched Hamilton's disciplined maneuver with a deepening sense of pride.

He now envisioned much more than simply another routine maneuver to secure a newly assigned advanced position in the newly dug parallel. He would not only demonstrate the prowess of his elite troops but also to send a stern message of Lord Cornwallis and his men, that they were no longer fighting untrained and inexperienced militiamen of the South.

During prisoner-exchange talks over the years, Hamilton had seen arrogant, condescending British officers up close, revealing the insidious nature of the arrogant class system of a global empire based on a sense of racial and cultural superiority to rule other people by force. Along with the fact that he had been a victim of a strict and oppressive ruling class system in the Caribbean while growing up without future prospects, he became especially contemptuous of these conceited British professional soldiers and upper-class officers.

Hamilton had first gained recognition for his drill expertise while in command of a volunteer student company at King's College in New York City in the spring of 1775. Here, Hamilton had not only gained his broad knowledge in the ancient classics from the end of 1773 to early 1776 but also learned some of the basic fundamentals of the military arts in drilling his novice student command.

Hamilton became more obsessed with perfecting the drill of his fellow students than in reading about the ancient sagas found in Homer's *Iliad* and *Odyssey* and other famous works. To Hamilton's precise instructions as he had learned from the diligent study of tactical manuals, young patriotic men of King's College, wearing green uniform coats and "Liberty or Death" caps, had performed the manual of arms with skill on the grounds of St. George's Church to small crowds, because of Hamilton's efforts.

At Yorktown, he wanted to prove that the situation of Cornwallis's troops was hopeless against such well-trained and highly motivated soldiers.[2] For almost the entirety of the lengthy advance, everything seemed perfectly in keeping with a traditional forward movement over the low-lying open ground when Hamilton and his Continentals finally reached the parallel, which afforded them ample shelter when closer to the enemy than ever before. Inside the sandy parallel whose sides were bolstered by logs and fascines, Hamilton then led his light battalion through the trench to their assigned advanced position. Here, Hamilton ordered the battalion's battle flag placed on the parapet, where it waved gently in the breeze of a pleasant Sunday morning.

To rudely greet the newcomers now that the occupation of the parallel was complete, British artillery opened up with a fire that swept Hamilton's new position, throwing up gushes of sand and dirt. In full view of hundreds of watching British, Tories, and Hessians, Hamilton suddenly ordered the troops of his light battalion to climb out of the new trench and to mount the parapet facing toward Cornwallis's line and in full view of the enemy.

Then, before the parapet, Lieutenant Colonel Hamilton directed his Continentals to align in a neat formation on the open ground before the wide trench of the first parallel within range of the British cannon. While other Continental soldiers watched in disbelief, Hamilton was taking his men directly into harm's way. Here, Hamilton deployed his troops in near perfect double ranks, as if they were on a drill field or preparing for a prestigious review by leading officers and Congressmen in Philadelphia instead of on a major battlefield.

Positioned near the national and unit banners as a member of the battalion's color guard, Pennsylvania's Captain James Duncan, age twenty-five, never forgot what had so suddenly and unexpectedly developed to surprise all: "Our next maneuver was rather extraordinary [to say the least.] We were ordered [by Hamilton] to mount the bank, front the enemy" in the inner works beyond the open ground leading to Yorktown.[3] Among Hamilton's battalion members who mounted the bank were Irish soldiers like Privates William Carr and Daniel Finn and black Continentals of the First Rhode Island Regiment. Meanwhile, fifer Oliver Mun and drummer boy Rufus Holdridge and other musicians played their instruments with spirit, as ordered by the lieutenant colonel, while standing in their assigned positions on the flanks of Hamilton's lengthy formation of young men and boys of all colors standing at attention, while brightly colored flags defiantly flew from the parapet.[4]

While his light infantrymen were fully exposed in the open before the deeply dug parallel and well within range of British cannon at a time when the British, Hessians, and Loyalists were watching their every move, Hamilton calmly stood before his troops under the bright

October sunshine, which illuminated colorful battle flags, including the Stars and Stripes, with thirteen stars on a blue field. He then turned to face his lengthy formation of soldiers and shouted out loud orders for his men to perform a series of complex various evolutions, including the manual of arms—specific instructions for handling their muskets in tight formations when soldiers were standing at attention when on parade—as long practiced according to Baron von Steuben's book of regulations. More specifically and partly thanks to Hamilton's forgotten contributions to the creation of this all-important instructional guide, von Steuben's manual, *Regulations for the Order and Discipline of the Troops of the United States*, had proved invaluable to the young American soldiers.

In shock, Captain Duncan said that "there was by word of command [to] go through all the ceremony of soldiery, ordering and grounding our arms," as if performing this often-rehearsed drill before an admiring crowd during a review at Williamsburg for the Virginia governor in a more innocent time on a lazy afternoon far from the nightmare and horrors of war.[5]

With his men evenly spaced and standing straight and tall at attention in the slight breeze blowing off the York River and Chesapeake, Hamilton continued to shout out an entire series of well-rehearsed commands for the brisk performance of the manual of arms, which his men had perfected by this time. It made no difference to Hamilton that he and his Continentals were well within the range of British and Hessian artillerymen, whose loaded guns were now pointed their way. Acting in mechanical-like fashion as long taught, and as the drummer boys at the either end of the long formation of perfectly aligned men furiously beat their drums in a steady cadence as ordered by Hamilton, these veterans put on an impressive display of drill precision for all to see.

Captain Duncan, who considered Hamilton to be "one of the first officers in the American Army," was somewhat anxious, however. After all, the young commander was clearly taking a gamble with the lives of his men. Hamilton calculated correctly that the watching

British, Tories, and Hessians, especially the artillerymen, would be initially too astounded by the bold display to open fire on such easy targets out in the open. One modern historian, without fully understanding or appreciating what Hamilton had in mind, labeled this drill exercise as nothing more than "a bizarre display of arms drill by Hamilton's battalion on the exposed parapet."[6]

To dazzle the crowds of Philadelphia, the well-uniformed French soldiers of the Soissonnais Regiment had recently given an equally impressive exhibition of their martial proficiency in the manual of arms to great applause. This was a popular way to demonstrate soldiery excellence, but never before on a battlefield when death could come at any moment.[7]

Hamilton's so-called bizarre display was a well-calculated decision that made good sense on multiple levels.

The act bolstered the morale among Washington's troops at this late stage of the war. This disciplined display was a subtle way to intimidate the enemy. There was absolutely nothing bizarre about it, because Hamilton's bold decision was calculated to demonstrate that these much-ridiculed American fighting men were every bit as good as, if not better than, the best trained British or Hessian regulars.

Meanwhile, the amazed enemy continued to watch Hamilton's audacious display of drill proficiency from their earthworks. With his troops fully exposed in the open minute after minute that seemed to last an eternity, Hamilton continued to demonstrate the considerably enhanced capabilities, training, and bearing of American soldiers to their opponent, who were now undergoing a crisis in confidence because of their commander's costly mistakes and their own recent setbacks of an ill-fated campaign that had seemed destined for glory in the beginning. As if the enemy was miles away, Hamilton's audacious exhibition of the manual of arms was performed flawlessly by his men, despite the omnipresent danger.

All the while, Hamilton's highly-visible demonstration infused greater confidence to large numbers of Washington's men, who watched the precise drill in an astonished breathless silence because this unorthodox display was typically American in many fundamental ways: a fact that one British historian misunderstood, as previously mentioned, by incorrectly labeling it "bizarre," which was certainly not the case, especially when the timing and circumstances of Hamilton's display of soldiery skill are better understood and appreciated in the overall context of the situation.

As mentioned, this was a new reality of the dawning of a new day that was partly the result of Hamilton's earlier efforts to guarantee that the Continental Army had gained a Prussian-inspired system of instruction (none had previously existed in the Continental Army) that had bestowed an enhanced level of discipline, because of his early support for a most "valuable man," in his own words, named Baron von Steuben.[8] In much the same way, especially in regard to lifting morale and spirits, Rochambeau had also fine-tuned his men and lifted their morale since his arrival in Newport, which were about to pay dividends at Yorktown.[9]

Hamilton's defiant drill exhibition of superior soldiery qualities of his elite fighting men became the talk of the army. The "devil-may-care young gentlemen of the army—those who wore their hats at a damn-your-eyes cock—were delighted by Hamilton's sheer bravado: here was a daring commander of dash and spirit who in exposing the lives of his men did not hesitate to put his own life to the hazard."[10] Hamilton's longtime desire for independent command and the need to now make a bold personal statement might have led to his death had the British artillery opened a concentrated fire while he presented himself as a target in the open just to prove the elite qualities of his crack fighting men. However, the knowledgeable former New York artillery commander had correctly gauged that the British artillery fire was overall ineffective at long range, because cannonballs had only kicked up sand and a thin layer of top soil without inflicting any serious damage.

That was partly because the British gunners were low on ammunition, which Hamilton did not know. However, an extra black powder charge for firing at a special target like Hamilton was well within the realm of possibility. For whatever reason, not a single cannon blast erupted from the artillerymen poised in the lengthy line of the British trenches and redoubts. In the words of Captain Duncan, "Although the enemy had been firing a little before, they did not now give us a single shot. I suppose in astonishment [which] must have prevented them" from opening fire on Hamilton's light battalion of Continentals.[11]

Most of all, in his youthful exuberance, Lieutenant Colonel Hamilton delivered a psychological blow to Lord Cornwallis's men by emphasizing the hopelessness of their situation.

Clearly, these soldiers were among Washington's finest troops and their audacious drill performance under the eyes and guns of the enemy had revealed as much. Especially with the naturally aggressive Lieutenant Colonel Hamilton at their head, these were among America's elite fighting men, who had survived the war's darkest days and the terrible winters at Valley Forge and Morristown, and they were extremely proud of having persevered for so long just so that they now possessed the opportunity to win it all and change the world at Yorktown.[12]

A Most Tragic Loss

Hamilton's taunting display continued to be dangerous for the young battalion commander the longer that he stood in the open before his troops. New Hampshire's Colonel Alexander Scammell, age thirty-four, the army's adjutant-general who commanded a light infantry regiment from New Hampshire, had recently died because he had been too bold at the wrong time and place. Scammel was one of America's best officers and the pride of Lafayette's Light Corps.

Washington's considerable faith in Colonel Scammell and his abilities had been revealed by his service as the army's adjutant-general, commander of the Light troops in Lafayette's absence in Virginia, and his assignment to rearguard service to protect the army. Scammell had excelled in commanding his troops in key situations. As the assigned officer of the day on September 30, the respected New Englander had inspected Cornwallis's recently-evacuated trenches on what seemed like a routine mission. Everything was going well until he was surprised by the sudden arrival of three of Banastre Tarleton's cavalrymen of the much-feared British Legion of Loyalists, who were known for their hatred of rebels and no-quarter proclivities. Making a fatal mistake, Scammel mistook Tarleton's dragoons for Americans. Tarleton's men were ruthless killers as they had long and fully demonstrated across South Carolina in 1780, including at the Waxhaws where Colonel John Buford's command of Virginia Continental troops was destroyed, and Fishing Creek, where Thomas Sumter's South Carolina partisan command was caught by surprise and utterly routed.

Taking full advantage of the opportunity, Tarleton's men quickly made Scammell, a hero of the great victory at Saratoga, a prisoner, while his handful of escorting New England horsemen hurriedly escaped. Scammell had no chance to fight or escape, after one of Tarleton's dragoons grabbed his horse's leather bridle and another one rode behind the revered Continental colonel with a drawn pistol. Colonel Scammell was then shot in the back at close range, while in the process of asking the identity of these men who had suddenly descended upon him when least expected.[13] He was then taken prisoner to Yorktown like a prized trophy to show off, while suffering from a mortal wound. A distraught Washington wrote to Cornwallis and requested the colonel's release to ensure that he received better care. To his credit, Lord Cornwallis felt empathy, allowing Scammell to be transported to Williamsburg for better care. Here, the popular colonel died on October 3, and Scammell's shocking death sent a dark pall of gloom over the Continental Army.[14]

In his journal in which he hoped in vain for the best for the wounded colonel, an embittered surgeon Thacher, who was Scammell's friend, was sickened by the senseless execution of the high-ranking New Hampshire officer at point-blank range, because while "reconnoitering the ground which the enemy had abandoned, was surprised by a party of their horse, and after having surrendered, they had the baseness to inflict a wound which we fear will prove mortal."[15]

Not only was Scammell's death tragic, but it was also an entirely unnecessary loss of a fine officer who was revered by the army. A polished, Harvard-educated attorney beloved by his New Hampshire men and the army in general, Colonel Scammell had been much like Hamilton in having decided to deliberately forsake safer duty for dangerous frontline service by willingly placing himself in harm's way. As Thacher explained, "For some time he sustained the office of adjutant-general to our army, but preferring a more active command and the post of danger, he was put at the head of a regiment of light-infantry [like Hamilton] for this enterprising campaign."[16]

Colonel Scammell's reputation had even spread to the French Army before his tragic death. Always sympathetic toward the plight and suffering of Washington's republican soldiers, Rochambeau's aide and nephew Lauberdiere described the needless loss: "Colonel Scammel of the light infantry and one of the finest officers of the Continental Army went out to reconnoiter and was taken prisoner. After his surrender, a British officer fired a pistol into his kidney and killed him. The Americans greatly regretted his loss."[17] Ironically, Colonel Scammell, when he had served as the army's adjutant-general at Morristown, had signed Hamilton's March 1, 1777 appointment to Washington's staff on one of the native West Indian's proudest days, when his future had seemed bright and almost limitless.[18]

Scammel's wound had been originally thought to have been survivable. In the words of Colonel John Lamb of Knox's artillery from an October 6 letter, "The worthy Colonel Scammell was wounded and taken Prisoner on Monday last, by three of Tarleton's Horse, as he was reconnoitering the Enemy's works. He is paroled and in a fair way to recover."[19] By universal agreement, Scammel was "a noble and gifted soul with an enviable future before him [and his tragic] fall was hardly less than a public loss."[20] At the beginning of a sad October 11 letter, Lieutenant Henry Dearborn wrote to his New Hampshire friend Meshech Weare:

I am very unhappy that the fore part of my letter is on so disagreeable a subject, but so it is. Our good friend Col. Scammell is no more. . . . He was visiting advanced picquits [*sic*] & reconnoitering the Enemies [abandoned] works when a small party of their horse made a sudden charge upon him & after making him prisoner one of them deliberately shot him, & after plundering him carried him into Town. . . . For several days his simtoms [*sic*] appeared favorable [but] very suddenly he altered for the wors [*sic*] [and] expired. . . . The New Hampshire [Continental] line is remarkably unfortunate in losing our best officers.[21]

Lingering Questions Raised about Hamilton's Sheer Audacity

Lieutenant Colonel Hamilton's daring exhibition on October 7 caused some concern among the light battalion's officers. After all, these men had not previously served together because they were members of a newly formed battalion of the Light Corps. Nevertheless, Hamilton completed his daring exhibition without the loss of a single man, and he ordered everyone into the safety of the trenches after his defiant display. His martial display of drill field expertise and perfection before the parapet of the first parallel revealed Hamilton's romantic side that had been partly fueled by his longtime study of the ancient classics in the golden age of battlefield heroes.[22]

As Hamilton only too well understood by this time, this war for the heart and soul of America had too often already demonstrated that life was frightfully cheap for both soldiers and civilians. Even now, a fatal disease, contracted in Valley Forge's cold and made worse by his endless physical exertions, was in the insidious process of steadily eroding the increasingly fragile health of Lieutenant Colonel Tench Tilghman. In consequence, the versatile Marylander so admired by Washington and Hamilton would die in 1786 at age forty-one from the arduous demands and lingering effects of his years of faithful service, including throughout the grueling Yorktown Campaign.[23]

Allied Artillery Roars

The completed first parallel now extended for more than a mile in a curved shape across level ground that lay before the ominous British defenses. For the next phase of the siege, the bulk of the French and American artillery, including sixteen French mortars and other siege guns from Admiral Barras, were laboriously dragged forward to their assigned positions. They were then positioned on newly built wooden firing platforms in the trenches and situated along the extensive line of earthworks, ready to open fire in unison on October 9. In the words of Lauberdiere,

> All the batteries of the parallel fired. Lord Cornwallis, having observed that we had not fired a single cannon for several days, took this occasion to encourage his troops, saying that he was informed that we had no siege artillery and that all our efforts would be in vain. His and their astonishment must have been great, as he was hardly able to respond after two hours of our firing.[24]

Nothing less than a minor miracle had occurred in having secured the French siege guns and moving them into place in their advanced positions in a timely manner. The story of the arrival of Admiral Barras's siege guns and their placement in the lines was an odyssey all in itself, while playing a key role in dooming Cornwallis and his army. Indeed, from the beginning, the French strategic plan of surprising Cornwallis had stemmed from the well-kept secret of the stealthy uniting of Admiral Barras's small squadron of eight vessels, which had carried the all-important siege guns all the way from Newport without mishap after having slipped away from all British warships on the prowl and bent on his destruction, with Admiral de Grasse's fleet—a success story that shocked the disbelieving British commander-in-chief to the core. And now the besieged British regulars, Hessians, and Loyalists were shortly about to pay a high price for the French having gained superiority at sea over the world's greatest navy.[25]

Thanks to his wide-ranging experience as a New York battery commander, Hamilton bestowed his own high level of expertise in enhancing the overall quality of the artillery positions and aiming cannon with pinpoint accuracy. The French siege pieces that had been brought more than 650 miles were heavier in caliber, like the big twenty-four-pounders, than Cornwallis's artillery, ensuring the ability to cause greater damage not only in casualties but also in tearing apart earthen defenses.

New Englander Joseph Plumb Martin, an experienced sergeant who held America's cause as holy like Hamilton who had been in the country for barely seven years at this point, described the situation:

> French, who were upon our left, had completed their batteries a few hours before us, but were not allowed to discharge their pieces till . . . the signal given to open the whole line of batteries, which was to be the hoisting of the American flag in the ten gun battery. About noon the much wished for signal went up. I confess I felt a secret pride swell my heart when I saw the 'star spangled banner' waving majestically in the very faces of our implacable adversaries; it appeared like an omen of success to our enterprise. . . . A simultaneous discharge of all our guns in the line followed; the French troops accompanying it with "Huzza for the Americans!"[26]

The fact that Washington had "put the match to the first [American] gun" (an eighteen-pounder in the American line on October 9 not long after the French artillery had opened fire), which unleashed a well-aimed fire to the chorus of American cheers, penned surgeon Thacher, was seen as a good omen for the siege's successful outcome—a much-publicized symbolic act that has fostered the myth that Washington initiated the first artillery fire when it had been the French.[27]

All the while, Hamilton became even more confident for success, especially because Cornwallis was outmatched by the large amount of French siege artillery. An almost gleeful Hamilton, who enjoyed the relentless pounding of the trapped army, wrote to Betsey, "Thank heaven, our affairs seem to be approaching fast a happy period [and soon] the enemy must capitulate."[28]

More than six hundred French artillerymen, who rightly considered themselves members of an elite corps, blasted away with their heavy siege pieces, including mortars, day and night. Now with allied guns positioned closer to Cornwallis's earthworks, as many as one thousand shells were hurled into Yorktown on a single night. After an intense bombardment, the massive array of long-arm firepower had early silenced the British guns during the daylight hours in a high complement to the efficiency of the veteran French artillerymen and their expertise in the art of the artillery arm.[29]

Lord Cornwallis wrote on October 11 about the awful truth that could no longer be denied: "We cannot hope to make a very long resistance."[30] As fate would have it, Cornwallis found himself "impaled [at Yorktown] not by the exercise of his own judgment but rather by orders from Sir Henry Clinton, a distant chief whom he could not disobey."[31]

Thursday October 11 was a significant day for a variety of reasons. First and foremost, the allies had to ease close enough to be able to charge out of the trenches to reach Cornwallis's line with the least distance to cover. Therefore, the construction of a second parallel, which would be about half the distance—around 350 yards—to Cornwallis's line, was absolutely necessary. Begun on the night of October 11, which was sufficiently dark to provide good cover, the second parallel was begun by American and French sappers and miners, and the hard work was destined to continue until the two remaining advanced British positions on the left stood tall on their own in defiance. And it was now clear to Rochambeau and Washington that Redoubts Number Nine and Number Ten southeast of Yorktown had to be reduced by storm as soon as possible for the second parallel to be completed.[32]

Cornwallis did not even realize how the ugliest of scenarios was now an inevitable reality because the sailing date of Clinton's expeditionary relief, at first so confidently promised by Sir Henry Clinton, had been in flux: first to October 5, then October 8, and finally to October 12, because of the delays in making repairs to the British vessels at the workshops on the New York City docks. As a cruel fate would have it, the British warships would not depart the deep harbor of New York City until October 17, when it was far too late for Cornwallis and his army.[33]

In October a British staff officer, Major Frederick MacKenzie, revealed the extent of the dysfunction resulting from the lack of good working relationships and rivalries that existed between the British Army and Navy: "If the Navy are not a little more active they will never get a sight of the Capes of Virginia before the end of this month, and then it will be a little too late. They do not seem to be hearty in this business, or to think that saving the army is an object of much material consequence."[34] As everyone realized, Lord Cornwallis was doomed if Clinton's promised forces failed to arrive as promised, especially now that Yorktown was sealed tight and completely cut off, because "all of its exits were guarded by the navy," in Lauberdiere's words.[35]

Baby on the Way

While in the frontline trenches with his men instead of located safely back in his headquarters where he might have stayed by choice to ensure his safety, Hamilton received a most pleasant surprise. His wife informed him by letter that she was pregnant with their first child, who Hamilton desperately wanted to be a male, which would be the case. He learned that his child was due to arrive in this world in January 1782. On October 12 from the "Camp before Yorktown," a truly happy Hamilton wrote a letter to his wife. Revealing his sense of humor and unable to conceal his sheer joy at his good fortune with the letter's unexpected arrival, Hamilton teasingly demanded of his young wife,

> You shall engage shortly to present me with *a boy*. You will ask me if a girl will not answer the purpose. By no means, I fear, with all the mother's charms, she may inherit the caprices of her father and then she will enslave, tantalize and plague one half the sex, out of pure regard to which I protest against a daughter. . . . In an instant my feelings are changed. My heart disposed to gayety is at one melted into tenderness. The idea of a smiling infant in my Betsey's arms call up [thoughts of joy and] In imagination I embrace the mother and embrace the child a thousand times. I can scarce refrain from shedding tears of joy. But I must not indulge these sensations; they are unfit for the boisterous scenes of war and whenever they intrude themselves make me but half a soldier.[36]

With his usual diplomatic tact and skill that promised a long-time happy union between the native West Indian with a murky past and one of the best possible partners from one of America's leading families, Hamilton also gently set his wife straight on another matter, while incorporating his refined sense of humor to take Elizabeth's mind off the brutally serious side of war:

> You complain of me my love, for not writing to you more often [but] Since I left Kings ferry [across Spuyen Duyvil Creek in the Bronx, New York] . . . I am constantly employed. Yet I am sure I have written to you during that period more than twenty letters. Don't image that this neglect will go unpunished.[37]

As he informed his wife in this same letter, he was already thinking about days of peace in November after the elimination of Cornwallis and his once-fabled army:

I hope to see you in three or four weeks from this time [because] Thank heaven, our affairs seem to be approaching fast to a happy period. Last night our second parallel commenced. Five days more the enemy must capitulate or abandon their present positions, if they do the latter it will detain us ten days longer; and then I fly to you. Prepare to receive me in your bosom. Prepare to receive me decked in all your beauty.[38]

But as much as he loved his wife and the couple's expected child, Hamilton was equally motivated, if not obsessed, to still win recognition for himself and his men. Throughout this most decisive of campaigns, he "squeezed every possible ounce of glory" out of every possible opportunity, like the recent drill exhibition out in the open on October 7.

Young Lieutenant Colonel Hamilton still felt that he had much to prove as the recently appointed commander of a new battalion of light infantry, but more to himself than anyone else. Indeed, it was not that long ago when he had cursed his ill-fated "Fortune [that had] condemned him," in his own words, to a bleak exile and unpromising future on Saint Croix. But the irrepressible Hamilton had overcome all the odds and a bleak future on a tiny Caribbean island to carve out his own special destiny and a distinguished name for himself in the midst of a people's revolution.[39]

Chapter VI

Leading the Headlong Charge on Formidable Redoubt Number Ten

Never before in the American Revolution was the factor of time more crucial than now during the dramatic showdown at Yorktown. Lord Cornwallis needed to buy precious time for the arrival of Clinton's reinforcements, and the allies needed to choke the life out of Cornwallis's Army as soon as possible, before Admiral de Grasse was forced to return to resume operations in the West Indies. Therefore, as much as for Rochambeau, the time factor had become a personal obsession to General Washington, who fully realized that he now had a long-elusive decisive victory that might win the war well within his grasp. He had even earlier expressed considerable concern that the French had been too cautious in not having earlier pushed Cornwallis harder, revealing the degree of the Virginian's impatience.

After all, Washington was fully aware that Cornwallis now was anxiously awaiting Clinton's promised arrival of the British fleet to provide his army with an escape from the Yorktown trap on the Virginia Peninsula. Therefore, the allies needed to force Cornwallis to surrender as soon as possible. Indeed, the increasingly worried Washington, who spent many a sleepless night during the course of this grueling and ever-unpredictable campaign, had already learned that thirty British ships would arrive to relieve Cornwallis in only seven days.[1]

The hard work of digging the second parallel, as designated by talented French engineers, about halfway between the first parallel and

Cornwallis's main line proceeded across a large stretch of flat, open ground known as the Pigeon Quarter, the most favorable natural avenue of approach located southeast of town and situated east of the tidal Yorktown Creek.

Two serious obstacles remained to fulfill the goal of completing the extensive expanse of the second parallel, however. Protecting the left of the British line, Redoubts Numbers Nine and Ten were poised on Washington's right flank, looming threateningly and high above the level ground that gently rolled toward the tidal York River. Of these two defensive bastions, Redoubt Number Ten, northeast of Redoubt Number Nine, was the key, because it anchored the left flank of Cornwallis's sprawling defensive line next to the York River and kept his vulnerable flank from being turned. The Americans extended the second parallel ever-closer to the York River, until enfiladed by the fire of these two redoubts located on Cornwallis's far left.

Positioned on cliffs located next to the river (which was about a half-mile wide at this point) to cover the sandy beach and protect Cornwallis's left flank, Redoubt Number Ten was a square-shaped bastion that stood about twenty feet high above the level ground.

General Washington knew that absolutely no time could be wasted by the usual siege process of reducing the two redoubts by a lengthy artillery bombardment. He also realized that once they were eliminated, fire could be directed on the remaining defenders of the small inner line that surrounded Yorktown, to force Cornwallis's surrender. So far, the fighting at Yorktown had consisted only of artillery exchanges at fairly long range, resulting in relatively light losses on both sides: the showdown at Yorktown was almost exclusively an artillery duel instead of a traditional battle proper. Ironically, Lord Cornwallis suffered higher losses from the ravages of disease than from the rain of allied projectiles, despite the bombardment's intensity. But now in this crucial situation with the clock ticking, two infantry assaults of elite light troops of both armies were required to eliminate the twin defensive bastions on Cornwallis's left as soon as possible.

Indeed, the key to placing Cornwallis in an even more critical situation to guarantee a hasty capitulation lay in capturing these two strategic redoubts situated near the York River. Located at the second parallel's eastern end, an epaulement (constructed nearby) offered an avenue from which to unleash an infantry assault on the two troublesome redoubts that defied the second parallel's completion. By retaining possession of these two strategic redoubts, Cornwallis held the key advantage that was guaranteed to slow siege operations and buy time. Given all that was at stake, the upcoming assaults on the two redoubts were the crucial turning point of the entire siege and campaign, if not the war itself.[2]

In the no-nonsense commonsense logic of the average fighting man in the ranks, Sergeant Joseph Plumb Martin said it best: "There are two strong redoubts held by the British, on their left [and] It was necessary for us to possess those redoubts, before we could complete our trenches" of the second parallel.[3]

Surgeon James Thacher, the aspiring son of a poor Massachusetts farmer who had completed his medical studies in 1775 and then enthusiastically joined the Massachusetts militia, recorded in his journal of the last remaining obstacles that effectively thwarted allied ambitions from achieving decisive success at Yorktown: "The enemy have two redoubts, about three hundred yards in front of their principal works, which enfiladed our intrenchment and impeded our approaches, it was resolved to take possession of them both by assault."[4]

As soon as he heard of the upcoming assaults on the two key defensive positions and despite a capable officer already having been chosen to lead the attack of the three light battalions on Redoubt Number Ten, Lieutenant Colonel Hamilton still saw a possible opportunity for himself. As had become his trademark by this time, he simply refused to be denied playing a leading role in the most climactic infantry assault of the war. Hamilton was determined to command the light infantry attack calculated to overwhelm the imposing redoubt situated closest to the York River, strategic Redoubt Number Ten. The Marquis de Lafayette and his Light Corps of three battalions had been assigned to the task of capturing Redoubt Number Ten, while the French were given the assignment of simultaneously reducing its sister redoubt, Redoubt Number Nine, located just to the southwest.

When Hamilton first learned that the Marquis de Lafayette had been chosen to orchestrate the attack, he took immediate action in his usual aggressive style. After all, Hamilton and Lafayette were warm friends and kindred spirits, and their close relationship was one marked by mutual respect.

Based on proper army protocol and seniority according to tradition, Lafayette had chosen his own former aide, Jean Joseph Sourbader de Gimat, to lead the assault on Redoubt Number Ten. A privileged member of the aristocracy like other French officers, Gimat was a respected French officer's son who had been early groomed for a general staff position. Lafayette's decision was also reinforced by the fact that he was close to Gimat, who had served capably on his staff and demonstrated loyalty to the marquis. However, Lafayette had been too partial in his decision-making, because he had violated Washington's personal desire, and thereby Rochambeau's wishes, to foster the image of perfect harmony existing between allies by designating one French column, headed by a French officer, and one American column, led by an American officer, to capture the respective redoubts.

Lieutenant Colonel Hamilton realized Washington's desires for the smooth working of the often-troubled alliance because he knew that an American officer was now needed to lead the attack on Redoubt Number Ten, which only made him more convinced that he was exactly the right man for the job instead of the highly-respected French officer, Gimat. After having waited so long for just such a golden opportunity to win distinction in a critical situation on the most important battlefield of the war, Hamilton was determined to go to considerable lengths, if necessary, to make that great dream come true. While many soldiers viewed the upcoming assault on the formidable redoubt and across a wide stretch of open ground with dread because of the high losses that were deemed inevitable, Hamilton instead only saw a golden opportunity.

Not in the least fearful of leading a risky frontal assault in such a key situation, the handsome lieutenant colonel was encouraged by the axiom that the tactical offensive "has a three-to-one chance of success," in his own words. These odds for success were well worth taking because Hamilton instinctively felt he could make a noteworthy contribution. Not even the fact that he was recently married with a pregnant wife was sufficient to deter the single-minded Hamilton. To overcome the imposing earthen bastion of Redoubt Number Ten, Hamilton once again relied upon an abundance of brainpower and nerve to get his own way and to right a wrong (a Frenchman instead of an American leading the attack on Redoubt Number Ten when jointed allied leadership was needed in symbolic terms for the two simultaneous assaults) in a highly sensitive and complex situation based on traditional army protocol when it came to choosing top personnel for the attack.

First, following proper army procedure, according to regulations, based on the premise that he would be officer of the day on October 14 which had been the time chosen to launch the twin attacks, Hamilton personally appealed directly to Lafayette in his bid to gain the coveted assignment of leading the assault of all three light battalions of American troops on Redoubt Number Ten. But Lafayette correctly followed standard army protocol, emphasizing that Washington, who was deferring to the French because of Rochambeau's expertise and vast experience (his fourteenth siege), already had approved of the decision to allow Gimat to lead the attack of all three battalions, but Hamilton would be at his own battalion's head as usual. Therefore, ignoring the memory of the unfortunate February 16 quarrel with Washington at New Windsor and hoping for the best, Hamilton took quill pen in hand. Once again, Hamilton was relying on the artfulness of his penmanship and keen reasoning that had so often produced dramatic results. He reasoned soundly and with precision. In this regard, Hamilton's nickname of the "Little Lion" was actually misplaced because his pen was mightier than his sword.

Like an experienced and gifted lawyer (his postwar civilian career ambition that was ultimately fulfilled in New York City) from the upper-class world of Charleston or Philadelphia, he smartly emphasized a legal technicality that might win his important case. Hamilton argued correctly that he was the predesignated officer of the day and a senior lieutenant colonel of the Continental Line, whereas the selection of Lieutenant Colonel Jean Joseph Sourbader de Gimat, who had first come to America with Lafayette in 1778 and now served as his personal aide-de-camp, revealed a level of bias. Therefore, Hamilton emphasized to Washington that it was actually now his legitimate and rightful turn to take command of the light infantry assault, while also appealing to the commander-in-chief's sense of Americanism and loyalty to him for having faithfully served for nearly four years as his indispensable chief-of-staff.

Hamilton was entirely within his right to lead the assault on Redoubt Number Ten because he already had been assigned officer of the day on Sunday October 14, which meant he was to lead operations on a tactical level. Hamilton had always been looking to play such a leading role, having revealed to his friend Ned Stevens in New York City of his frustration from his bleak, unpromising Saint Croix exile on November 11, 1769: "My ambition is prevalent. . . . I wish there was a war."[5]

Hamilton boldly took his appeal directly to General Washington at army headquarters, going over the Marquis de Lafayette's head in a direct violation of the traditional rules of a strict chain of command.

Because Lafayette was also a best friend of Hamilton, this was an overall sensitive and delicate situation, but just the kind that the native West Indian could finesse with his usual skill and savvy. Fortunately for Lieutenant Colonel Hamilton, feelings of friendship rather than egos rose to the fore in the case of both Washington and Lafayette. No delicate Gallic feathers of the ever-sensitive French were ruffled. It is not known, but perhaps Lafayette, who often acted like an advisor and sounding board for Hamilton, might have made the suggestion for Hamilton to personally present his case to Washington.

But knowing Hamilton's aggressive style of problem-solving and his marked penchant for dealing directly with the source of any existing problem to reap the best results as soon as possible, he certainly needed no advice from the Marquis de Lafayette in this regard.

Winning His Bold Appeal

As could be expected, Lieutenant Colonel Hamilton also relied on the argument that his honor and reputation (even that of father-in-law General Philip Schuyler and his family but, of course, to a lesser degree) would be damaged throughout the army and America, if he was passed over for such an important assignment of leading the charge of all the American light troops—not just his battalion—on strategic Redoubt Number Ten. Fortunately for Hamilton, no one more than Washington, who keenly understood such pressing concerns of a fellow gentleman and talented officer, fully understood as much. In this sense, Hamilton had his finger on Washington's pulse.

Thanks to Hamilton being senior to Gimat, Washington readily agreed that Hamilton possessed a legitimate argument and right to command the attack because he was the previously assigned officer of the day.

General Washington then went to Lafayette's headquarters to explain the delicate situation to his beloved Frenchman. The commander-in-chief explained Hamilton's position in detail. Of course, the Marquis de Lafayette then officially relented in favor of his friend, which was a rather easy decision for him under the circumstances. Clearly, for once in his controversial career, Hamilton now benefited from friends in high places and the three men saw eye-to-eye in all regards.

Hamilton still had to overcome strict army bureaucratic ways tied to tradition. As mentioned, the young man's keen attorney-like arguments were indeed correct, and they could not be denied in regard to his legitimate claim and right as the leading Continental officer of the day on October 14. In addition, in strictly personal terms,

Washington also realized that his support for Hamilton's final request was the best way to patch up the lingering hard feelings between him and his headstrong former chief-of-staff, whose brash and unorthodox ways of doing things, especially when he was right, were somewhat unsettling to a proper gentleman-planter of the Virginia upper class elite but yet somewhat admirable at the same time: a classic case of the irrepressible "Little Lion" roaring off the battlefield, despite the odds against success.

Finally getting his way that actually resembled a belated payment of sorts for his nearly four years of faithful service to Washington as the head of staff, Hamilton was now given command the column of all three light battalions chosen to attack Redoubt Number Ten at the "post of honor": a leadership decision entirely in keeping with Washington's original desire that one attack column should be French and the other American in a symbolic gesture to display the unity and equality that existed between allies. In the end and to his credit, for a commander who always went by the book and was a slave to then proper dictates of army protocol and gentlemanly conduct, Washington could not deny Hamilton's main points that were irrefutable.

Clearly, Hamilton's recent lucky streak, including his marriage to pretty Betsey Schuyler, easy entry into one of New York's leading families, and the securing of his own command in Lafayette's crack Light Corps, continued unabated. To placate Lieutenant Colonel Gimat, the aristocratic Frenchman was designated to lead his own battalion at the assault column's head. Meanwhile, Major Nicholas Fish was chosen by Hamilton to lead his old battalion and the ever-reliable John Laurens, the aristocratic South Carolinian of French Huguenot descent, the other battalion. For the upcoming attack on Redoubt Number Ten, Hamilton could not have possessed a better or more hard-hitting team than with Fish and Laurens, two of his best and oldest friends, and Gimat, who took the sudden change of command in stride in the spirit of harmony between allies.

Gaining this coveted assignment showed Hamilton's aversion to caution. Hamilton always shared the same hardships as his men and led the way by example, which endeared him to them.

General Washington also knew that Hamilton possessed the tactical and leadership skills needed for a successful assault, realizing that if anyone was to capture imposing Redoubt Number Ten, it was fiery Lieutenant Colonel Hamilton. Hamilton now embraced with considerable enthusiasm "one of the most dangerous missions of the war."[6]

But in doing so, Hamilton overlooked the considerable risks. He never dwelled on the dangers, because he simply did what he had to do under the circumstances. When Hamilton first learned that he had won the coveted assignment, the excited young man hugged a much-surprised Major Fish, shouting, "We have it! We have it!"[7]

After the war, enemies of Hamilton, including none other than John Adams, the second president of the United States, circulated the ugly rumor that he had blackmailed Washington to get the key assignment to lead the most famous American charge of the American Revolution.

Of course, this was not the case. The rumor was only a case of angry and jealous political rivals attempting to tarnish Hamilton's reputation.[8] To his credit, "Washington had decided it was finally time to give two of his most promising American officers [Hamilton and Laurens] the opportunity they deserved."[9]

A Pregnant Wife in Faraway Albany

As early as before mid-July and not long after taking command of his light battalion, Hamilton had first learned of the move south by unknown sources, almost certainly from a friend of the commander-in-chief's staff, because Washington kept his secret. However, Washington might have early given a hint to Hamilton at some point about what to expect. In an earlier letter to Elizabeth, Hamilton wrote for the express purpose of comforting his wife, writing there existed "little prospect of activity," when the overall strategic situation was indicating quite the opposite.[10]

Not long before the attack on Redoubt Number Ten, Hamilton then wrote Betsey what might be his final letter to her, if he was killed in the upcoming offensive effort. But Hamilton was haunted by no gloomy thoughts or premonitions of impending doom like some other members of the storming party almost certainly were, despite planning to lead the way over the wide stretch of open ground. As usual, Hamilton remained upbeat and confident, as if already knowing that he had nothing to fear and that no British, Loyalist, or Hessian bullet was meant for him. So far in this war, he had never been seriously wounded, despite often riding in the most exposed positions on the battlefield, including at the Battle of Monmouth when rallying hard-hit troops and serving on the front lines. Hamilton was the kind of dynamic commander who seemingly everyone knew would never become a tragic figure in this war by falling to an enemy bullet or cannonball.

At this time, Betsey was five months' pregnant in Albany with her family, which certainly gave Hamilton a great deal of comfort in knowing that she was safe in upper New York. And after the British had shifted their ambitions south in 1780, the New York theater remained relatively quiet, and Albany was not under serious threat like in the past, especially during the Saratoga Campaign. Revealing his sense of humor and high spirits, Hamilton wrote to his wife, "You shall engage shortly to present me with a boy. You will ask me if a girl will not answer the purpose."[11]

The feeling of an inevitable success continued to grow throughout the army. In an October 11 letter, Lieutenant Colonel Henry Dearborn wrote a letter to a friend in New Hampshire:

Our army is making regular approaches to the Enemies Works [and now] our works are within less than five hundred yards of their main work . . . their resistance has not been great as yet;—from what we can hear from them [deserters] their principal dependence is on [the arrival of] a superior Fleet, which I think they must fail in [and] if we should succeed in taking Corn Wallis, & Gen. [Nathanael]

Green [*sic*] continues successful in Carolina, it will have a great tendency to put an end to his distressing war, & give liberty to us in the field once more to come peacible [*sic*] citizens.[12]

On October 12 a confident Lieutenant Colonel Hamilton confided in his wife, "Thank heavens, our affairs seemed to be approaching fast to a happy period. Last night out second parallel commenced. Five days more the enemy must capitulate or abandon their present position."[13]

A Host of Harsh Realities

As a married man with a wife and a child on the way in Albany, Hamilton should have been worried a great deal in his somewhat irresponsible eagerness to lead such a dangerous attack. Anchoring the left of Cornwallis's lengthy defensive line atop a cliff next to the York River, Redoubt Number Ten was one of the most powerful defensive positions at Yorktown.

An infantry assault across more than four hundred yards against such a strong earthen bastion as Redoubt Number Ten guaranteed high losses and perhaps disastrous results. Quite simply, Hamilton was now responsible for what seemed almost impossible.[14]

Indeed, Hamilton now faced a daunting tactical dilemma that seemed to have no solution unless he developed a very good innovative, if not unorthodox, tactical plan. Like so often in the past, he again relied upon his reservoir of experience and resourcefulness to develop an innovative tactical solution to increase the odds of achieving success in a seemingly no-win situation. Hamilton realized early that the true key to overwhelming this timbered and earthen bastion was the element of surprise and stealth instead of the headlong onslaught that could be easily repulsed by the defenders bolstered by an ample number of artillery pieces—seven cannon in the case of Redoubt Number Ten—if they were alerted in time to man the parapet.

Hamilton planned a concentrated assault column of all three light infantry battalions, under Laurens, Fish, and Gimat, launched under the protective cover of darkness not long after sunset on October 14 to minimize losses and exploit the element of surprise. In total, he planned to lead the assault with a relatively small group of attackers, only around four hundred picked men, who were chosen because they were the best soldiers of his light battalion, while the French struck Redoubt Number Nine to the southwest and on the left of Redoubt Number Ten. Everyone, especially Washington and Hamilton, knew that the key to success was a swift attack with the bayonet in the darkness to get as many men as quickly as possible across the killing ground, before volleys and cannon fire erupted. Most important in overall tactical terms, Hamilton planned an innovative pincer movement by striking each flank of the redoubt simultaneously with one battalion and the third one striking from the rear.

Hamilton felt fortunate to have the Continental soldiers of the First Rhode Island, consisting of a large number of black troops, in his battalion, reasoning that these seasoned veterans under the capable Captain Stephen Olney would be badly needed for the upcoming challenge, which was indeed the case. Hamilton's soldiers were tough Continental veterans, including survivors of more than half a decade of military service. These seasoned New York, Connecticut, and Rhode Island men, including Captain Olney's African American troops, were determined to make the maximum effort to overwhelm the most formidable defensive bastion that they had ever seen.

Hoping to catch the defenders by surprise, Hamilton wanted no attacker to fire a single shot so that the defenders would not be alerted to summon timely reinforcements. They were to rely solely on the bayonet. Hamilton's light troops now relished the exact same kind of bayonet work that had terrified so many rookie American soldiers.

Hamilton wisely calculated that no unnecessary risks were to be taken because he knew that a single mistake, even a small one, might well sabotage the ambitious plan of attack. Therefore, Hamilton made thorough and meticulous preparations for the risky attack.

No musket was to be loaded by any of Hamilton's men, eliminating any possibility of an accidental firing of a weapon from the dropping of a loaded flintlock or a soldier tripping and falling. Revealing his abolitionism and past advocation of employing black troops to fight for America, Hamilton almost certainly felt a sense of pride in the well-uniformed black and mixed-race fighting men of the First Rhode Island Continental Regiment.

Clearly, a good deal of discipline, courage, and iron nerve were now required among Hamilton's light troops. This earthen bastion that anchored Cornwallis's left flank was now the key to the defense of Yorktown, and both sides fully realized as much.

No matter what Hamilton devised in overall tactical terms to guarantee a stealthier approach, it would still take time for his men, black and white, to weave their way through the thick layer of felled timber and the row of sharp stakes that had been erected on the redoubt's slope aligned in a neat row in about the middle to impale attackers. This entangled array of abatis was guaranteed to slow, if not entirely stop, the attackers, especially if the garrison was alerted in time and poured forth volley after volley into the interlopers.

Of course, reaching the massive earthwork with seven cannon without his troops getting cut to pieces was Hamilton's primary tactical objective. Some of Hamilton's Continentals, no doubt including the lieutenant colonel, had trouble sleeping the night before the great assault. The rising autumn sun of October 14 reflected off the murky waters of the Chesapeake to illuminate the extensive arc of American, British, and French defenses. October 14 was beautiful in the Virginia Tidewater and part of a traditional Indian summer. Best of all, Cornwallis and his men had their backs to the York River and there was now no place for them to run or hide, so they were doomed if Sir Henry Clinton's reinforcements failed to arrive in time. As noted, all of the British redoubts of the original ten were now lost to the allies except Redoubts Number Nine and Number Ten and the second parallel was nearly complete by this time. And now only the two redoubts, standing firm and high in menacing fashion, had succeeded in halting the completion of the second parallel.

The red ball of the morning sun on October 14 had slowly lifted over the York River to reveal the most decisive showdown of the war. But this fall morning became cool and overcast, providing the hint of rain later in the day and the inevitable arrival of harsher fall weather. Already, flocks of chevron-shaped formations of honking Canadian Geese were flying high in the sky, making their annual way south down the Chesapeake.

Nevertheless, the brightness of the early autumn morning sun had almost seemed to proclaim that Hamilton's special day of destiny, like that of the Continental Army, had arrived at long last. The young man who had once served as Washington's head of staff now basked in the knowledge that he had won a golden opportunity in what might be the war's final battle of major importance. At long last, Hamilton finally possessed his chance to win battlefield glory to wipe away his past of having served as an unknown—in America in general rather than in the army—desk officer on Washington's staff in a too subservient role to "His Excellency" year after year for the overall good of the nation, when it went directly against his independent nature and ambitious longings to make a name for himself, especially when the commander-in-chief had lost his temper that resulted in the unfortunate New Windsor incident rather than from Hamilton's fault as expounded by admiring Washington biographers.

Perhaps early on October 14, Hamilton had been reminded of the beautiful sunrises of his youth far away in the West Indies that most of the men—more Americans than Frenchmen—at Yorktown had never seen, when the piercing sun's rays had sparkled like diamonds off the Caribbean's turquoise waters.

But now on the low-lying eastern edge of the Virginia Tidewater in the Chesapeake Bay far from the Caribbean's natural beauty, Hamilton was about to face his greatest challenge that he well might not survive. Most important, he fought for a new day in which the common man, like when he had been living in the Caribbean, was never again solely judged by their family background, occupations, financial worth, levels of education, and political and social connections, because of the rise of a new world of new republican value systems where every man had value, including individuals of the lowest class in a society of free citizens. It is not known what exactly the former artillery officer and chief-of-staff was thinking right before the assault on Redoubt Number Ten. Hamilton might have thought back on the fact that he would have been sitting in Hugh Knox's old Presbyterian Church on this Sunday October morning in faraway Christiansted, if he had never migrated to America.

Back at the ivory tower of King's College in New York City where he had been friends with Nicholas Fish, Hamilton had been known for his devout qualities, including kneeling in prayer and praising God for his many blessings, especially in having escaped an unpromising future in the Caribbean. The young man's Presbyterian faith had never left him because it had been the faith of his Scottish father, who had been proud of his family and the time-honored Celtic traditions of the old country across the sea never seen to Hamilton. Lieutenant Colonel Hamilton had never been more religious than when he had been back in the islands, but now on October 14 he possessed ample good reason to become considerably more devout and pray for survival.

With a great deal on his mind, Hamilton had gotten up early on this cool late morning of October 14. He continued to make final preparations for the nighttime assault. He carefully worked out the final tactical details of the attack, while readying his men of three light battalions of the Continental Light Corps. The initial frontal assault was to be launched in column and then separate into two strike forces upon reaching the thick bed of abatis protecting Redoubt Number Ten, with one light battalion (under the irrepressible Lieutenant Colonel John Laurens) moving to the left and Gimat, who now commanded Hamilton's battalion since Hamilton possessed overall command of all three light battalions, shifted to the right to hit the redoubt's right flank (from the attacker's viewpoint), while Fish moved to the west upon encountering the abatis to strike the redoubt on the other, or left, flank. While Gimat commanded the right column with Lieutenant Colonel Hamilton at its head, Laurens led the left column of seasoned light troops, who were then shortly followed by Fish's battalion to strike the redoubt's left flank in conjunction with Gimat on the redoubt's other side.

Laurens's light battalion of two companies was to circle wide to the west, or left, to gain a position in the redoubt's rear to intercept the enemy's retreat and strike the defenders of Redoubt Number Ten, under the command of Scotsman Major Patrick Campbell, from behind to deliver the final blow. The battle plan was complex, especially for a night assault and for troops in their first battle together as a unit and under a young commander who had never before led them into battle. Lieutenant Colonel Hamilton's innovative pincer movement required the three light battalions to move swiftly and with tactical precision in the darkness to strike a hard-hitting blow for which there would be no escape for the British and Hessian garrison. Timing had to be almost perfect in all phases of the assault, because all three formations of attackers were to simultaneously hit their respective targets. Hamilton felt greater confidence for success because his best friend, John Laurens, was leading the left column.

They were now once again about to risk their lives together on a battlefield like on the field of Monmouth and other hard-fought battles, when they had served together on Washington's staff. Almost miraculously, Hamilton and Laurens would somehow survive the upcoming attack (only Gimat would fall wounded that night during the assault) in leading the way at the forefront, but the dashing South Carolinian was destined to lose his life in a needless exhibition of heroics in the eastern lowlands of his native state in 1782, a tragic loss that made little sense.

Like when he had spoken to his young New York artillerymen to inspire them before Washington's surprise attack on the Hessian garrison on the early morning of December 26, 1776, Hamilton encouraged his Rhode Island, New York, Connecticut, and Massachusetts soldiers of all three Continental light battalions, now situated in the sandy trenches and poised to attack, with inspiring words that raised spirits and confidence for a successful outcome. However, no cheers as usual came in response to Hamilton's words of encouragement so as not to alert the enemy.

Throughout this mild autumnal Sunday in the tidewater, the worship of God was no longer a top priority because of the absence of proper church services, although the private soldier's prayers said to themselves had dramatically increased when on the verge of unleashing the attack. Lieutenant Colonel Hamilton had been the very embodiment of energetic activity in making final preparations for the great assault Hamilton's attack was planned for not long after the October 14 sun of this autumn day finally dropped. After having waited years for just such an opportunity and having worked hard to obtain it, Hamilton nervously awaited the arrival of the comforting veil of darkness and the cooler temperatures of an early autumn night. October 14 might well have been the longest day in Hamilton's short life that would become considerably shorter if he was fatally cut down, which seemed quite likely. But for Lieutenant Colonel Hamilton, thoughts of self-preservation were entirely secondary to the chance of reaping a dramatic success and doing what he believed that he had to do, although he must have wondered if he would ever see his son in the future.

Indeed, on this day of destiny in the Chesapeake country, Hamilton also was consumed by other thoughts that had nothing to do with war. Back at the stately two-story Schuyler Mansion in Albany that overlooked the Hudson, Hamilton's wife was already past her midterm with his first child. Elizabeth was still obsessively concerned about her husband's fate. If dark thoughts of leaving a grieving widow on her own tugged at his conscience, then Hamilton pushed such gloomy thoughts aside by only focusing on the positive and in the final details of orchestrating a successful attack.

But of course, if he was killed in the upcoming assault, then Hamilton's repeated requests for active command would certainly have been seen as the epitome of folly, especially after he had married extremely well in America's upper crust of an old New York family.

However, in his most reflective mood, Hamilton might have thought that his first child might well have to grow up fatherless like himself in the West Indies, enduring the same painful upbringing that he had suffered in the Caribbean and that still haunted him to this day. Indeed, despite all of his successes in life, young Hamilton still possessed old scars from having endured a difficult childhood without a father on King Street in the town of Christiansted on Saint Croix. Of course, that possible tragic fate Hamilton naturally desired to avoid at all costs, perhaps more for his expected first-born's sake rather than his own.

October 14th's Sun Drops over the Horizon and the Artillery Opens Fire

After what seemed like an eternity to Lieutenant Colonel Hamilton on a busy, nerve-wracking day, the sun of October 14 finally descended over the tree line on the western horizon, while Hamilton's light troops waited in the eerie silence and the levels of tension reached new highs in the trench among the hushed soldiers, who tightly gripped their flintlock muskets with fixed bayonets. Hamilton's veteran men were ready for the final order to attack. Crouched and lying low in the darkened trenches in the blackness, some of Hamilton's soldiers were in a foul mood. They were still angry and eager for revenge because of the senseless killing of the popular Colonel Alexander Scammell at age thirty-four. Scammel was the highest-ranking Continental officer to die at Yorktown.

Finally, the time had come. Experienced American and French engineers had reasoned that the two redoubts had been sufficiently damaged by the massive artillery bombardment to allow for successful assaults on both redoubts. In preparation, American and French batteries opened a heavy fire to additionally soften up their targets not long after sunset. The intense artillery barrage was concentrated on the earthen defensive bastions not only to eliminate as many defenders and artillery pieces as possible but also to blow holes in the abatis entanglements to clear the way for Hamilton's light infantrymen, as ordered by Washington, and for the French troops, who had targeted Redoubt Number Nine. Of the two, Redoubt Number Nine was the larger earthen structure, with a garrison of around 120 British and Germans, but Redoubt Number Ten was the most strategically important. Meanwhile, Redoubt Number Ten possessed a smaller garrison of Hessians and British, while both redoubts were strengthened by cannon. Because Redoubt Number Nine was larger, it held more cannon (more than a dozen versus seven in Redoubt Number 10), which must have come to a great relief to Hamilton and his men.

At the other end of the line to the northwest upriver, French artillery pieces also unleashed their wrath on the Fusilier Redoubt situated atop the high ground of the river bluff located northwest of town. Of course, this pounding of the Fusilier, or the Star Redoubt, located on Cornwallis's far right that overlooked the little tobacco port on the northwest, was a clever ruse. The intense artillery barrage directed on the star-shaped defensive bastion was calculated to take Lord Cornwallis's attention away from the true targets on his left. Indeed, Cornwallis knew that if the Fusilier Redoubt, positioned on the cliff overlooking the wide expanse of the York River, was taken, then Yorktown would be subjected to artillery fire pouring down into the town from his right flank. But the more exciting tactical possibilities with the capture of Redoubts Nine and Ten offered a far greater advantage for the victors.[15]

Hamilton described his tactical plan of a pincer movement in charging forward

> in two columns with unloaded arms, the right composed of Lt. Col. [Jean Joseph Sourbader de] Gimat's battalion and my own [battalion] commanded by Major [Nicholas] Fish, the left of a detachment [of two light companies] commanded

by Lt. Col. [John] Laurens, destined to take the enemy in reverse, and intercept their retreat.[16]

Hamilton's own battalion was under the immediate command of dependable Major Nicholas Fish, and there was no one who could serve more capably as Hamilton's replacement. Upon reaching the maze of felled timber of the abatis, Fish had been directed to shift west, like Laurens earlier in targeting the redoubt's rear, to strike the redoubt's right flank (from the defender's view).[17]

Hamilton also relied heavily on dynamic Lieutenant Colonel Francis Barber, who was the division inspector of Lafayette's Division of Light Troops. Born in Princeton, New Jersey, in 1751, where he had graduated from today's Princeton University in 1767, he was a gifted intellectual who had profoundly influenced young Hamilton not long after his arrival in America. Barber was Hamilton's former ancient classics instructor from the Elizabethtown Academy at Elizabethtown, New Jersey, where he had served as the rector from 1769 to 1776. Barber began the war as an ensign of the Third New Jersey Continental Regiment, before becoming a staff officer (adjutant general) for General William Maxwell and then for Lord Sterling while advancing in rank by way of merit, like Hamilton. Barber had already performed with distinction in this war, having fallen wounded at the daylong Battle of Monmouth, New Jersey, during the summer of 1778 and at Newton, New York, on August 29, 1779, during General John Sullivan's expedition to chastise Native Americans and Tory raiders. Only five years older than Hamilton, Barber was destined to fall wounded in the upcoming assault on Redoubt Number Ten. Sadly, he would die tragically in a bizarre accident—the falling of a tree would crush him—at the army's encampment at Newburgh, New York, before the war's conclusion.[18]

Lieutenant Colonel Laurens, the most intense and combative leader of the three battalions, had been given command of a light battalion after Colonel Alexander Scammell had been killed and his New Hampshire regiment was then divided by Washington into two light battalions. Laurens had been handed the key assignment of striking the redoubt's rear partly because of having led his attack column in the bloody assault, which had been doomed after devastating losses, on Savannah's defensives in October 1779. Once again, these two best friends and brother republicans had been recently reunited just in time for the climactic showdown at Yorktown.[19]

Like his best friend and kindred spirit from the tropical island of Saint Croix, Laurens could not have been more highly motivated in leading his own experienced light battalion on October 14, when the stakes were exceptionally high for America. Revered by Washington because of his tireless work with the "family" of staff officers and even more diehard in his sheer combativeness and staunch republican convictions, which was no small achievement, than Hamilton partly because he was not married, Laurens now desired either a "Glorious Death, or the Triumph of the Cause in which I am engaged," in his own words.[20]

These two young officers were much more than typical leading Continental officers of Lafayette's Light Corps, because they were among the best and the brightest of an elite cadre and of America. When Hamilton had informed Laurens of his innovative remedies for all that ailed America (financially, politically, and militarily) that were ahead of their time and right on target, Lieutenant Colonel Laurens had responded with a sage warning that these radical solutions that revealed Hamilton's impatience for improvement "would not go down at this time." In response to Laurens's timely warning, Hamilton had emphasized with insight how America's future fate and the possibility of a bright future depended upon these bold solutions that he advocated with such insight and passion: "Necessity must force them down [because] If they are not speedily taken, the patient will die."[21]

The daredevil South Carolinian, whose bravery and audacity before the enemy regardless of the odds would result in his death in less than a year deep in the South Carolina lowlands, was ready for his key assignment of leading eighty hand-picked men (roughly two companies) of his light battalion on a bold flank movement to the west to circle around to gain Redoubt Number Ten's rear and hit the redoubt from behind to eliminate all escape and thwart any arriving reinforcements to complete the victory. He would then lead his troops through the redoubt's entrance (a sloping earthen ramp) in the rear, while Hamilton struck the redoubt's left flank from the right with Gimat's light battalion of experienced Continental troops, and Fish's battalion was to shift west, or to the left, to strike the other, or right flank, of the redoubt.[22]

Meanwhile, Lieutenant John Mansfield, Fourth Connecticut Regiment, was in command of the so-called forlorn hope of around twenty volunteers who would lead the way for the right column. With Mansfield were the sappers and miners under Captain John Gilliland. This ad hoc unit of some of the most experienced veterans of the forlorn hope was to hurriedly form in front of the assault column before Gimat's battalion, which was leading the way with Hamilton at its head, when a designated (by Hamilton) advanced point was reached about halfway of around two hundred yards to Redoubt Number Ten.[23] In honor of the Frenchman's service to America and as Lafayette's faithful aide-de-camp, Lieutenant Colonel Gimat's battalion had been granted "the honored point position" of leading the way.[24]

Significantly, the reassuring knowledge that Hamilton prepared to lead the American assault column in person encouraged not only his men but also Washington's other troops. In the complimentary words of surgeon James Thacher in his journal, "The advanced corps was [to be] led on by the intrepid Hamilton, who had commanded a regiment of light-infantry during the campaign, and assisted by [Lieutenant] Colonel Gimat," who had been born in Gascony, southwest France.[25]

Like other Frenchmen on October 14, the Marquis de Lafayette was proud of the fact that this fellow countryman, Gimat, was leading the attack as the vanguard in command of his own battalion. At this time, Gimat's battalion of light infantry consisted of five Connecticut companies, two Massachusetts companies, and one company of the First Rhode Island Continental Regiment, under Captain Stephen

Olney, that included African American soldiers, as if to verify Hamilton's and Laurens's early wisdom of advocating for black troops to fight for their own and America's freedom.[26]

Lieutenant Colonel Hamilton was also assisted by another respected French officer, Marquis Charles de la Rouerie Armand. Despite being a veteran cavalry officer who had led Colonel Charles Armand Tuffin's First Partisan Corps (known simply as Armand's Legion that consisted of mostly foreign volunteers in French service) with distinction in the Southern theater and having narrowly escaped General Gates's blundering that resulted in the Camden, South Carolina, fiasco in August 16, 1780, when the hero of Saratoga became the goat of the South, Armand requested that Hamilton allow him to join in the assault on Redoubt Number Ten. Armand was now a leader without a command and was nearly as desperate to see action and win distinction as Hamilton.

By this time, Armand's Legion was no more after having been formed in 1778. Like so many other ill-fated commands, the legion had been cut to pieces by Cornwallis's troops at Camden, when General Horatio Gates's Southern Army had been destroyed in mid-August 1780. This eager French leader, therefore, had an old score to pay with his lordship. Not only Armand but also some of his men volunteered to join the attack, which later earned Hamilton's thanks in his official battle report to the Marquis de Lafayette. With a display of proper French manners, Hamilton courteously assented to allow Armand to serve as a "volunteer" in his light infantry command. Hamilton knew that he needed as many veteran officers as possible for the assault.

Therefore, Chevalier Jean de Fontvieux, Armand's close friend, also served in Hamilton's assault column to provide an extra measure of solid leadership. Idealistic children of the Age of Enlightenment who had been partly influenced by bold French Enlightenment thinkers, or the *philosophes*, like Jean-Jacques Rousseau and Voltaire, these two zealous French volunteers chose to serve with Hamilton, instead of under Lieutenant Colonel William de Deux-Ponts. This fine experienced officer of distinction had been chosen to lead the French assault northwest on Redoubt Number Nine, which was located around 330 yards southwest of Redoubt Number Ten.[27] In overall strategic terms, the upcoming assaults northwest on Redoubt Number Nine and Redoubt Number Ten, in Rochambeau's words of October 13, invoked an appropriate analogy: "We shall see tomorrow if the pear is ripe."[28]

Fortunately for Hamilton and those in his officer corps, he could count on some very good experienced men in the enlisted ranks. Sergeant Joseph Plumb Martin, who now served in the Continental Army's Corps of Sappers and Miners (now attached to Lafayette's Division from General Henry Knox's artillery command and located at the head of the assault column) after having recently joined this elite unit at Annapolis, Maryland, was one such dependable veteran. The young New Englander concluded in a matter-of-fact manner about the daunting challenge that lay ahead on the night of October 14: "There were two strong redoubts held by the British, on their left [and] It was necessary for us to possess those redoubts, before we could complete our trenches [and therefore] We arrived at the trenches a little before sunset."[29]

In the safety of the trenches before Redoubt Number Ten to the northwest, the sappers and miners of this veteran regular Continental company were commanded by Captain James Gilliard, an experienced New Yorker of French descent and his top lieutenant of Scotch-Irish descent, Captain David Kirkpatrick. At this time, Hamilton's men were still unaware of the exact location of their ultimate target on October 14, which had been kept a closely guarded secret. Not even these invaluable soldiers under Captain Gilliard who were to serve in "the van," under Lieutenant John Mansfield, Fourth Connecticut Continental Regiment, of leading the assault column (before Gimat's battalion, which would be at the head of the attack because it was the oldest light battalion and, therefore, possessed the right of seniority) on the right possessed knowledge of their objective.

Security was exceptionally tight to guarantee that Redoubt Number Ten's British and Hessian soldiers could be caught completely by surprise. Appreciating the supreme importance of secrecy from his old chief of intelligence officer days at Washington's headquarters, Hamilton prudently did not inform his men of their tactical objective to eliminate additional risks.

About to be assigned to the head of Gimat's right column with the other sappers and miners, Sergeant Martin described his late discovery of the perilous nature of the upcoming mission that came as a shock:

> I saw several officers fixing bayonets on long staves [as ordered by Hamilton and] I then concluded we were about to make a general assault upon the enemy's works; but before dark I was informed of the whole plan, which was to storm the redoubts, the one by the Americans, and the other by the French. The sappers and miners were furnished with axes, and were to proceed in front and cut a passage for the troops through the abatis, which are composed of the tops of trees, the small branches cut off with a slanting stroke which rendered them as sharp as spikes.[30]

After the sun of October 14 finally went down to leave no trace of any autumn daylight on the distant western horizon, even more of a cool autumn veil of blackness settled over the low-lying Chesapeake Bay country. Naturally, Hamilton felt the same growing anxiety like his men, knowing that the decisive moment of beginning the attack was drawing ever-closer. Consequently, the tension in the sandy trenches was high and nerves were as taut as a hemp rope on the deck of a French warship. But as a savvy veteran, Hamilton was experienced in such high pressure life-or-death situations since the early days of the struggle for America's liberty. With confidence and whispering reassuring words, he walked slowly along the line to encourage his men and to give last minute tactical instructions and perhaps make a joke or two to relieve the mounting tension among his anxious soldiers.

Young men in Continental uniforms were inspired by Hamilton's well-spoken words that still carried a dim accent of the Caribbean islands and the experience of an old artillery officer. Then, with deep respect and glowing words, he formally introduced General Washington to his men, who listened intently to the commander-in-chief's final words before the attack to lift spirits. Washington encouraged Hamilton's troops with inspiring words to ensure a maximum effort.

No one knows exactly what young Lieutenant Colonel Hamilton was thinking before he ordered the assault. But to be sure, Hamilton was anxious like everyone else before his greatest battlefield challenge. Because he had studied the ancient classics, including Homer's immortal *Iliad*, at American colleges, perhaps Hamilton thought briefly about the courage and sacrifice of the ancient heroes of the Trojan War, like Achilles, Hector, Paris, Nestor, and Odysseus in a heroic age that had been reconstructed during the American Revolution by the republican-minded soldiers of America. In many ways, the basic realities of warfare, especially the war's surreal horrors and the seemingly endless deaths among the common soldiers, had not really changed since ancient times; including that Hamilton and his men had to master their personal doubts and fears just before the launching of this all-important assault.

But he was determined to lead his troops at their head all the way to Redoubt Number Ten and even inside the defensive bastion where hand-to-hand combat was sure to erupt in full fury, if not first shot down. Minute after minute, Lieutenant Colonel Hamilton waited in the gloomy trenches beside his men, while the night air felt colder without a trace of Chesapeake humidity or summer warmth that had long since vanished with the dying summer. Like the dropped curtain of darkness, the slight breeze from the cold Atlantic to the east brought a chill to the men in thin and light uniforms and with little gear so as to not impede movements, but the deepness of the trench offered some slight protection and comfort on the verge of the assault.

However, most of Hamilton's men were northerners who had never seen the Caribbean or had ever experienced the early fall weather this far south in their lives. They, consequently, were more accustomed to cooler weather than Southerners and, of course, Hamilton before his arrival in America from the West Indies. If any of Hamilton's soldiers now touched their steel bayonets, which had been silently fixed on the end of flintlock muskets, in the blackness, then these instruments of death felt colder than usual. This escalating chill of the early night brought no comfort to the troops standing quietly in the trenches and awaiting Hamilton's signal to go over the top. Naturally, some soldiers now feared to hear the inevitable signal to advance from the young lieutenant colonel, knowing exactly what kind of horrors awaited them in the lengthy charge across such a wide stretch of open ground and toward the imposing redoubt that stood high and silent like a cold wall of stone.

Meanwhile, Hamilton walked slowly up and down the ranks, whispering words of encouragement to his men, including those soldiers who were about to be killed. These veterans had never served under such a young commander or one who looked so young. Hamilton also almost certainly went through the routine of checking the flintlock muskets of his men and to make sure that everything was ready. But these Continental veterans already knew what was needed in the upcoming attack, which made Hamilton's job in making thorough preparations easier. And, of course, Lieutenant Colonel Hamilton also certainly thought about Elizabeth and his first child who had yet to be born, when he had a spare moment to reflect upon his life in the darkened trench. At some point, Hamilton now must have wondered if would live to see that child, after he led his men over the top? Would his first child (Elizabeth was now around five month's pregnant) be a girl or a boy and was the child's future destined to be bright or dark?

Boding well for the success of the upcoming assault, Hamilton's luck had miraculously held firm in this war so far, and he had never suffered a serious wound, which might have made him believe that he was practically untouchable, after having quite a few close calls in past battles. Seemingly countless projectiles, both bullets and cannonballs, had whizzed close to him for years, including at the Battle of Monmouth, but none had found their target. He could not possibly have imagined that the bullet that would finally take his life would be fired by a former Continental officer who had once served on Washington's staff and was an abolitionist like himself. But that unnecessary tragedy was more than twenty years in the future and now Lieutenant Colonel Hamilton was solely focused on capturing Redoubt Number Ten, because he knew that October 14 was his day of destiny that he had seemingly awaited his entire life.

At last, Hamilton ascertained not long after sunset that exactly the right time had finally come. Taking a deep breath, he ordered his men up and out of the trench as silently as possible and led them out into the vast expanse of no-man's-land of at least a quarter mile under veil of darkness at 8:00 p.m. With Hamilton leading the way northwest through the light ground fog and lingering smoke from shell explosions of the recent heavy bombardment, these Continental veterans raced forward with fixed bayonets as silently as possible, after the usual load of gear and accoutrements had been left in the sandy trenches behind to ensure faster movements.

While each second lingered like an eternity, they advanced deeper into October's cool blackness. Hamilton's previously issued order that none of the usual war-cries were to be unleashed at the attack's beginning was now faithfully obeyed by his onrushing troops.

After advancing a good distance, Hamilton suddenly ordered his troops to halt. As previously arranged by him, they then laid in this advanced position on the level terrain within easy striking distance of the quiet redoubt, waiting for the prearranged signal of three cannon shots fired high into the sky from the designated nearby battery.

By this time, the young lieutenant colonel felt relieved by the fact that he had early smartly appealed directly to Washington, which had meant going over Tench Tilghman's head, to secure the best equipment and supplies, including sturdy leather shoes, for his men. To his credit, Washington had agreed with Hamilton's request.

Hamilton already had informed his men that the watchword was "Rochambeau," in honor of a dynamic leader of the French expeditionary force. To make sure that no accidental firing of a musket occurred prematurely to alert the redoubt's garrison and as mentioned, Hamilton's men still carried empty muskets and would continue to do so even when they would go over the top of Redoubt Number Ten, if they were so fortunate to have survived to reach the defensive bastion. These New York, Rhode Island, and Connecticut veterans under Hamilton now realized that they must rely solely upon the eighteen inches of their steel bayonets, which they knew how to use from previous battles with the hated redcoats, Hessians, and Loyalists, including some of these same men who now served under Lord Cornwallis.

Also providing inspiration to the men of the light battalions, they recalled General Washington's recent words to inspire them to greater exertions at the moment of truth. Like Hamilton, they realized that decisive victory at Yorktown now depended upon their combat prowess and what they could accomplish on the chilly night of October 14. Like their young commander, these veterans of the Light Corps sensed that they now possessed the golden opportunity to win the most decisive victory of the war in its climactic battle, which then well might end in the independence of the United States. Everything, consequently, was now at stake for them and their infant republic. In this key situation, Lieutenant Colonel Hamilton and his troops felt the burden and heavy pressure in regard to what was about to transpire, knowing that their moment of destiny had come at long last.

Desperate Race of Death

Finally, blasts from three cannon suddenly signaled that now was finally the time for the assault's unleashing in full force. Hamilton abruptly ordered his troops to rise up from the level ground before the imposing redoubt.

With drawn saber that he had worn and flashed on previous battlefields, Hamilton led the charge of his young soldiers, who rushed forward with fixed bayonets and far more courage than fear, moving as silently as possible northwest across the open ground and through the night's coolness. On the right, meanwhile, a "van guard of twenty men" (volunteers from each Continental light company, including experienced First Rhode Island black soldiers under Captain Stephen Olney) headed by Connecticut's Lieutenant Mansfield and the all-important "detachment of sappers and miners," (under Captain James Gilliland and including Sergeant Martin, who was among the 110 men who were officially part of Brigadier General Henry Knox's artillery brigade), in Hamilton's words from his report. This small vanguard led Gimat's and Fish's column forward over the level terrain.

At a good pace, Hamilton led his disciplined troops over the wide expanse of open ground. Lieutenant Colonel Hamilton realized that any tactical mistake or loud noise would now alert the British Seventy-First Regiment (Fraser's Highlanders) and Hessians.

These veteran defenders of the most strategic bastion were protected by a formidable array of obstacles from front to back, or south to north: first, a wide defensive field of abatis of sharpened tree limbs, then a timbered palisade or wooden fence, then a deep ditch, and then a wall of closely placed stakes with sharpened ends pointed toward the attackers. These stakes were positioned about midway up the steep earthen slope of the redoubt leading to the parapet, having been implanted deeply into the side of the square-shaped earthen bastion by skilled British engineers to impede anyone attempting to scale it. Quite simply, the overall engineering design and position of the sharpened stakes was calculated to impale as many men as possible. As if this was not enough, the redoubt's steep earthen sides that towered above a deep ditch to impede attackers were slick from the recent rains.

All the while, the deepening sense of anxiety continued to mount among Hamilton's fast-moving troops while they pushed northwest across the open ground of sandy soil, which helped to muffle the noise of hundreds of pounding feet. Hamilton continued to hope that the enemy garrison would not hear the pounding feet from so many infantrymen.

Hamilton and his light infantrymen only too well realized that a concentrated, close-range volley might erupt out of the blackness at any moment to cause widespread destruction, riddling the compact ranks with a hail of .75 caliber bullets from "Brown Bess" muskets. So far, the silence of the fast-paced advance failed to alert the enemy. Of Scottish heritage on his father's side, Hamilton had no idea that Redoubt Number Ten was now held by mostly Scottish Highlanders and that a mini-Celtic civil war was about to be played out once the two sides met in mortal combat.

Upon nearing the dense abatis of felled timber without detection, Hamilton suddenly called a brief halt just before the wide field of a thick abatis to organize his assault column on a prearranged signal for the final maneuvers. Here, based on Hamilton's precise tactical plan, the main assault column now split in its predesignated different parts with separate missions.

Lieutenant Colonel Laurens's command had moved out first and turned west to dash across the redoubt's right flank because it had the longest distance to travel in circling around to gain the redoubt's rear. Then, in the foremost on Hamilton's command, Lieutenant Mansfield's forlorn hope advanced as the vanguard on the double-quick. Meanwhile, Gimat's battalion swung to the right to hit the redoubt from that side opposite of Laurens's two companies of hardy veterans. All the while, Hamilton led the way in front of Gimat's surging battalion of onrushing troops. Meanwhile, Fish's battalion of light infantry was ready to shift to the left, or west, once it reached the thick field of abatis.

While Hamilton's troops descended upon the comatose redoubt, the other arm of the pincer movement, under Lieutenant Colonel Laurens, continued to move swiftly farther to the left, or west, and then shift north to gain the redoubt's rear. Fortunately, for Lieutenant Colonel Laurens and his troops, they were about to encounter no reserve force of British or Hessian troops stationed on the right flank or behind Redoubt Number Ten, after they turned east toward the York River.

By this time, the men of all three light battalions of infantry were on the move at a brisk pace.

The Dense Maze of Abatis Entanglements

Meanwhile, Lieutenant Colonel Hamilton had already made a bold decision that proved wise in saving lives and catching the veteran British regulars and Hessians of Redoubt Number Ten by even greater surprise. Unlike the French attackers, whose sappers were using axes to laboriously cut through abatis before Redoubt Number Nine, Hamilton knew the proper procedure would take too long.

The foremost attackers of the main body (Gimat's battalion) overtook the small detail of sappers and miners, who were in front with Lieutenant John Mansfield's vanguard. Therefore, to save time, Hamilton's troops would now have to make their way through the sharpened limbs as best they could on their own without the usual work of the miners and sappers, while hoping not to betray their close proximity and making as little noise as possible.[31]

Hamilton's ambitious tactical plan was working to perfection so far. Hamilton felt more confident for success in having covered so much ground without receiving any fire from Redoubt Number Ten, after

> Major Fish with the batalion [sic] under his command, who when the front of the column reached the abatis, unlocking his corps to the left [or west to attack the redoubt on its right after following in Laurens's tracks because troops had earlier followed the same route], as he had been directed, advanced with such celerity, as to arrive in time to partici-pate in the assault.[32]

In the rear of Hamilton's column to assist the men who were about to fall wounded whenever the inevitable first volley exploded out of the night from imposing Redoubt Number Ten, surgeon Thacher and other medical personnel had been intently watching since "the assault commenced at eight o'clock in the evening" on October 14.

All the while out in front with the advanced guard, Lieutenant Colonel Hamilton continued to encourage the experienced soldiers of Gimat's column onward through the abatis with his waving sword to the right, or east, of the silent redoubt, while boldly leading the way through the sharpened tree limbs and hoping that the first volley from the enemy would not erupt out of the blackness.[33] As mentioned, some Continentals possessed a burning desire to obtain revenge because of the respected Colonel Scammell's needless death at the hands of his merciless captors, who had long reasoned that the only good rebel was a dead rebel like so many of their heartless comrades who wore their distinctive green jackets with pride—ironically, fellow Americans of Lieutenant Colonel Tarleton's command, the infamous British Legion, which had wiped out one patriot command after another in South Carolina in bloody 1780 to win some of the most impressive, but bloodiest, battles of the war.[34]

Hamilton feared that the defenders were about to open fire because his fast-working soldiers now could not help making noise in their frantic efforts of picking their way through the sharp tangles of abatis that tore uniforms and cut through trousers to lacerate the skin on legs. But most important, Hamilton had already saved invaluable time and lives at this point when so near to Redoubt Number Ten, while avoiding detection by immediately charging with his men through the abatis as best they could.

Before Hamilton and his soldiers pushed entirely through the abatis and reached the deep ditch at the foot of Redoubt Number Ten, a Hessian sentry atop the towering earthen redoubt heard the noise and promptly issued the challenge "Wer da?" ("Who goes there?"), which, of course, was not answered.

The Explosion of the First Close-Range Volley

All of a sudden, the German and Highland defenders aligned along the parapet in a great hurry to the commands of shouting officers. Here, behind good protection, they finally unleashed a volley that spat fire out into the midst of the hundreds of Americans struggling through the abatis. Finally breaking Hamilton's order for absolute silence, the Light Corps soldiers unleashed a spirited cheer that split the night air to echo over the York River, which helped to unnerve the defenders. This raising chorus of war cries that was heard by General Washington and his men to the rear informed them that the "Little Lion" had indeed roared in his attack and that a desperate fight to the death was erupting in full fury at Redoubt Number Ten.

Meanwhile, Gimat's men of the Light Corps struck from the right and Fish's troops, Hamilton's old battalion, from the left in a classic pincer movement, while the soldiers of Laurens's battalion continued to swing wide to the west to circle around the redoubt in a bid to gain its rear. On Hamilton's orders not to waste precious time by adhering to standard procedures for an attack, the sappers and miners at the head of the right assault column under Gimat had not frantically cut through the abatis like in the French sector at Redoubt Number Nine. More eager to carry muskets rather than wielding axes, these men had begged Hamilton to be allowed to join the headlong charge. Knowing at this crucial juncture that he now needed every man in the attack to secure his great prize, Hamilton responded, "Then go to the devil if you will," which revealed his ready acceptance.

Now ready for the final sprint to scale the high parapet and reach the redoubt's fiery top before they were cut to pieces, Hamilton shouted for his men, including the miners and sappers, to charge to go over the top. In one bold rush and with Hamilton leading the charge with a drawn saber, the first soldiers to reach the redoubt began to laboriously climb over the timbered palisade at the redoubt's base, while cheering wildly in the hope of unnerving the Highlanders and Hessians, who continued to blast away as fast as possible.

Unseen by Hamilton's attackers in the darkness until they reached them, gaping holes had been torn open in the earth from the shell explosions which caused some onrushing men to stumble and fall into black depths before the redoubt, wasting more time and causing additional difficulty. But they quickly scrambled out of shell holes and continued onward. After climbing over or knocking down the palisade, Lieutenant Colonel Hamilton encouraged everyone onward by inspiring example, leading his troops into the ditch's eerie depths, where bodies now lay, that seemed deeper than anyone had previously imagined.

Without stopping to rest in the deep ditch, the foremost light infantrymen had still to confront the array of pointed stakes located about midpoint on the redoubt's steep sides, as the defenders continued to fire at point-blank range and began to throw hand grenades. The deep ditch proved precarious for the attackers by becoming a death trap if one lingered too long. If Hamilton did not get everyone quickly out of the deep ditch and up the redoubt's slick earth and sandy slope, then the soldiers might be slaughtered.[35]

One Hessian defender never forgot how Hamilton's attackers "made such a terrible yell and loud cheering that one believed the whole wild hunt had broken out" upon Redoubt Number Ten.[36] All the while, the onrushing mass of attackers continued to shout the password "Rochambeau," which became an inspirational battle cry. One soldier realized that this battle cry was effective because it symbolically "sounds like 'Rush-on-boys' when pronounced quick."[37]

While waving his sword, an animated Hamilton encouraged additional soldiers onward up the redoubt's slippery slope, shouting, "The fort's our own!" and "Rush on, boys!" Hamilton was about to be the first man to make significant progress in scaling the slippery slope of the redoubt's face. Meanwhile, twenty-six-year-old (the same age as Hamilton) Captain Stephen Olney led the troops of his crack First Rhode Island Regiment that was now in the vanguard and close behind Hamilton. In amazement, Olney saw that Hamilton was rising splendidly to the challenge and his example inspired everyone else.

With catlike agility and holding tight to his saber after an exhaustive effort, Hamilton successively climbed over the palisade of pointed stakes halfway up the slope. The sharp points of the stakes tore at the skin and lieutenant colonel's resplendent blue uniform during his desperate scramble ever higher. Finally reaching the smoke-wreathed top of Redoubt Number Ten and assisted in gaining the high parapet by two sturdy soldiers, a breathless Hamilton reached the top of the smoke-shrouded parapet, while the men of Gimat's battalion followed close behind, Fish's battalion struck on the left flank, and Laurens was closing the back door.

Crossing Bayonets in the Night

After scaling the around twenty feet of the redoubt's earthen slope, Hamilton then went over the top and straight into the enemy's very midst with a slashing saber, which he worked with a furious finesse against the fiercely resisting defenders, who now seemed everywhere. Hamilton was the first American fighting man to enter the fiery redoubt. By achieving this remarkable feat at the risk of his life, Hamilton had fulfilled another lofty, but most dangerous, ambition that bordered on sheer recklessness in complete accordance to his aggressive style of command and daredevil qualities.

The inspiring sight encouraged his men to even greater exertions. Immediately upon entering the earthen redoubt full of red coats and Hessians, a bloody bayonet fight erupted in cramped quarters. Hamilton had numerous close calls in the confusing fighting at close range.

Not far behind Hamilton, the oldest captain in the attack, Captain Olney, was the third American soldier to mount the smoke-lined parapet, after Lieutenant John Mansfield, leading the vanguard. Olney was the second man over the top. Here, amid the confusion and din, he frantically shouted for ten to twelve of his foremost men, including black fighting men from Rhode Island, to quickly form a line and load muskets to unleash a volley to cut down the nearest defenders.

Now a completely exposed target atop the parapet, Captain Olney simultaneously dodged bayonet thrusts from half a dozen British soldiers. Fortunately, Hessian and British soldiers had no time to reload their Brown Bess muskets after unleashing their initial volley—a factor that almost certainly saved both Olney and Hamilton from injury or death.

The hard-fighting Captain Olney was not so fortunate as his commanding officer, however. Like Lieutenant Mansfield, he also suffered serious bayonet wounds. Olney screamed when the long steel blade of a defender tore through the flesh of his thigh. Making broad swipes with their bayonets, other soldiers, especially a Scottish Highlander, ripped open Olney's lower abdomen, causing the intestine to protrude from the gaping wound. But Olney ignored his ugly wound and searing pain from multiple wounds to continue playing a spirited role.

Indeed, the elder Rhode Island captain continued to encourage his men over the parapet's top while holding the intestine inside his lower body cavity with blood-stained hands that trembled in pain. As additional elated Americans reached the parapet and began to open fire after having quickly loaded muskets that had been unloaded during the attack, the feisty defenders resisted for some time. Since he was in the charge's forefront and the first inside, Hamilton was most fortunate to have escaped injury from not only the initial volley fired by the enemy at close range, but also the flurry of furious bayonet thrusts.

The second-highest-ranking Continental officer after Captain Gilliland, Captain David Kilpatrick, second in command, also fell wounded in the wild combat inside the suffocating redoubt. Hamilton was impressed by the courage of the hard-fighting Kilpatrick. Finally overpowered after savage hand-to-hand combat that cut down some of the best fighting men on both sides, the surviving German and Highlander soldiers began to either flee down the redoubt's steep northern river side or surrender.[38]

Laurens and his detachment of light troops struck from the rear to capture defenders and close the back door on the redoubt, while Hamilton had struck the redoubt from the right flank and Major Fish from the left flank, which overwhelmed resistance in relatively short order. From beginning to end, the swiftness of Hamilton's capture of Redoubt Number Ten, which had once seemed all but impossible, had consumed less than ten minutes of bloody combat, after an advance that took about the same amount of time.

Delighted to have his best friend with him, Hamilton wrote with admiration, "Lt. Col. Laurens distinguished himself by an exact and vigorous execution of his part of the plan, by entering the enemy's work with his corps among the foremost" of the attackers.[39] Watching intently the amazing success of his former chief-of-staff whom he had finally allowed to excel on the field on his own, Washington exclaimed, "This work is done, and well done."[40]

Amazed by the young man's audacity in defying death and the odds, surgeon Thacher described how Hamilton and his light infantrymen

> bravely entered the fort with the point of the bayonet without firing a single gun. We suffered the loss of eight men killed, and about thirty wounded, among whom General Gimat received a slight wound in his foot, and Major [Caleb] Gibbs, of his excellency's [body]guard [and described as "a good-natured Yankee"] and two other officers [Barber and Kirkpatrick], were slightly wounded. Major [Patrick] Campbell, who commanded in the fort, was wounded and taken prisoner, with about thirty [British] soldiers.[41]

The remainder made their escape out of the hellish redoubt as best they could, until Laurens's column cut-off their line of retreat from the rear.

Laurens and his troops had so completely surprised the British-Hessian garrison that the South Carolinian personally captured

Highlander Major Campbell, who commanded the redoubt and had been caught napping.[42] Sergeant Martin never forgot the sight of desperate escapees fleeing from the smoking cauldron of Redoubt Number Ten and heading north toward the York River: "I saw a British soldier jump over the walls of the fort next to the river and go down the bank, which was almost perpendicular, and twenty or thirty feet high."[43]

Despite the redoubt's capture in record time, the bloodletting was still not over. With Major Campbell cut down with a wound and the "Stars and Stripes" being raised above Redoubt Number Ten to a chorus of cheers while the Union Jack was lying in the dust, some victorious Americans were still not satisfied with their sparkling tactical success, possessing revenge in their hearts.

After following Hamilton's attackers with fixed bayonets up the earthen slope, surgeon Thacher finally reached the inside of the smoking redoubt strewn with the bodies of a good many young men and boys on both sides. Here, he was astounded to discover that an angry

> captain of our infantry, belonging to New Hampshire [a special friend of Scammell who hailed from the same state], threatened to take the life of [the captured] Major Campbell, to avenge the death of his favorite, Colonel Scammel; but Colonel Hamilton interposed, and not a man was killed after he ceased to resist.[44]

If any man should have desired to see Campbell killed, it would have been Hamilton. However, because of his humanity, sense of honor, and desire for no stain on his good name if an atrocity were committed by men under his command, Hamilton interceded to save Campbell and a number of his helpless men from a grim retribution. Hamilton's actions were that more remarkable because he had personally liked the polished Scammell, who had been his immediate superior in the Light Corps, respected friend, and "an officer and a gentleman."[45]

After saving Major Campbell's life by placing himself between the injured captive and the enraged New Hampshire captain and some of his vengeful New England followers, Hamilton made sure that all British and Hessian soldiers, at least twenty men, were treated properly as prisoners-of-war and that no insult or harm would come to them.[46]

Meanwhile, the French attackers had risen magnificently to the fore at Redoubt Number Nine. Mirroring Hamilton's sparkling success to the northeast, disciplined French grenadiers and chasseurs of the Royal Deux-Ponts Regiment and the Regiment Gatinois, captured nearby Redoubt Number Nine in a gallant effort. After a bloody melee of French, Scottish, German, and English soldiers, including hand-to-hand combat, the victorious French planted the gold fleurs-de-lis on the white Bourbon flag on the body-strewn parapet to a chorus of victory cheers. Some infantrymen, who spoke German because of their Teutonic heritage and wore the standard 1779 white uniforms of the Royal Deux-Ponts Regiment, captured Hessian prisoners, whose war was now finally over, after a mini–civil war had been waged.

Unlike Hamilton's men, the Gallic attackers had been detected early, as the French officers insisted that the abatis be cleared away, according to military procedure. The Hessian sentry atop Redoubt Number Nine had been alerted by the sapper's noisy work and quickly sounded the alarm to rouse garrison members to hurriedly form on the parapet from where numerous volleys were then unleased at close range. Consequently, French losses (almost a hundred men) were nearly three times higher than those suffered by the Continental attackers.[47]

Young Lauberdiere, of Rochambeau's staff, described the attack on Redoubt Number Nine, writing that

a few sappers [advanced] at the head of this detachment to open passage in the abatis and to cut the fraises. The enemy began firing at a distance of 150 toises [but] We did not respond with a single musket shot. The march was rapid [and the French] penetrated the redoubt. We did not have any need for ladders. The same zeal, the same bravery animated the commander and the soldiers and we took the work sword in hand. There were 160 men to defend it. We only took 73 prisoners. The rest jumped over the parapet . . . when the first French grenadiers entered [Redoubt Number Nine.][48]

In fact, during the entire siege and in the attack on Redoubt Number Ten, the Continental troops had only twenty-four men killed and had another sixty-five wounded.[49]

Reaping the Laurels

As could be expected, Hamilton basked in the swift effectiveness of Redoubt Number Ten's capture and his relatively few losses. As he penned in his battle-report, "As it would have been attended with delay and loss to wait for the removal of the abatis and palisades the ardor of the troops was indulged in passing over them."[50] With pride in his men, Hamilton emphasized to the Marquis de Lafayette, "The rapid and immediate success of the assault are the best comment on the behavior of the troops. . . . I do but justice . . . when I . . . assure you, there was not an officer nor soldier whose behaviour, if it could be particularized, would not have a claim to the warmest approbation."[51]

But most of all, the true reason why formidable Redoubt Number Ten was so quickly captured with relatively light losses was Lieutenant Colonel Hamilton's outstanding tactical skill and leadership ability. With a modesty that was actually misplaced under the circumstances, Hamilton explained in his battle report, "There was a happy coincidence of movements. The redoubt was in the same moment invelopped [*sic*] and carried on every part [even though] The enemy are intitled [*sic*] to the acknowlegement [*sic*] of an honorable defence [*sic*]" of Redoubt Number Ten.[52]

Lieutenant Colonel Hamilton was especially proud that his men proved to be of a moral soldiery in a highly volatile and combustible situation inside the redoubt when consumed by chaos, despite the fact that it had taken his own frantic efforts to halt what might have resulted in a massacre of some prisoners, including Major Campbell. As Hamilton wrote, "Incapable of imitating examples of barbarity, and forgetting recent provocations, the soldiery spared every man, who ceased to resist."[53]

For ample good reason, Hamilton lavishly praised Lieutenant Colonel John Laurens for his leading role in capturing the imposing defensive bastion by closing the back door in a timely manner. To the Marquis de Lafayette, the native West Indian wrote, "Lt. Col. Laurens distinguished himself by an exact and vigorous execution by his part of the plan, by entering the enemy's works with his corps among the foremost" in the assault that overwhelmed Redoubt Number Ten.[54]

One of Washington's officers never forgot the dramatic sight of "a detachment of French and one of American troops took possession of the enemy's works, and planted on the epaulements the standards of the two nations."[55] General Washington fully realized that Hamilton's capture of Redoubt Number Ten (along with its sister redoubt by the French to the southeast) doomed Yorktown in short order. He wrote that, with the twin defensive bastions on Cornwallis's left now in friendly hands, "from them we shall enfilade the enemy's whole line" of defenses.[56]

After having overwhelmed the last hard-fighting defender and with the American flag flying proudly over Redoubt Number Ten, Hamilton was not taking any chances. He quickly formed his men for action, just in case the British launched a counterattack, refusing to take anything for granted in opposing a talented commander like Cornwallis. But thankfully for the weary victors and to Hamilton's great relief, the expected counterattack never came.[57]

Hamilton was extremely proud of what he had accomplished. But he was even more proud of the men of the light battalions. In Hamilton's own words that revealed his deep admiration for the young men and boys of his cherished light infantry battalion who he had led to such an astonishing victory, especially his "soldiers [who] spared every man who ceased to resist."[58]

Amazed at what had been accomplished by his former chief-of-staff, General Washington wrote in glowing terms and without exaggeration about Hamilton's remarkable success on the night of October 14: "The bravery . . . was emulous [and] Few cases have exhibited stronger proofs of Intrepidity, coolness and firmness than were shown upon this occasion."[59]

Chapter VII

Siege of Yorktown Continues Unabated

Early on Monday October 15, most of Hamilton's victors were finally relieved by a fresh battalion of Continental troops, while more than a hundred allied guns continued to relentlessly pound the British defenses. To stem off the inevitable, rows of British artillery shelled Redoubt Number Ten and the menacing second parallel with a vengeance and a new sense of desperation. Hamilton and his men endured the intense British bombardment while American soldiers labored to advance the second parallel to link with the captured redoubts. To ensure that Hamilton never lost his grip on what had been won, Redoubt Number Ten was bolstered with some of General Knox's cannon in case the British counterattacked. Lieutenant Colonel Hamilton and the redoubt's new defenders continued to ready themselves.

During the intense British cannonade of the redoubt, Hamilton and Henry Knox, Alexander's old artillery commander who was now setting up guns to enfilade the foe's line from the newly acquired commanding high ground perch, engaged in an animated discussion. In an ongoing debate, Hamilton discussed the wisdom of dodging incoming cannonballs and shells. They talked over General Washington's recent directive for his soldiers to yell "a shell" as a warning to save lives. Because of the righteous tone of Knox's inflexible opinions that were partly rooted in a Scotch-Irish intransigence, Hamilton might have wondered if Washington's best artilleryman was related to his equally single-minded and headstrong Saint Croix friend Reverend Hugh Knox of the Presbyterian faith.

But what now weighed heavily on Hamilton's mind was the true meaning of courage that has obsessed mankind since time immemorial, including ancient writers like Homer who focused on this timeless subject in the *Iliad*. Hamilton wondered if perhaps Washington's order was not causing excessive unsoldierly conduct among the men because it resulted in an undignified dodging for cover like rabbits scurrying away from a hungry fox or coyote. Such behavior based upon the simple laws of survival and natural instinct seemed incompatible with Hamilton's idealized view of a virtuous republican soldier's conduct.

After all, Hamilton was thoroughly imbued with Age of Enlightenment ideology and the loftiest romantic sentiments about the nature of courage and the proper actions of men engaged in this most noble and righteous of struggles. Therefore, an ever-idealistic Hamilton complained about the inherent indignity of Washington's order. A commonsense New Englander whose own sense of romanticism had long since faded away because of the war's horrors, Knox voiced no qualms about the necessity of crying, "a shell," so that the men had time to scurry for cover before the inevitable explosion.[1]

During this heated discussion between Hamilton and Knox inside Redoubt Number Ten, two British shells suddenly screamed overhead and dropped into the redoubt. With yells of "A shell, A shell!" in keeping with Washington's recent directive, savvy veterans instantly raced for the best cover, lest exploding projectiles were to tear them to pieces. Together, Lieutenant Colonel Hamilton, slender and slight, and General Knox, rotund and sturdily built like a bull, struggled to simultaneously get behind the same nearest protective cover. Born of a mutual panic, this highly undignified scramble for safety resulted because Hamilton had prudently decided "to be yet more secure held on behind Knox [and] Upon this Knox struggled to throw Hamilton off and in the effort himself [now] rolled over and threw Hamilton off toward the shells."[2]

As quick as a cat, Hamilton then "scrambled back again" behind the shelter where Knox was now secure, just before the two shells exploded to hurl iron fragments "in all directions." General Knox, well known for his keen sense of humor, now gained the last word to settle the spirited debate once and for all: "Now, now what do you think, Mr. Hamilton, about crying 'shell'? But let me tell you not to make a breastwork of me again!"[3] No doubt shocked by the sharp retort from the usually merry, light-hearted general, Hamilton's response was not recorded in the historical record and perhaps for very good reason.

The capture of the last two strategic redoubts allowed for the completion of the second parallel, which additionally sealed Cornwallis's fate and left no hope remaining for the doomed army. With the bitter end now only a matter of time, a distraught Lord Cornwallis knew that it was over, writing Clinton in New York City, "My situation now became [absolutely] critical [for we] shall soon be exposed to an assault in ruined works, in a bad position, and with weakened numbers."[4]

With summer already having died a slow death in the Virginia Tidewater and the meadow grass having already started to turn brown, Cornwallis never regained the strategic redoubts. Redoubt Number Ten remained firmly in Hamilton's hands, and he never relinquished his tight grip on his hard-won prize. After the capture of the two strategic redoubts on the British left, the besiegers pressed their tactical advantage to tighten the noose around Cornwallis and his rapidly-dwindling garrison. As surgeon Thacher wrote in his journal,

> Our second parallel line was immediately connected with the two redoubts now taken from the enemy, and some new batteries were thrown up in front of our second parallel line [and now] it must convince his lordship that his post is not invincible, and that submission must soon be his only alternative.[5]

Most importantly, Hamilton played a key role in delivering a fatal blow to the once-bright hopes of the best British commander in America to hasten the most humiliating end for Cornwallis and his entire army, thwarting "a modern Hannibal" in General Nathanael Greene's estimation, and his lordship's "evil genius," in the words of another contemporary that was equally appropriate.[6] As early as October 10, a desperate Cornwallis had written to Clinton to give a most prophetic analysis of his eventual fate: "Nothing but a direct move to York River—which includes a successful naval action—can save me."[7]

In earlier having lamented the "folly" of inefficient American efforts to galvanize a united resistance effort against the invader and after suffering one miserable defeat after another in the South, Hamilton's on-target words to Laurens on June 30, 1780, now rang true: "If we are saved France . . . must save us."[8]

Cornwallis's lines to the northwest up the south bank of the York River were fatally compromised and enfiladed, especially from the high ground of the two captured redoubts that dominated the British left flank. Sensing decisive victory more than ever before, the two dissimilar allies of Old and New World now commanded the river between Yorktown and Gloucester Point, which was located upriver on the river's north side opposite the powerful Fusilier Redoubt on the British right flank. Therefore, the surrender of Cornwallis's entire army was shortly forthcoming.

Lieutenant Colonel Hamilton began to feel a bit guilty about his considerable risk-taking in having led the charge, as if suddenly realizing that he possessed considerable family obligations. Therefore, he finally wrote a short note to his pregnant wife back at the Schuyler home at Albany, which now seemed like a world away from the dank Virginia Tidewater's lowlands and the struggle for possession of America.

Back in upper New York at Albany, Betsey was now fretting under considerable stress and anxiety about the safety of the sometimes irresponsible father of her first child, who was expected to be born in only a few months. She was also concerned about her unborn child's condition and her own health. Although a married man and father-to-be, Hamilton still thought much like a single man when it came to his own career and reputation.

In a rather remarkable letter, Hamilton wrote with heartfelt sincerity and a sense of creeping regret. After all, Betsey was now six months pregnant and she suffered alone without the man of her dreams when she most needed him. A healthy and handsome dark-haired son Philip Hamilton was destined to be born on January 22, 1781.

Hamilton underplayed the great dangers involved in leading the assault on Redoubt Number Ten by leaving out key details for the overall sake of his wife's sensibilities and for future martial harmony:

> Two nights ago, my Eliza, my duty and my honour obligated me to take a step in which your happiness was too much risked. I commanded an attack upon one of the enemy's redoubts; we carried it in an instant, and with little loss. You will see the particulars in the Philadelphia papers. There will be, certainly, nothing more of this kind [and] if there should be another occasion [for an attack], it will not fall to my turn to execute it.[9]

Clearly, Lieutenant Colonel Hamilton was excessively modest to his own wife, saying nothing about the strategic importance of Redoubt Number Ten, and how it was the key to the possession of Yorktown, allowing America's journalists from the nation's leading newspapers to sing his praises that were sure to come. And, of course, he made no mention that he had led the attack in person on the powerful defensive bastion in this letter to Elizabeth. Clearly, Hamilton embodied a paradoxical nature in so often relentlessly seeking the greatest glory in an almost irresponsible way, but then declining to elaborate upon what he accomplished of such a significant nature to the closest person to his heart, while also being a gambler by instinct and considerable risk-taker by nature—a side of her husband (the "Little Lion" side) that Elizabeth had not known about when they married, after a whirlwind romance. Hamilton never lied about his actions to his wife, but he just conveniently failed to mention all the relevant facts and details to keep matrimonial harmony intact, which demonstrated his wisdom and tact on the matrimonial front. Ever-the-diplomat who always knew exactly what to say and write to give the best impression, especially when it came to the ladies, Hamilton wisely knew what to tell his wife and what not to tell her.

However, a proud General Washington filled in the gap about Hamilton's stirring performance on October 14 in his official report. He described Hamilton's "bravery" in leading the assault on the defensive bastion that had to be captured at any cost, as Washington and Rochambeau fully realized without any doubt because of the crucial time factor. Then, Washington concluded his impressive tribute to his former chief-of-staff without exaggeration or hyperbole: "Few cases have exhibited stronger proofs of intrepidity, coolness and firmness" than Hamilton in having played such a key role at Yorktown.[10]

The Bitter End Finally Comes for Lord Cornwallis

Thanks largely to the two redoubts' falls and Cornwallis's failed attempt to evacuate his force by sea on the night of October 16, a brave drummer boy in a neat scarlet uniform climbed atop the earthen parapet of the battered defenses to the shock of onlookers on both sides on the following hot tidewater morning at around 10:00 a.m., while a British officer waved a white handkerchief. The young man, an unknown musician of the British Army, then beat the traditional signal for a parley on October 17.

Synchronistically, this golden day—a most memorable Wednesday—was the four-year anniversary of General Burgoyne's surrender at Saratoga that had garnered the crucial Franco-American alliance of 1778, which had finally come to full maturity at Yorktown. After twenty days of siege and more than a week and a half of constant artillery bombardment from more than one hundred American and French cannon, Lord Cornwallis was about to surrender his entire army in the greatest British debacle of the war.

Unluckily for the British, this Wednesday morning along the York River was the same balmy autumn day that thousands of Clinton's reinforcements began to board their ships in New York City for the belated mission of attempting to rescue Cornwallis. This vital mission called for a week's journey down the East Coast, if everything went according to plan.

Finally, hundreds of French and American artillery pieces ceased their incessant roar at Yorktown and an eerie calm settled over the war-torn port town on this most eventful of fall mornings. Washington's terms were harsh because Cornwallis possessed no other options and especially because of the mounting concern about the possible arrival of Clinton's reinforcements at any time. On October 18 Hamilton wrote his wife of the good news that caused all of America to rejoice: "Tomorrow Cornwallis and his army are ours [and] In two days after, I shall in all probability set out for Albany and I hope to embrace you in three weeks from this time."[11]

A Great Dream Comes True on Friday, October 19

Appropriately, Lieutenant Colonel John Laurens was one of the peace commissioners who finalized the terms of capitulation at the two-story Augustine Moore House. When finished after much arguing with hardheaded and proud British officers, the document was then sent to Washington, who stood waiting in Hamilton's Redoubt Number Ten, for final approval. After minor alterations were made by Washington to the document, Cornwallis signed the final articles of capitulation under Washington's threat that the bombardment would resume by 11:00 a.m., after granting his lordship only two hours to sign, because of the fear of the arrival of Clinton's reinforcements. Symbolically, Washington received the signed papers at Redoubt Number Ten and placed his final signature to paper along with Rochambeau and Admiral Barras, who represented Admiral de Grasse, while a little mound of dirt stood beside the strategic redoubt to mark a row of graves for Hamilton's men who had fallen in capturing the key position.

Led by Brigadier General Charles O'Hara, thousands of sullen, angry, and exhausted British, Loyalist, and Hessian troops did the unimaginable. They marched out of the battered array of defenses at 2:00 p.m. on October 19 and along Hampton Road to hand over twenty-four prized battle-flags and two hundred British artillery pieces. In total, Cornwallis surrendered around eight thousand men, including naval personnel, of the combined garrisons at Yorktown and Gloucester Point located on the north side of the York River.

Meanwhile, an embittered Cornwallis, a victim of his own soaring ambitions, hubris, and utter contempt for the American fighting man, had been stricken with a bout of dysentery like so many of his men, after three bouts with malaria. Although a sick man who had been worn down by disease, stress, and seemingly endless pressures, Cornwallis had demonstrated his mettle and commitment to his men by gamely remaining in command, when almost any other British general would have earlier retired to Charleston to recover from his aliments. In this regard, Cornwallis was not unlike Hamilton because of his desire to share the fate of his men.

Contrary to popular myth that has long been enthusiastically embraced by Americans of the day and generations of historians, Cornwallis was not feigning illness to avoid the ultimate humiliation of surrendering himself and his vanquished army. However, handing over his prized sword to a former Virginia militiamen and Mount Vernon agriculturalist was unthinkable to the proud aristocratic earl, who was a favorite and friend of the king of England. Consequently, the Ireland-born General Charles O'Hara, the most faithful of top lieutenants and brigadier general, now carried the earl's sword to surrender it to the commander of the Franco-American Army, General Washington.[12] Like his anguished men, O'Hara now sullenly realized that "America is irretrievably lost."[13]

A detailed American account that appeared in the pages of the *New-York Journal*, New York City, revealed the final dramatic scene, after

> about one o'clock, the articles of capitulation were signed and interchanged, and about two o'clock p.m., the British garrison of York, led on by General [Charles] O'Hara (Lord Cornwallis

being indisposed) were conducted by General [Benjamin] Lincoln through the combined army, drawn up in two lines to a field, where, having grounded their arms, and stripped off their accoutrements, they were reconducted through the lines, and committed to the care of a guard. At the same time and in the same manner the garrison at Gloucester was surrendered [and] Previous to this, a detachment of French, and one of American troops, took possession of the British horn works, and planted on the epaulements the standards of the two nations.[14]

A colonel of the Virginia militia wrote the following in a letter on October 26:

I had the happiness to see that British army which so lately spread dismay and desolation through our country, march forth . . . at 3 o'clock through our whole army, drawn up in two lines about 20 yards distance and return disrobed of all their terrors, so humbled and so struck at the appearance of our troops, that their knees seemed to tremble, and you could not see a platoon that marched in any order. Such a noble figure did our army make, that I scarce know which drew my attention most. You could have heard a whisper or seen the least motion throughout our whole line, but every countenance was erect, and expressed a serene cheerfulness. . . . Their own officers acknowledge them to be the flower of the British troops, but I do not think they exceeded in appearance our own or the French [and] Finer troops never saw [in Rochambeau's white-uniformed men and] His Lordship's defence [*sic*] I think was rather feeble. His surrender was eight or ten days sooner than the most sanguine expected, though his force and resources were much greater than we conceived.[15]

As could be expected in a long, bitter war of attrition, the proud British were in the foulest of moods throughout the surrender ceremony. In the words of one French officer, "The British were sorry to surrender their weapons to the Americans, for whom they had the worst contempt. They called to our soldiers and offered them their guns . . . adding that they would rather break them in a thousand pieces than leave them to the Americans."[16]

Symbolically, Lieutenant Colonel Hamilton was appropriately "mounted close to Washington [because] it was justice. He had been at Washington's side at headquarters during four years, expressing— and many times sharing in—his superior's decisions. Then, only five days before, his capture of an enemy redoubt has been preclude to the surrender."[17]

In an embarrassing but symbolic episode, O'Hara attempted to hand over Cornwallis's sword to Rochambeau since he believed that the finely uniformed Frenchman and nobleman was the overall commander, because he certainly looked and acted the part. General Rochambeau pointed toward Washington, and the dignified Irishman rode over to the Virginian, who diplomatically refused to accept Cornwallis's sword. Instead, he directed O'Hara to hand over his lordship's saber to Major General Benjamin Lincoln, who was second in command. Lincoln gained an appropriate satisfaction because he had been forced to surrender Charleston in May 1780 on humiliating terms in what was the greatest American disaster of the war.[18]

In his journal on October 19, Surgeon James Thacher wrote with unrestrained joy:

This is to us a most glorious day; but to the English, one of bitter chagrin and disappointment [because] Preparations are now making to receive as captives that vindictive, haughty commander, and that victorious army, who, by their robberies and murders have so long been a scourge to our brethren of the Southern states.[19]

One idealistic American officer never forgot the sight of the

brilliant appearance of the allied army, the joy which diffused itself from rank to rank, contrasted with the mortification, the despondence, and unsoldierly behavior, of the British troops, formed one of the most pleasing prospects a patriot can behold, or even his fancy depict . . . an army, thus cemented by affection, created by a union of interests and the intercourse of good officers, and animated by an attachment of the rights of mankind, could not fail of triumphing over a body of troops, enlisted under the banner of despotism, and led on by the hopes of plunder.[20]

Witnessing a sight that he thought that he would never see, a mounted surgeon Thacher described how the tall (generally taller than the French, Britons, and Hessians)

Americans were drawn up in a line on the right side of the road, and the French occupied the left. At the head of the former, the great American commander, mounted on his noble courser, took his station, attended by his aids [and] The Americans, though not all in uniform [mostly in brown hunting and riflemen shirts of coarse undyed wool], nor their dress so neat, yet exhibited an erect, soldiery air, and every countenance beamed with satisfaction and joy [and] it was in the field, when they came to the last act of the drama . . . their mortification could not be concealed. . . . We are not to be surprised that the pride of the British officers is humbled on this occasion, as they have always entertained an exalted opinion of their own military prowess, and affected to view the Americans as a contemptible, undisciplined rabble. . . . Cornwallis has fallen! And our country is not subjugated.[21]

General Charles O'Hara was thankful for gaining especially good treatment that he received partly because of an earlier promise he had made with Hamilton, in case either one would be captured, during the prisoner exchange mission in April 1778. Hamilton continued to demonstrate that he was a man of his word and a humane one.

After British, Hessian, and Loyalist arms had been laid down in a broad grassy field along the Hampton Road, it was time for the colors of more than two dozen proud British regiments to be surrendered. However, a complication in the customary surrender proceedings developed when twenty-four of Cornwallis's officers, who carried the twenty-four colors (six British and eighteen German) to be surrendered, suddenly balked, causing a delay in the solemn ceremony bound by protocol and tradition. These officers "brought forward their colors, to surrender to the representatives of the American Army, but when these officers found that they were confronted by a like number of sergeants [instead of officers], they hesitated and stood motionless with their encased colors."[22]

Again relying on one of his most dependable officers, Washington immediately dispatched Hamilton to ride down the long line to ascertain the exact source of the problem. Hamilton then learned from British officers that they would only surrender their prized silk colors to officers of equal rank, according to proper European military tradition and protocol. Lieutenant Colonel Hamilton reported their "wishes and feelings" to Washington, who assigned a detail of officers to accept the colorful banners.[23]

While watching the unforgettable scene with pride while on horseback near Washington, Hamilton basked in the glow of America's greatest success and his most outstanding tactical performance at Redoubt Number Ten during "the war's greatest strategic coup."[24] Hamilton could hardly believe the fruits of victory because Cornwallis's surrender was an absolute disaster for British arms and the major blow that was destined to eventually break the domestic and political will of the British people, including King George III.[25]

As Hamilton, after having just talked to some angry British officers and learning of their desire for revenge, wrote to a leading French
officer, "I have seen that army [of British, Loyalists, and Hessians] so
haughty in its success; not an emotion of the soldiers escap'd me; and
I observed every sign of mortification with pleasure."[26] In a sense of
triumph in which his strong feelings for revenge, which he usually
kept hidden, were satisfied, Hamilton wrote, "Cruel in its vengeance,
England will not believe that every project of conquest in America
is vain."[27]

General Rochambeau's staff officer and nephew, Lauberdiere,
described not only the bitter end of an entire army but also the abrupt
conclusion of a most distinguished military career and a tragic end for
England's best commander in North America:

> Such was the end and the fate of Lord Cornwallis after seven
> campaigns in America where he had nothing but victories.
> He contributed the most of General [William] Howe's suc-
> cess and he personally won several battles. He was well-liked
> by his troops whose hardships he shared with much courage
> and pleasure. . . . Against Mr. the Count de Rochambeau, he
> forgot the maxim which is to never ask how many are they
> but where are they? to beat the charge and to charge. He never
> gave enough credit to the Americans who are brave and that
> is what Mr. de Rochambeau taught him at York (because he
> was said to be ill) the day of the signing of the capitulation.
> My Lord was humbled and kind. Our general consoled him,
> pitied him, encouraged him and engaged him especially to
> appreciate and even like Mr. Washington who must inspire
> his enemy by his life and his actions, his feelings.[28]

After doing all that he could for Washington and America for more
than half a decade, Hamilton, age twenty-six, had won the kind of
battlefield fame that exceeded the widespread recognition that he had
first won as a New York artillery officer at Chatterton's Hill, the Raritan

River, Trenton, Princeton, and then at Monmouth in the summer of 1778, while then a member of Washington's staff—a string of stirring and impressive performances from 1776 to 1778. The dramatic victory reaped at Yorktown by the allies caused one American newspaper to print the bold-lettered, gleeful headline "How Are the Mighty Fallen!!"[29]

As appearing in the pages of the *New-York Journal* on November 12, 1781, one American officer described the extent of the remarkable success that Hamilton had made possible by having captured strategic Redoubt Number Ten with his prized light troops:

> No returns have been handed in, but from the accounts of the British officers, there are between five and six thousand prisoners, including sick and wounded [and] Near one hundred vessels, with their sailors and marines, have fallen into the hands of the French fleet under the capitulation. The British loss during the siege, they allow to be very considerable, the loss of the allied army does not exceed three hundred killed and wounded.[30]

Symbolically, Colonel Tench Tilghman, Hamilton's old Maryland friend, carried the surrender papers and the glorious news of Cornwallis's surrender to Congress, after an arduous journey by land and water of more than three hundred miles to Philadelphia. Tilghman arrived in America's capital in the early morning hours of October 22, but he shortly came down with a fever for his exhaustive effort and became bedridden. Appropriately, Congress voted to present Tilghman with a new horse (he certainly now needed one after his long, epic journey), bridle, leather saddle, and an ornamental dress sword.[31] Tilghman also now deserved a reward because he had refused to take any pay for serving longer than Hamilton or anyone else on Washington's staff and had even refused a well-deserved promotion.

Idealistic and dedicated like Hamilton because he believed in the egalitarian faith of true republicanism as the most noble of reasons to fight against Old World oppressors, Tilghman wrote the following in

a prophetic February 22, 1777, letter: "I have the happiness and satisfaction of feeling that I have contributed largely by my personal appli-
cation to the Cause in which I am engaged and which I am certain will
end in the Freedom of this Country."[32] Tilghman paid a high price for
his revolutionary zeal. The young Marylander's health was broken by
his years of exertions, including the long ride to Philadelphia to bring
the news of Yorktown to Congress, and he died of a fatal disease three
years after the war's end at age forty-two.[33]

In a letter, Hamilton briefly summarized the Yorktown Campaign
to the Vicomte De Noailles:

> After the junction with the French troops from the West
> Indies, the number of the two armies, and their excellent dis-
> position, amounted to a certainty of success [and] the cause
> of our victory [lay] in the superior number of ground and
> regular troops, in the uninterrupted harmony of the two
> nations, and their equal desire to be celebrated in the annals
> of history.[34]

The pages of the *New York-Journal* printed an account that was
more revealing than Hamilton's relatively brief description:

> Never was a plan more wisely concerted, or more happily
> and vigorously executed, than the present. The wisdom,
> perseverance, and military talents of our illustrious com-
> mander, shone with superior lustre on this occasion, and . . .
> The well-concerted and animated support of the Count de
> Grass [*sic*], was essentially conducive to the completion of
> this glorious event, and deserves the warmest thanks of his
> own country, and the grateful plaudits of every American.
> The exertions of the Count de Rochambeau, and all the offi-
> cers and soldiers of the French army, can never be excelled
> [because they were] the finest body of men in the world. The
> only contention which subsisted during the siege between the

troops of the two nations, was the glorious one of excelling each other in operations against the common enemy, and in doing justice to each others' merits.[35]

In anguish, Lord Cornwallis penned a short letter to Clinton that contained the tortured words which emphasized that the bitter end had come at last for his soaring ambitions of winning the war:

Sir, I have the mortification to inform your Excellency that I have been forced to give up the posts of York and Gloucester and to surrender the troops under my command by capitulation on the 19th instant as prisoners of war to the combined forces of America and France.[36]

After receiving the news of the elimination of an entire army under the nation's best commander at Yorktown, Lord North cried, "Oh God, it is all over!"[37]

In contrast, Washington's letter to the Continental Congress contained the most joyous words ever written by the Virginian in his finest hour:

I have the Honor to inform Congress, that a Reduction of the British Army under the Command of Lord Cornwallis, is most happily effected. The unremitting Ardor which actuated every Officer and Soldier in the combined Army in this Occasion, has principally led to this Important Event, at an earlier period than my most sanguine hopes had induced me to expect.[38]

Like so many of his fellow soldiers, including Hamilton, the prayers of Captain Joseph Bloomfield, 3rd. New Jersey Continental Infantry, were now in the process of being answered, thanks to the great victory at Yorktown: "God Grant that the United efforts of the

Colonies may be crowned with success & that they may be made a free[,] great and happy People."[39]

A Rendezvous with Destiny

Lieutenant Colonel Hamilton had finally achieved his lofty goal, "my object to act a conspicuous part in some enterprise that might perhaps raise my character as a soldier above mediocrity."[40] After having finally escaped Washington's giant shadow while serving on the Virginian's staff, he now became an authentic American hero for his achievements at Yorktown, especially in the capture of Redoubt Number Ten.

For years hardly known outside of Washington's staff and virtually unknown to the Congress and the American public, Hamilton established on October 14 a reputation far and wide as "a romantic, death-defying young officer, gallantly streaking toward the ramparts [of Redoubt Number Ten]. Take away that battle, and Hamilton would have gone down [in history] as the most prestigious of Washington's aides, but not a hero."[41]

For the young man who had been "one of the first Americans of the War of Independence to unlimber a cannon" when in command of his New York battery before he joined Washington's staff on March 1, 1777, he planned to resign his commission and then finally go home to Albany and his new family.[42] The fulfillment of Hamilton's longtime ambition of playing a leading role in the long-awaited delivering of a mortal wound to America's enemy on an important battlefield brought a measure of contentment to this restless, ever-ambitious soul. Hamilton's distinguished role was almost certainly "the most satisfactory minutes of his life."[43]

Now Hamilton's ambition was focused on his future life in his first true home and his own personal priorities for the first time since his difficult childhood days in the West Indies. Feeling that he had a new lease on life after his close calls at Yorktown, he only wanted to rejoin his wife Elizabeth in time to witness his first child's birth in Albany. Less than a week after Cornwallis's surrender to ensure the independence of America, Lieutenant Colonel Hamilton prepared to ride off to be once again by the side of his beloved wife, which is where he knew that he belonged.[44]

As he had recently written to his wife, "It is my object to be happy in a quiet retreat with my better angel." In the future, Hamilton planned to resume the study of law "to avoid inferiority [therefore he] must be laborious," in his words that revealed his insatiable ambition that had now been transferred in full from the battlefield to the civilian field. For Hamilton, there was destined to be no rest or relaxation in the future because he was about to carve out a remarkable political career on the national scene with President Washington.[45]

Desiring most of all to make up to Elizabeth for his past somewhat irresponsible and selfish behavior in having repeatedly risked his life when their child was on the way, Hamilton's wild race across country, which exhausted his horses to the point that they had to be repeatedly replaced, to Albany brought a joyous reunion. But like his friend Tench Tilghman, the long years of exhaustive campaigning and faithful service to his country had left Hamilton weary and ill by the end of December. He spent most of the next two months in bed at the Schuyler home on the Hudson, recovering. Finally, on January 22, 1782, Hamilton became the father of a son with the birth of Philip Hamilton.[46]

He had departed the army forever with no regrets, after more than six years of service. After Hamilton had said good-bye to Washington, members of the "family," especially his best friends the Marquis de Lafayette and Tench Tilghman, and leading officers and men of his beloved light battalion, Hamilton only desired the opportunity to enjoy civilian life to the fullest and take advantage of the opportunities on the national scene in the political realm, when the right time came.[47]

After Redoubt Number Ten's capture and Cornwallis's surrender, Hamilton had no regrets about his desire to end his military career. As noted, he was now consumed by one thought and priority that was for once not war-related: enjoying life with his lovely wife and their new son, Philip. Secretary of War Benjamin Lincoln and Congress hoped to retain Hamilton because his merits were now fully appreciated. Congress passed a January 1782 resolution that praised Hamilton's "superior abilities & knowledge of his profession." In fact, on the final day of December 1780, Congress had even taken the step of voting to retain Hamilton until the war's conclusion. However, after Yorktown, Hamilton already had made up his mind. Indeed, once Hamilton had come to a final decision about his life and future, nothing could change his mind, as Washington had already learned.[48]

From Philadelphia on March 1, 1782, Hamilton felt the need to clarify his thoughts in order to officially explain his final decision to depart his country's service, while making a special request of Washington for inactive status because he did not want to officially resign his commission:

> As I have many reasons to consider my being employed hereafter in a precarious light, the bare possibility of rendering an equivalent will not justify to my scruples the receiving any future emoluments from my commission. I therefore renounce from this time all claim to the compensations attached to my military station during the war or after it. But I have motives which will not permit me to resolve on a total resignation. I sincerely hope a prosperous train of affairs may continue to make it no inconvenience to decline the services of persons, whose zeal, in worse times, was found out altogether useless [therefore] I am unwilling to put it out of my power to renew my exertions in the common cause, in the line, in which I have hitherto acted. I shall accordingly retain my rank [Lt. Col.] while I am permitted to do it, and take this opportunity to declare, that I shall be at all times ready to obey the call of the public, in any capacity civil, or military [role].[49]

Therefore, as emphasized to Washington in this letter, Hamilton remained on the officer inactive list to be called up only in the case of national emergency—basically a reserve officer—with the new nation now on its own in a dangerous world of international predators eager to exploit any advantage for their own gain. In this sense, Hamilton was only semiretired, but he had renounced his military pension like a true republican soldier while retaining his lieutenant colonel's rank.[50]

At long last, the war (which still continued for America until 1783 when the Treaty of Paris was finally signed in early September) for the gifted young man so far from his native Caribbean homeland was finally over.[51] Surrounded by family and friends in Albany, Hamilton blossomed as a father, gaining new maturity and insights about what was most important in life. Of course, Hamilton's son brought the greatest joy to the proud father. He jokingly wrote to Lafayette that "I have been employed for the last ten months in rocking the cradle" of son Philip.[52] Now with a family of his own and far from the war's horrors, Hamilton became truly happy for the first time in his life. He wrote to a friend, "You cannot imagine how entirely domestic I am growing [and] I lose all my taste for the pursuit of ambition. I sigh for nothing but the company of my wife and baby." Hamilton was a doting father in part because he had been abandoned by his own father. Hamilton was fascinated by his son's rapid growth and development.

In one letter, he emphasized how his son "has a method of waving his hand that announces a future orator." Then, Hamilton joked that little Philip lacked proper coordination in attempting to stand "rather awkwardly and his legs have not all the delicate slimness of his father's [and therefore] It is feared he may never excel as much in dancing" as his debonair father, who danced with an enthusiasm and endurance hour after hour that brought admiration among men and women. The dashing Hamilton had long captivated women by his grace, boyish handsomeness, and winning ways that had become legendary in the army leadership circles, especially among the members of Washington's staff.[53]

Although no longer a soldier fighting his country's battles, Hamilton's hatred of America's invaders failed to diminish in part because England continued to be America's primary enemy long after the American Revolution, as evident in the outbreak of the War of 1812.

In a letter to the Louis-Marie-Antoine de Noailles, one of Rochambeau's top lieutenants who he addressed as Vicomte De Noailles during the winter of 1781–1782, Hamilton explained his feelings about facing the soldiers of the world's foremost leaders of imperialism and colonialism: As "for myself, I disclaim the loss of animosity, certain that a constant and eternal hatred is the only method to humble our enemy—like Rome who inflexible in her enmity, even after the destruction of Carthage, could not forgive her former glory."[54]

Hamilton's strong sense of morality and humanitarianism once again came to the fore during a headquarters crisis stemming from a war atrocity. An extremely unlucky American officer, New Jersey–born Captain Joshua "Jack" Huddy, had met a cruel fate. While being transported to a prisoner exchange, he was hanged by a captain at the head of a party of Loyalists, who sought revenge for a Tory's death, on April 12, 1782: the year Hamilton was elected to Congress from the State of New York. When General Washington learned about the hanging of an American officer by a fellow American, he faced a policy and morality crisis. What kind of response was now most appropriate and necessary so that other captive Americans did not suffer the same tragic fate at vengeful Loyalist hands?

Therefore, from his Newburgh, New York, headquarters, Washington sought the advice of top officers, including Hamilton, whose sage opinions continued to be indispensable to the commander-in-chief. Almost all twenty-five officers responded that the Tory officer responsible—American Richard Lippincott—should be handed over by Sir Henry Clinton, who commanded and led the British war effort from New York City, for harsh American justice. Washington accepted this vindictive solution of executing the officer responsible for Captain Huddy's death, if Clinton turned him over to the patriots. At this time, Washington's Army was positioned outside New York City, watching Clinton just in case he moved his forces into the interior or received reinforcements in an attempt to unleash the offensive.

Taking an unpopular minority position, Hamilton strongly argued against the harsh retaliation that so many of his fellow officers so righteously advocated and against Washington's own hard-line policy. This policy's ugliness became more obvious when a captured British captain, Charles Asgill, was chosen to pay the price for Huddy's murder instead of Captain Richard Lippincott, who naturally was not turned over by Clinton or he would have been hanged. Only age nineteen and from a respected family, Asgill was innocent of all crimes.

Correctly gauging that General Knox was not comfortable with Washington's unfair retaliation and that he perhaps could change Washington's mind, Hamilton wrote from Albany to his former artillery commander, "If we wreck our resentment on an innocent person, it will be suspected that we are too fond of executions. . . . I address myself to you upon this occasion, because I know your liberality and your influences with the General," who greatly admired his top artillery commander since nearly the war's beginning. Hamilton's nonprejudicial and fair-minded initiatives eventually paid dividends when, combined with the French agreeing with the young man's opinion, applied pressure on Washington for leniency. Therefore, in the end, Asgill's life was spared, and the brutal retaliation policy, which would have led to the inevitable reprisals to prompt an endless cycle of atrocities, was thankfully scrapped. Perhaps partly because he had been an immigrant to America's shores not long before the start of the American Revolution, Hamilton continued to be a strong advocate for a fair and lenient policy toward the Loyalists, who were after all fellow Americans, in order to bind the new nation's wounds during America's first civil war, especially in the South where this civil war had most fiercely raged.[55]

But unlike the extremely lucky Asgill, the life of Hamilton's best friend, Lieutenant Colonel John Laurens, was not spared by the harsh realities and brutalities of this war. Laurens was killed in a meaningless skirmish in a remote backwater region of South Carolina, when nothing was at stake but a trivial matter of pride and honor—one of the war's most needless sacrifices of a promising young man of so much talent. When Laurens and a small group of American cavalry-men discovered a British landing party on a relatively harmless sortie to secure provisions in the Combahee River country, he could not resist striking a blow.

Instead of prudently awaiting the arrival of nearby reinforcements that already were on the way, Laurens immediately ordered an attack with a few followers against a larger force located in a lightly fortified position. On this tragic Tuesday, August 27, 1782 during his mad dash to punish the redcoat interlopers who were only members of a foraging party, Laurens, age twenty-seven and slightly younger than Hamilton, was shot off his horse, falling with a mortal wound. Amid the remote-ness of bleak Chehaw Neck deep in the subtropical vegetation-covered South Carolina low country, the life of one of America's shining stars and true revolutionary heroes came to a tragic end when the war was all but over.[56]

As could be expected, Hamilton took the news of Laurens's death extremely hard. After all, Laurens was a best friend and kindred spirit. Hamilton's numerous warnings to the impetuous and hot-headed Laurens were not heeded in the end. In a letter to General Nathanael Greene and with heartfelt sadness, Hamilton penned an almost pro-phetic observation that applied to his own life in the end:

I feel a deepest affliction at the news we have just received of the loss of our dear and [inesti]mable friend Laurens [and now] His career of virtue is at an end. How strangely are human affairs conducted, that so many excellent qualities could not ensure a more happy fate? The world will feel the loss of a man who has left few like him behind, and America of a citizen whose heart realized that patriotism of which others only talk. I feel the loss of a friend I truly and most tenderly loved, and one of a very small number.[57]

And to the Marquis de Lafayette, without any exaggeration whatsoever, a grief-stricken Hamilton wrote painful words in regard to the only member of Washington's "family" to die in battle, of "Poor Laurens [who] has fallen a sacrifice to his ardor in a trifling skirmish. . . . You know how I truly loved him."[58]

He had lost a part of himself because of this senseless tragedy during a meaningless skirmish in South Carolina, when the mounted Laurens, with a flashing saber as if leading the attack on Redoubt Number Ten, had charged on the British practically by himself. In written form, Hamilton's close and intense feelings for Laurens had been revealed as early as April 1779. From Middlebrook, in east central New Jersey, Bridgewater Township, at the Continental Army's encampment, the normally reserved Hamilton had begun his letter to Laurens, who had departed Washington's staff for service in his native South Carolina, with a sincere confession that caught the essence of the day's romantic and fraternal spirit:

> Cold in my professions, warm in my friendships, I wish, my Dear Laurens, it might be in my power, by action rather than words, to convince you that I love you. I shall only tell you that 'till you bade us Adieu, I hardly knew the value you had taught my heart to set upon you. Indeed, my friend, it was not well done.[59]

What had been truly well done had been the mercurial (like Hamilton) John Laurens's diplomatic mission in France, where he not only secured invaluable aid from King Louis XVI but also played a key role in gaining French naval superiority in America's waters to help to pave the way for decisive victory at Yorktown. Along with obtaining the much-needed "gift" funding to purchase supplies for the badly depleted Washington's Army in time for the Yorktown Campaign, Laurens had directed his main efforts, as instructed, to gain a high-level French promise to employ the nation's West Indies fleet (under Admiral Comte de Grasse that had arrived to save the day for America) in American waters for combined offensive operations between allies—the key to decisive victory in this war. In this sense, the Hamilton-Laurens team played invaluable roles on and off the battlefield for years and on both sides of the Atlantic in helping to pave the way to the decisive success at Yorktown.[60]

Throughout his life, Hamilton never lost his faith in the great dream of America and its limitless potential and promise, which he had exploited to the fullest in the immigrant tradition. As he grew older, he always remembered the dramatic events in which he played a part in the war that had saved America: the dangerous crossing of the ice-clogged Delaware River on a stormy late December night and transporting his New York guns safely across the river's swirling waters in the cold blackness with his friend Henry Knox, who orchestrated the perilous river crossing during a winter storm; his New York artillery pieces roaring and delivering a well-aimed fire from the snowy heights that overlooked Trenton and punishing the Hessian garrison of a full brigade—three regiments—that had been caught by surprise by Washington's surprise attack early on the morning of December 26, 1776; playing a key role in helping to reverse the tide by his tirelessness to rally hard-hit American troops during the hard-fought battle at Monmouth by helping to stem a rout and then at the head of spirited counterattacks against Lord Cornwallis's men in New Jersey during one of the hottest days of the summer of 1778; and serving with distinction as Washington's chief-of-staff from early 1777 to early 1781, while making multiple invaluable contributions to the war effort. No matter what he later accomplished in life, Hamilton most of all cherished the fond memories of his men of the light battalion and especially his sparkling success at Yorktown.

Like during the war years, Hamilton's strong opinions and brash style continued to gather new enemies in the years after the war. This situation was just a continuation of when he had served as principal protector of Washington's much-derided reputation and the Machiavellian activities of insidious rivals, when his outspokenness—especially against the incompetence of a wholly ineffective Congress that had long caused the army so much suffering and death—earned him countless enemies in high places, including leading generals and politicians. But Hamilton had managed to escape the fatal consequences of their wrath by good fortune and his own adroit maneuvering, in addition to Washington's protection.

But Hamilton became more vulnerable after Washington ended his service as a two-term president in 1797. As could be expected, Hamilton's personal and political enemies fully exploited the opportunity when Hamilton's criticisms about Vice President Aaron Burr's lack of character and morality were printed in newspapers. Hamilton's sharp and on-target words infuriated President Thomas Jefferson, members of his administration, and his legion of supporters during the first term of the "sage of Monticello."

Of course, Hamilton refused to retract anything that he had said or written about Burr, because it was all true. This situation eventually spiraled and set Hamilton on a fatal collision course with the former Continental officer who also had won distinction during the war. Eventually, Hamilton felt that he had no choice but to accept Burr's challenge to settle matters in an affair of honor that had become an established custom of the day among America's elite.

However, Hamilton could have easily declined the invitation to engage in a duel, but he could not be convinced by either sound reason or common sense from friends and family. In truth, the proud Hamilton could not decline any more than he could have declined to lead the attack on Redoubt Number Ten, because it was not in his makeup. On the early morning of July 11, 1804, on the Hudson's west bank at Weehawken, Bergen County, New Jersey, Hamilton faced Vice President Burr in one of the most famous showdowns in American history. Of course, Hamilton viewed this duel as still another issue of personal honor because he was convinced that it was necessary to protect his good name from the criticisms and smears of his rivals, like during the war years.

Hamilton and Burr were much alike except in political terms and their respective visions of America's future. Burr had briefly served as

Washington's aide-de-camp, but these once-close bonds of a revolutionary brotherhood were no more. Both of these remarkable men were northeastern lawyers who had won recognition for their daredevil heroics on the battlfield. Hamilton was no stranger to facing death. However, during the war years, he had never imagined that the bullet that would take his life would come from a fellow countryman, who also had fought the British with a passion.

Even more ironic, before meeting Burr, the sitting vice president, on the dueling grounds of New Jersey in an ill-fated showdown with a matching pair of smoothbore flintlock pistols of small caliber, Hamilton had earlier penned how he was morally and philosophically opposed to dueling to settle personal differences, as he had advised son Philip. Nevertheless, Philip had already bravely gone to his dueling death after having deliberately wasted his shot rather than kill his opponent. Therefore, in moral terms and even after his son's death, Hamilton was determined to freely "expose [his] own life" instead of "taking the life of another" human being according to his philosophical reasoning, when about to meet a more cynical and non-philosophical man who had murder in his heart. Like when he had been Washington's "Little Lion" on America's battlefields, Hamilton faced Burr with his usual courage on the dueling grounds at exceptionally close range, because he felt that he had no choice. Here, at Weehawken on a ledge of land that overlooked the Hudson River and New York City on the river's east side, destiny itself had seemed to have brought Hamilton, the former capable secretary of the treasury for Washington, to this point. He simply felt that he had no choice but to defend his honor and name.

Hamilton would have never come under Burr's expert aim on July 11, 1804, had he not been so successful and famous in life. Hamilton knew he had to to act on his personal beliefs and principles. He, consequently, wasted his first shot in the reasonable and honorable gentleman's expectation that Burr would do the same to settle this matter with customary dignity. But for once, Hamilton had seriously errored in his usually sage judgment, making a gross miscalculation about the man who opposed him. It would cost him his life.

But still recalling Hamilton's scathing testimony to protect Washington's reputation against his beloved commander General Charles Lee during the England-born general's court martial proceedings in 1778 when Washington had charged him with cowardice at the Battle of Monmouth, Burr had other ideas about the precise definition of honor and its true meaning. Burr, who possessed a host of deep character flaws, was not the type of man to forgive and forget like the high-minded Hamilton, who had now met an entirely different kind of man than he had imagined.

Unlike Hamilton who had never allowed himself to be consumed by bitterness or hate except in regard to the cruel actions of the British enemy, Burr had succumbed to his strong personal passions. They overruled his reason to an inordinate degree and the day's established code of honor when it came to dueling, violating the native West Indian's most sacred personal principle that he was upholding by having wasted his shot by firing into the ground like his son Philip. The seemingly endless list of sparkling successes and impressive achievements of Hamilton's past, especially in preserving Washington's reputation and lofty position as the Continental Army's commander and the symbolic leader of the revolution, now came back to haunt him in the same state, New Jersey, as the Washington-Lee incident at Monmouth with a cruel vengeance, when he found himself suddenly staring down the barrel of Burr's dueling pistol, in the open at close range. Clearly, there was not going to be a reasonable settlement of differences between gentlemen on the Weehawken dueling ground as Hamilton had fully anticipated, because Burr was intent on killing him without either hesitation or qualms.

To this day, Hamilton's last thoughts are unknown. Despite his cynical but realistic nature, a look of astonishment, if not profound sadness, must have raced across the well-chiseled features of Hamilton's handsome face when Burr squeezed the trigger of his dueling pistol.

Just before he was fatally struck down by Burr's .54 caliber bullet, perhaps Hamilton became stoically reconciled to his tragic fate: dying needlessly, like his best friend John Laurens and his own promising son Philip, who was fatally cut down on the same dueling field of Weehawken at age nineteen on November 24, 1801.

Hamilton had cautioned his son, who was defending his father's good name from politically based slanders and had been educated in Trenton where his father had so magnificently risen to the battlefield challenge during Washington's surprise attack on a snowy December morning near the end of 1776, to fire his dueling pistol into the ground in a token gesture, according to the gentleman's code of honor. However, another talented lawyer, like Burr, had thought otherwise and fired a fatal bullet at close range from his dueling pistol.

Ironically, Hamilton was fatally cut down on the soil of New Jersey, where he had survived some of the war's most fierce battles, like Trenton, Princeton, and Monmouth, without receiving so much as a scratch. The dueling pistol was manufactured in England, and Hamilton had escaped harm from the large number of projectiles from British-made weapons on numerous battlefields from New York to Virginia.

While he lay dying on the dueling ground of Weehawken, perhaps the forty-nine-year-old Hamilton momentarily flashed back on the many close calls of past battles. The heavily bleeding Hamilton might have now thought back on his golden moment in the sun when he had led his crack light troops in the mad scramble up the formidable earthen defensive bastion to capture Redoubt Number Ten on the night of October 14 to ensure America's and Washington's greatest success at Yorktown.

On the following day, July 12, 1804, Hamilton died with a certain peace of mind in knowing what he had accomplished for America, General Washington, and his beloved Continental Army. Ironically, after having had so many close calls during the war and as mentioned, he had received his fatal wound from a former Continental officer in peacetime in a duel that went against his personal beliefs.

Few people, if any, at the time of Hamilton's death even remembered that he had played leading roles in having saved Washington's position as commander-in-chief and in making the Virginian a better general. One of America's brightest shining lights was extinguished in one of the most needless and unnecessary of deaths. Just before the tragic end came and before the final journey to the graveyard of Trinity Church on Broadway in Lower Manhattan, New York City, to be buried near his beloved son Philip on July 14, 1804, Hamilton must have realized that he had done all in his power to ensure that America not only won its independence but also was placed solidly on the right road to becoming a great republic with a bright future, including as a world power by the twentieth century, when the world was threatened by the rise of fascism and totalitarianism.

Before he finally breathed his last in New York City on July 12, Hamilton might have thought back to when he had so proudly worn an officer's uniform of blue as a diehard republican soldier during what he had solemnly considered to have been a sacred struggle and holy war for an infant nation's freedom during the world's first successful independence struggle against a major European Power.

When Hamilton was fatally cut down on July 11, 1804, by the shot fired by Burr, no founding father (except, of course, Washington) had accomplished more both on and off the battlefield to ensure America's ultimate victory than the one who had the most inauspicious and dismal start in life and the most tragic ending. Nevertheless, even after the war, he was still looked upon by many Americans, especially his many enemies whose numbers had continued to grow year after year, as nothing more than a detested "foreigner" with a trace of black blood (a persistent but false rumor), who was undeserving of the revered name of American, despite the fact that very few of his generation made more impressive achievements to America both on and off the battlefield than the native West Indian. However, when Hamilton died in New York City to the disbelief of his friends and supporters, his faith of a bright future for America did not die with him. Most important, he left behind enduring political, military, and economic legacies, including laying the foundation of the United States becoming a superpower in the twentieth century, as everlasting gifts to America and her people.[61]

Indeed, like no other founding father, Hamilton had left more of his permanent mark on America in more significant and fundamental ways. America would never be the same, thanks in no small part to Hamilton's many invaluable contributions in war and peace over the course of three decades. From beginning to end, he was a shining star and an innovative, bold free-thinker, who was well ahead of his time and perhaps, was destined to burn out early because his aura was so bright like a fiery comet streaking across the sky. As demonstrated more by his actions rather than words like most other people not long after his arrival on America's shores in 1773 just before the American Revolution's beginning, this enterprising immigrant from the West Indies was actually more truly American than most Americans, whose families had been living in the New World for generations, including the first settlers on the *Mayflower*.

With his trademark open-mindedness and ever-flexible lofty level of thinking unencumbered by ancient rules and prejudices, Hamilton repeatedly stood tall on moral principle to go against conventional and traditional thought, especially in regard to his most radical proposal in conjunction with John Laurens who hailed from a large South Carolina slave-owning family: advocating for the use of black troops to fight for America and their own freedom in order to replenish the army's limited manpower in the South nearly 140 years before African Americans were officially incorporated into an integrated United States military during the post-World War II period. Hamilton's position certainly did not sit well with the aristocratic Virginia elite, especially slave owners. Of course, Washington was included among the large slave-owning elite of Virginia, and the two men of radically divergent backgrounds possessed radically different views about slavery and its future in America.

No single wartime role played by Hamilton was more important to America's fortunes during the American Revolution than that of Washington's brilliant chief-of-staff and primary adviser and confidant to the commander-in-chief year after year, when the two men forged a truly "unbeatable" team second to none during the war years. The heady intellectual Hamilton was the model chief-of-staff for General Washington from beginning to end, establishing a template for the development of a permanent modern chief-of-staff position in today's America's military establishment. As the brilliant Louis-Alexandra Berthier was to Napoleon Bonaparte as a longtime chief-of-staff and right-hand man throughout numerous successful campaigns across Europe, most of which the native Corsican conquered, so Hamilton was the same guiding force to Washington from 1777 to early 1781. Napoleon wisely understood the supreme importance of a chief-of-staff in the indispensable Berthier who was the forgotten genius behind the most famous military man in history, and Washington likewise benefited greatly from Hamilton's multi-faceted contributions and talents on many levels for nearly four years.

In a strange twist of fate, Berthier was destined to die as tragically and prematurely as Hamilton. The gifted Berthier, who served during the Yorktown Campaign and was one of Rochambeau's top officers, fell from a window of a house and onto the cobblestone street in Bamberg, Germany, under mysterious circumstances that continue to be debated by historians to this day. In the end, Napoleon blamed his Waterloo defeat on not having the gifted Berthier, who earned a marshal's baton, by his side.

Hamilton's late 1772 arrival in the colonies as a hopeful immigrant not long before the American Revolution's beginning was still another sign from above that America's sacred cause was indeed blessed by a kind "Providence [which] is for some wise purpose," as Washington firmly believed to his dying day.[62]

Perhaps Hamilton's old Presbyterian minister, Hugh Knox, from Saint Croix said it best in regard to the strong religious faith of Washington and his Continental officers, including Hamilton, which largely explained his nearly four years of faithful service to Washington on his personal staff: "I feel . . . under a strong Impulse, to *prophesy* that Washington was born for the Deliverance of America; that [the will of] Providence will Shield his head in every Day of Battle [Washington was never wounded in battle], *Will Guide* him to See America *free, flourishing & happy.*"[63]

General Washington paid a rare tribute (although considerably understated) to Hamilton: "There are few men to be found, of his age, who has a more general knowledge than he possesses; and none, whose soul is more firmly engaged in the cause, or who exceeds him in probity and sterling virtue."[64] But even more, "save for Hamilton's intelligence gathering, Washington could well have fallen from power," to change the course of not only the American Revolution but also American history.[65]

Perhaps Colonel Timothy Pickering, Washington's trusty adjutant for a period of time, said it best in regard to Hamilton's many contributions of supreme importance: "During the long series of years, in war and peace, Washington enjoyed the advantages of Hamilton's eminent talents, integrity and felicity, and these qualities fixed [Hamilton] in [Washington's] confidence to the last hour of his life."[66] Nevertheless and unfortunately, after the war, "few men would remember redoubt 10" and what its all-important capture meant at Yorktown in overall strategic terms.[67]

As usual, Washington has long exclusively garnered the laurels, dominating the field of American Revolutionary War historiography and America's much-embellished creation story. After all, how could a lowly and young immigrant with a shadowy background in the Caribbean have possibly played such a vital role?

However, Washington's actions have spoken much louder than his words. Continuing the close teamwork of a dynamic partnership that had been forged in the crucible of the war years, Washington chose Hamilton as his secretary of the treasury when he became the president of the United States of America in 1789. Even more and although largely forgotten, Hamilton made another significant impact on the nation's history by having been in large part responsible for first convincing a reluctant Washington to serve as the nation's first president and then for a second term. Thereafter, the old war-time team of Washington and Hamilton was reunited during his presidency, continuing a remarkable success story from beginning to end—one of the most important alliances not only of the American Revolution and the early republic but also in American history.

Significantly, Hamilton also continued to be responsible for writing Washington's speeches, including his famous farewell address, throughout his presidency because Washington lacked the necessary formal education and writing skills. Like during the war years at headquarters, Hamilton became the first president's chief political advisor.

As America's first secretary of the treasury, Hamilton served as the chief architect of the modern American banking system and stronger centralized government. But of course, none of these successes would have been possible had not Washington and Hamilton first evolved into a highly successful in wartime. Quite simply, the most effective high-level military partnership and team during the Revolutionary War then became the equally effective political team for the key collaboration that led to the creation of the Constitution and a "more perfect Union" in the end.

For good reason, Washington sincerely referred to himself in a 1797 letter to Hamilton as "your sincere friend, and affectionate H[umble] Servant." Indeed, Hamilton was the forgotten key player behind many of the impressive successes of Washington as not only a general but also as a president year after year, because the Virginian relied more on Hamilton than any other individual in war and peace over the course of four decades. Of course, these were also some of the fundamental reasons, especially the close relationship between the two men who made each other better when working together, why Hamilton was hated, including by other founding fathers and especially by Aaron Burr, because of jealousy and envy stemming from his lofty abilities and achievements. Most telling of all, when it appeared that war between the United States and revolutionary France would erupt in 1798, Washington only considered taking charge of the army if the guiding light of Hamilton was by his side as his vital "coadju-tor," or second in command.[68]

One modern historian made the appropriate connection between Hamilton's vital position in Washington's administration and his contributions from 1777 to 1781: "This supremely confidant and extraordinarily able young man threatened to dominate the executive and to emerge as a kind of Prime Minister, with Washington as a kind of limited constitutional" head.[69]

But while the native West Indian's accomplishments were for-gotten in regard to his invaluable chief-of-staff role under General Washington, Hamilton's wife, Elizabeth, who lost her beloved hus-band and son Philip at Weehawken, New Jersey, perhaps said it best when she correctly informed one of his political foes about her hus-band's most enduring legacy that has survived to this day, not long after he died in New York City thirty-six hours after having been shot: "Never forget that my husband *made* your government" of the United States of America. Hamilton's final words to his wife were some of the most heartfelt that he had ever written by one of the most prolific men in America, because he wished for "the sweet hope of meeting you in a better world. Adieu, best of wives and best of Women. Embrace all my [eight] darling Children for me."[70] Hamilton lamented in a most prophetic September 12, 1780, letter to his best friend John Laurens, "The truth is I am an unlucky honest man."[71]

His legions of detractors could never take away Hamilton's lengthy list of achievements that he made on and off the battlefield, especially at Yorktown and Redoubt Number Ten. Emphasizing exactly why he had risked his life on fields of strife across America and struggled so passionately for America's liberty and often risked his life where the bullets flew the thickest, Hamilton penned these October 1787 words imploring the American people to adopt the proposed United States Constitution, because what was truly at stake was nothing less than "the fate of an empire in many respects, the most interesting in the world [and if not adopted then such an egregious mistake] deserve[s] to be considered as the general misfortune of mankind."[72]

In some strange, inexplicable cosmic equation, it was almost as if Hamilton's life had been ordained to meet an early tragic end because he had been blessed with so many exceptional gifts shared by few, if any, and especially at such an early age. As he sincerely lamented with some anguish because of a heightened awareness of the corrupt world operating on self-serving and dishonest principles, Hamilton was indeed not made for the cynical, harsh world that surrounded him and treated him so unfairly. In the end, Hamilton's remarkable life played out much like a classic Greek tragedy that he knew so well, but also like an authentic American tragedy for the most brilliant and gifted founding father in America's epic saga.

Epilogue

Today, very little evidence of young Alexander Hamilton's stirring role that he played in the most decisive battle of the American Revolution can be found at the Yorktown battlefield, including at Redoubt Number Ten, which is part of the National Park Service's Colonial Historical Park. Today, there are no remainders of Hamilton's vital role at Yorktown in the traditional form of a heroic statue, a paradox similar to the many in his life. The only physical reminder of Hamilton's glory day on October 14, 1781, can be seen today in the modern reconstruction of Redoubt Number Ten.

However, Hamilton's true legacy lies today in the everyday workings of modern America and not on the Yorktown battlefield. He had long opposed Thomas Jefferson's idealistic and utopian vision of a future American economy based on what it had primarily rested upon in the beginning of settlement in Virginia, the South, and even New England, where first Native American and then black slavery thrived, from the beginning: an insidious institution as old as mankind itself, slavery. Those views revealed how Hamilton was a moral and righteous man well ahead of his time and on the right side of history in not only political, social, and economic matters but also humanitarian concerns because he early possessed the enlightened vision of America's bright future without the curse of slavery, unlike Washington and Jefferson.[1]

Clearly, Hamilton's two finest hours of the war were during the Yorktown Campaign and in promoting black equality and freedom. Even during the war years, he bestowed America with a future vision of a nation without slavery by advocating the use of black troops battling for their own freedom and that of America, because he was convinced of the equality of the black man, an unimaginable concept to the vast majority of white Americans at the time and long afterward.[2]

From the beginning to the end of his remarkable life, Hamilton still remained a son of the sunny Caribbean, the islands of Nevis and Saint Croix, but not a true son because of his abolitionism, which opposed the world's most evil institution upon which the island societies and economies were based. He had come so far in life that it must have seemed improbable for anything in his life to go so profoundly wrong, because good fortune and the fickle gods of war had always smiled upon him until that fatal day of late November 1801, when his beloved son Philip was killed in an unnecessary duel at Weehawken.

Since that terrible day, Hamilton's personal fortunes had gradually sunk until he somehow found himself of all places on the same dueling grounds where Philip had been killed. An incredible case of the twisting turns of the hands of fates and personal fortunes coming full circle, almost as if these dual tragedies were somehow necessary to compensate for so many of Hamilton's past successes of an extraordinary nature, including in leading the assault that captured strategic Redoubt Number Ten. Ironically, Hamilton had given his life and his all for the winning of the war fought over the heart and soul of America, which ultimately betrayed him and his son in the cruelest possible manner in the end.

Most important and seldom emphasized by historians partly because of the excessive idolization of the more famous founding fathers, especially slave owners Jefferson and Washington, Hamilton was the most enlightened racial thinker and the most abolitionist of all the founding fathers. Proving that he was on the right side of history by his actions and not words, Hamilton saw slavery as the greatest disgrace and moral blemish on the young republic's egalitarian values and enlightened principles at a time when the robust and highly profitable institution was fully accepted by seemingly every nation of the world and thriving virtually everywhere around the globe like in the days of ancient Rome.

Significantly, Hamilton knew that slavery as the primary foundation of the American economy was not morally right, and he had acted accordingly, including as a founder of the New York Manumission Society, during his relentless pursuit to create a better America for all of its people, regardless of color. Clearly, Hamilton, who additionally verified that he was "one of the most brilliant men of his age," was once again no the right side of history and humanity, when it came to his hatred of slavery and efforts to end America's greatest curse.[3]

However, it was not Hamilton's antislavery vision that prevailed in post–Revolutionary War America but the idealistic Jeffersonian vision of an agrarian utopia to ensure a long life for the institution of slavery for future generations and more than halfway into the next century. In one of the great ironies of American history, the amazing victory at Yorktown, in which black soldiers from Rhode Island fought for liberty, ultimately placed the infant republic on the road to another bitter struggle to determine slavery's future.[4]

Endnotes

Chapter I

1. Ron Chernow, *Alexander Hamilton* (New York: Penguin Books, 2004), pp. 3–6, 62–125, 139, 149–52; Bruce Chadwick, *George Washington's War: The Forging of a Revolutionary Leader and the American Presidency* (Naperville, IL: Sourcebooks, 2005), pp. 426–27; Phillip Thomas Tucker, *Alexander Hamilton's Revolution: His Vital Role as Washington's Chief of Staff* (New York: Skyhorse Publishing, 2017), pp. 1–285; Jini Jones Vail, *Rochambeau: Washington's Ideal Lieutenant, a French General's Role in the American Revolution* (Tarentum, PA: Word Association Publishers, 2013), pp. 78–80; Broadus Mitchell, *Alexander Hamilton: The Revolutionary Years* (New York: Thomas Y. Crowell Company, 1970), pp. 29, 217–26; Jack Rakove, *Revolutionaries: A New History of the Invention of America* (Boston: Houghton Mifflin Harcourt, 2010), p. 406; L. G. Shreve, *Tench Tilghman: The Life and Times of Washington's Aide-de-Camp* (Centreville, MD: Tidewater Publishers, 1982), pp. 127–28.
2. Nathaniel Philbrick, *In the Hurricane's Eye: The Genius of George Washington and the Victory at Yorktown* (New York: Viking, 2018), pp. 155, 216.
3. Chadwick, *George Washington's War*, p. 427.
4. Ibid., pp. 428–29; Rakove, *Revolutionaries*, p. 406.
5. Chernow, *Alexander Hamilton*, p. 152; Shreve, *Tench Tilghman*, pp. 138–139.
6. Chadwick, *George Washington's War*, p. 428.
7. Ibid., p. 154; Shreve, *Tench Tilghman*, p. 138.
8. Tucker, *Alexander Hamilton's Revolution*, p. 285.
9. Mitchell, *Alexander Hamilton*, p. 226.
10. Tucker, *Alexander Hamilton's Revolution*, p. 9.

11. Mitchell, *Alexander Hamilton*, p. 1.
12. *Maryland Gazette*, Annapolis, Maryland, October 25, 1781.
13. Oswald Tilghman, *Washington's Loyalist: Lt. Col. Tench Tilghman's in the American Revolution* (private printing: 2016), p. 110; Shreve, *Tench Tilghman*, p. 23.
14. Vail, *Rochambeau*, p. 54.
15. Ibid., pp. xv, 54.
16. Tom Shachtman, *How the French Saved America: Soldiers, Sailors, Diplomats, Louis XVI, and the Success of the Revolution* (New York: St. Martin's Press, 2017), pp. 1–9.
17. Shreve, *Tench Tilghman*, p. 108.
18. Vail, *Rochambeau*, pp. xvi, xx–xxi, 3–12, 19, 22–33, 43, 46, 55–95.
19. Ibid., pp. 32–33.
20. Ibid., pp. 32–33, 41, 116.
21. Holger Hoock, *Scars of Independence: America's Violent Birth* (New York: Crown, 2017), p. 270.
22. Vail, *Rochambeau*, p. 41; Claude Manceron, *The Wind From America, 1778–1781*. vol. 2, *Age of the French Revolution*, vol. 2, (4 volumes, New York: Touchstone Books, 1989), pp. 236, 342; Norman Desmarais, *America's First Ally: France in the Revolutionary War* (Havertown, PA: Casemate Publishers, 2019), p. vi; Mark Mayo Boatner III, *Encyclopedia of the American Revolution* (New York: David McKay Company, 1966), p. 992.
23. Vail, *Rochambeau*, p. 95.
24. Ibid., p. 64.
25. Ibid., pp. 56–58; Manceron, *Wind From America*, p. 342.
26. Vail, *Rochambeau*, p. 57.
27. Ibid., p. 81.
28. Manceron, *Wind From America*, p. 340; Stanley D. M. Carpenter, *Southern Gambit: Cornwallis and the British March to Yorktown* (Norman: University of Oklahoma Press, 2019), p. 144; Mitchell, *Alexander Hamilton*, pp. 236–37.
29. Carpenter, *Southern Gambit*, pp. 216–19; John S. Pancake, *This Destructive War: The British Campaign in the Carolinas, 1780–1781* (Tuscaloosa: University of Alabama Press, 1992), pp. 222–23; Chadwick, *George Washington's War*, pp. 433–34; Mitchell, *Alexander Hamilton*, pp. 29–30, 237.
30. Carpenter, *Southern Gambit*, pp. 142–261; Tucker, *Alexander Hamilton's Revolution*, pp. 30–33; Mitchell, *Alexander Hamilton*, pp. 30–33.

31. Tilghman, *Washington's Loyalist*, pp. 1, 4–6, 8–9, 114.
32. Philbrick, *In the Hurricane's Eye*, p. 75.
33. *New Jersey-Gazette*, Burlington, New Jersey, August 15, 1781.
34. Philbrick, *In the Hurricane's Eye*, p. 218.
35. Ibid., p. 75.
36. Ibid.; Henry P. Johnston, *The Yorktown Campaign and the Surrender of Yorktown—1781* (New York: Harper and Brothers, 1881), p. 152.

Chapter II

1. Brendan Morrissey, *Yorktown 1781, The World Turned Upside Down* (Oxford: Osprey Publishing, 1997), pp. 8–9; Carpenter, *Southern Gambit*, pp. 233–45.
2. Don Cook, *The Long Fuse: How England Lost the American Colonies, 1760–1785* (New York: The Atlantic Monthly Press, 1995), p. 315.
3. David K. Wilson, *The Southern Strategy: Britain's Conquest of South Carolina and George 1775–1780* (Columbia: The University of South Carolina Press, 2005), pp. xiii–265; James K. Swisher, *The Revolutionary War in the Southern Back Country* (Gretna, LA: Pelican Publishing Company, 2008), pp. 111–116.
4. Johnston, *Yorktown Campaign*, p. 18.
5. Swisher, *Revolutionary War in Southern Back Country*, pp. 111–41; Chadwick, *George Washington's War*, p. 389.
6. Chadwick, *George Washington's War*, p. 389.
7. Carpenter, *Southern Gambit*, pp. 256–58.
8. William C. Stinchcomb, *The American Revolution and the French Alliance* (Syracuse: Syracuse University Press, 1969), pp. 134–35; Vail, *Rochambeau*, pp. 30–49, 69–73.
9. Swisher, *Revolutionary War in Southern Back Country*, pp. 143–68; Lawrence S. Kaplan, *Alexander Hamilton, Ambivalent Anglophile* (Lanham: Rowman and Littlefield, 2001), p. 31; Willard Sterne Randall, *Alexander Hamilton* (New York: Harper Perennial, 2014), p. 149.
10. Wayne Lynch, "Unlucky or Inept? Gates at Camden," *Journal of American History*, May 1, 2014, Journal of American History Online.
11. Vail, *Rochambeau*, p. 55.
12. Carpenter, *Southern Gambit*, p. 213; Robert Harvey, *"A Few Bloody Noses," Realities and Mythologies of the American Revolution* (New York: Abrams Press, 2002), p. 392; Russell F. Weigley, *The American Way of War:*

A History of United States Military Strategy and Policy (Bloomington: Indiana University Press, 1977), pp. 27–30.

13. Swisher, *Revolutionary War in Southern Back Country*, pp. 168–72; Wilson, *Southern Strategy*, p. 264; Harvey, *"A Few Bloody Noses,"* p. 392.

14. Wilson, *Southern Strategy*, pp. xiii, xv; Carpenter, *Southern Gambit*, pp. 167, 259–61.

15. John Buchanan, *The Road to Guilford Courthouse: The American Revolution in the South* (New York: John Wiley and Sons, 1997), pp. 221–41, 234–35; Carpenter, *Southern Gambit*, pp. 216–18, 223, 257–60; Robert L. Tonsetic, *1781, The Decisive Year of the American Revolution* (Philadelphia: Casemate Publishing, 2013), p. 7; Walter Edgar, *Partisans and Redcoats: The Southern Conflict That Turned the Tide of the American Revolution* (New York: William Morrow, 2001), pp. 139–45; Swisher, *Revolutionary War in Southern Back Country*, pp. 168–69, 294–322; J. David Dameron, *King's Mountain: The Defeat of the Loyalists, October 7, 1781* (New York: Da Capo Press, 2003), pp. 9–83, 92; Robert D. Bass, *Gamecock: The Life and Campaigns of General Thomas Sumter* (Orangeburg, SC: Sandlapper Publishing Company, 2000), pp. 62–216; Ron Gragg, *By the Hand of Providence: How Faith Shaped the American Revolution* (Brentwood: Howard Books, 2012), pp. 175–76; Harvey, *"A Few Bloody Noses,"* pp. 389–91; Weigley, *American Way of War*, pp. 27–30; Lucien Agniel, *The South in the American Revolution* (Myrtle Beach, SC: Artpress International, 1980), p. 109; James Webb, *Born Fighting: How the Scots-Irish Shaped America* (New York: Broadway Books, 2004), pp. 169–72.

16. Johnston, *Yorktown Campaign*, p. 23.

17. Ibid., p. 26; Cook, *Long Fuse*, p. 334.

18. Johnston, *Yorktown Campaign*, p. 29.

19. Cook, *Long Fuse*, p. 336.

20. Morrissey, *Yorktown 1781*, p. 9.

21. Carpenter, *Southern Gambit*, pp. 214–18; Pancake, *This Destructive War*, pp. 222–23; Johnston, *Yorktown Campaign*, pp. 29, 32–33; Vail, *Rochambeau*, pp. 32–33.

22. Agniel, *South in the American Revolution*, p. 110.

23. Morrissey, *Yorktown 1781*, p. 17; Vail, *Rochambeau*, pp. 32–33.

24. Tilghman, *Washington's Loyalist*, p. 121; Vail, *Rochambeau*, pp. 32–33.

25. Chernow, *Alexander Hamilton*, p. 154; Mary-Jo Kline, *Alexander Hamilton, A Biography in His Own Words, Founding Fathers*, volume 1,

(2 vols: New York: Harper & Row, 1973), p. 97; Chadwick, *George Washington's War*, pp. 427–29.

26. Kline, *Alexander Hamilton*, p. 97.
27. Chernow, *Alexander Hamilton*, pp. 154–55; Randall, *Alexander Hamilton*, p. 226; Milton Lomack, *Odd Destiny, The Life of Alexander Hamilton* (New York: Farrar, Straus & Giroux, 1969), p. 75.
28. Mitchell, *Alexander Hamilton*, p. 238.
29. Chernow, *Alexander Hamilton*, p. 155; Randall, *Alexander Hamilton*, p. 226; Boatner, *Encyclopedia of the American Revolution*, p. 634; Mitchell, *Alexander Hamilton*, p. 239; Shreve, *Tench Tilghman*, p. 124.
30. Rakove, *Revolutionaries*, pp. 399–400.
31. A. J. Langguth, *Patriots, The Men Who Started the American Revolution* (New York: Simon & Schuster, 1989), p. 519; Chernow, *Alexander Hamilton*, p. 155; Randall, *Alexander Hamilton*, p. 226; Rakove, *Revolutionaries*, pp. 406–7; Lomask, *Alexander Hamilton*, p. 75; Stephen F. Knott and Tony Williams, *Washington and Hamilton, The Alliance that Forged America* (Naperville: Sourcebooks, 2016), p. 99; Mitchell, *Alexander Hamilton*, pp. 240–41.
32. Rakove, *Revolutionaries*, pp. 400, 407; Randall, *Alexander Hamilton*, pp. 218, 226; Kaplan, *Alexander Hamilton*, pp. 26–33; Douglas S. Freeman, *Washington* (New York: Simon & Schuster, 1995), p. 465.
33. Mitchell, *Alexander Hamilton*, pp. 29–30.
34. Ibid.
35. Alexander Hamilton to George Washington, May 2, 1781, Alexander Hamilton Papers, National Archives, Washington, DC; Chernow, *Alexander Hamilton*, p. 158; Mitchell, *Alexander Hamilton*, pp. 240–41.
36. Mitchell, *Alexander Hamilton*, p. 241.
37. Alexander Hamilton to George Washington, May 2, 1781, Alexander Hamilton Papers, National Archives, Washington, DC.
38. Randall, *Alexander Hamilton*, p. 226.
39. Rakove, *Revolutionaries*, p. 403.
40. Randall, *Alexander Hamilton*, p. 226.
41. Rakove, *Revolutionaries*, p. 403.
42. Randall, *Alexander Hamilton*, p. 227; Tonsetic, *1781*, p. 71; Gregory D. Massey, *John Laurens and the American Revolution* (Columbia: University of South Carolina Press, 2015), pp. 173, 176–78, 186; Freeman, *Washington*, p. 464; Carpenter, *Southern Gambit*, p. 233; Knott and Williams, *Washington and Hamilton*, p. 413; Vail, *Rochambeau*, pp. 86–87, 89–92, 98–101; Shachtman, *How the French Saved America*,

pp. 86, 228–31, 237; Mitchell, *Alexander Hamilton*, pp. 227, 231; Vail, *Rochambeau*, pp. 74–80, 86; Shreve, *Tench Tilghman*, pp. 132, 142.

43. Mitchell, *Alexander Hamilton*, p. 238.
44. Ibid.
45. Pancake, *This Destructive War*, p. 223; Carpenter, *Southern Gambit*, pp. 220–21; Agniel, *South in the American Revolution*, pp. 110–11.
46. Mitchell, *Alexander Hamilton*, p. 237.
47. Carpenter, *Southern Gambit*, p. 218; Agniel, *South in the American Revolution*, p. 111.
48. Vail, *Rochambeau*, pp. 86, 96–98; Agniel, *South in the American Revolution*, pp. 111–12.
49. Mitchell, *Alexander Hamilton*, pp. 241–42.
50. Ibid., p. 242.
51. Shreve, *Tench Tilghman*, pp. 142–43.
52. Ibid., p. 144.

Chapter III

1. Chernow, *Alexander Hamilton*, p. 159; Langguth, *Patriots*, p. 519; Chadwick, *George Washington's War*, pp. 428–29; Rakove, *Revolutionaries*, p. 407; Shreve, *Tench Tilghman*, p. 62; Kline, *Alexander Hamilton*, pp. 97–98; Randall, *Alexander Hamilton*, pp. 176, 182–85, 218, 227–30, 236; Freeman, *Washington*, p. 465; John C. Miller, *Alexander Hamilton, Portrait in Paradox* (New York: Barnes & Noble Press, 2003), pp. 72, 242.
2. Mitchell, *Alexander Hamilton*, p. 244.
3. Chernow, *Alexander Hamilton*, p. 159; Mitchell, *Alexander Hamilton*, pp. 244–45.
4. Mitchell, *Alexander Hamilton*, p. 245.
5. Robert K. Wright, *The Continental Army* (St. John's Press, 2016), p. 167; Chadwick, *George Washington's War*, pp. 428–29; Langguth, *Patriots*, p. 519; Miller, *Alexander Hamilton*, p. 73; Johnston, *Yorktown Campaign*, pp. 113–14.
6. Kline, *Alexander Hamilton*, pp. 97–98.
7. Randall, *Alexander Hamilton*, pp. 175, 236–37; Mitchell, *Alexander Hamilton*, p. 245; Tonsetic, *1781*, p. 200.
8. Mitchell, *Alexander Hamilton*, p. 246.
9. Ibid., p. 250.

10. Ibid., pp. 75–76; Mitchell, *Alexander Hamilton*, p. 246; Randall, *Alexander Hamilton*, pp. 218, 226, 237; Shreve, *Tench Tilghman*, p. 84; Robert A. Geake, *From Slaves to Soldiers: The 1st Rhode Island Regiment in the American Revolution* (Yardley, PA: Westholme, 2016), p. 79; Morrissey, *Yorktown, 1781*, p. 35.

11. Mitchell, *Alexander Hamilton*, p. 246; Johnston, *Yorktown Campaign*, p. 114.

12. Randall, *Alexander Hamilton*, p. 237.

13. Mitchell, *Alexander Hamilton*, p. 225.

14. Kline, *Alexander Hamilton*, p. 98.

15. Robert Middlekauff, *The Glorious Cause, The American Revolution, 1763-1789* (Oxford: Oxford University Press, 2007), p. 687.

16. Henry Steele Commager and Richard B. Morris, T*he Spirit of 'Seventy Six,' The Story of the American Revolution As Told by Participants* (New York: Da Capo Press, 1988), p. 1202.

17. Carpenter, *Southern Gambit*, p. 235.

18. Pancake, *This Destructive War*, pp. 223–24.

19. Ibid., p. 225; Carpenter, *Southern Gambit*, pp. 221, 236.

20. *Pennsylvania Packet*, Philadelphia, Pennsylvania, July 14, 1781.

21. Vail, *Rochambeau*, pp. 96–97.

22. Johnston, *Yorktown Campaign*, p. 95.

23. Ibid.

24. Vail, *Rochambeau*, pp. 56–57, 76–78; Stinchcombe, *American Revolution and French Alliance*, pp. 135–37.

25. Stinchcombe, *American Revolution and French Alliance*, pp. 137–38.

26. Ibid., p. 138; Tonsetic, *1781*, pp. viii, 8, 73–74; Mark Puls, *Henry Knox, Visionary General of the American Revolution* (New York: St. Martin's Press, 2010), p. 146; Piers Mackey, *The War for America, 1775-1783* (Lincoln: University of Nebraska Press, 1993), p. 413; Vail, *Rochambeau*, pp. 76–78, 89–90, 98–99.

27. Stinchcombe, *American Revolution and French Alliance*, p. 138; Harvey, *"A Few Bloody Noses,"* p. 395.

28. Stinchcombe, *American Revolution and French Alliance*, pp. 138–39; Harvey, *"A Few Bloody Noses,"* pp. 394–96.

29. Stinchcombe, *American Revolution and French Alliance*, pp. 138–39; Harrison Clark, *All Cloudless Glory, The Life of George Washington* (Washington, DC: Regnery Books,1998), p. 505; Puls, *Henry Knox*, p. 146.

30. Tonsetic, *1781*, pp. 74, 99–100; Stinchcombe, *American Revolution and French Alliance*, pp. 138–40; Harvey, *"A Few Bloody Noses,"* p. 397;

Clark, *All Cloudless Glory*, p. 505; Vail, *Rochambeau*, pp. 86–87; Massey, *John Laurens and the American Revolution*, pp. 173, 176–78.

31. Vail, *Rochambeau*, pp. 86–87.
32. Vail, *Rochambeau*, pp. 96, 98–99; Tonsetic, *1781*, pp. 100, 109–10; Mackesy, *War for America*, p. 413.
33. Tonsetic, *1781*, p. 110; Maskesy, *War for America*, pp. 413–14.
34. Cook, *Long Fuse*, p. 342.
35. Vail, *Rochambeau*, pp. 96–97.
36. Stinchcombe, *American Revolution and French Alliance*, pp. 138–40; Commager and Morris, *Spirit of 'Seventy-Six*, p. 717; Randall, *Alexander Hamilton*, pp. 217–18.
37. *Maryland Gazette*, August 2, 1781; Mackesy, *War for America*, pp. 428–429.
38. Harvey, *"A Few Bloody Noses,"* pp. 391–93; Pancake, *This Destructive War*, pp. 223–25; Mackesy, *War for America*, pp. 411–12; Tonsetic, *1781*, pp. 125–26, 128, 132; Vail, *Rochambeau*, p. 92; Agniel, *South in the American Revolution*, p. 111; Cook, *Long Fuse*, p. 339.
39. Pancake, *This Destructive War*, p. 225.
40. James Thacher, *Military Journal of the American Revolution* (Cranbury: Scholar's Bookshelf, 2005), p. 264; Harvey, *"A Few Bloody Noses,"* p. 398; Howard C. Rice and Anne S. K. Brown, translaters and editors, *The American Campaigns of Rochambeau's Army 1780, 1781, 1782, 1783*, (2 vols, Princeton: Princeton University Press, 1972), vol. 2, p. 7; Vail, *Rochambeau*, pp. 118–20, 123, 129, 132.
41. *Maryland Gazette*, July 13, 1781; Rene Chartrand, *The French Army in the American War of Independence* (London: Osprey Publishing Limited, 1991), p. 36; Tonsetic, *1781*, p. 128; Mackesy, *War for America*, p. 413.
42. Mitchell, *Alexander Hamilton*, p. 255.
43. Randall, *Alexander Hamilton*, p. 168.
44. Ibid.; *Maryland Gazette*, September 20, 1781; Mackesy, *War for America*, p. 413
45. Alexander Hamilton to Colonel Hugh Hughes, July 25, 1781, Papers of Alexander Hamilton, https://founders.archives.gov/documents/Hamilton/01-26-02-0002-0066, Editor Harold C. Syrett. Charlottesville: University of Virginia Press, Rotunda, 2011.
46. Carpenter, *Southern Gambit*, p. 253.
47. *Maryland Gazette*, August 2, 1781.
48. Alexander Hamilton to George Washington, August 7, 1781, Alexander Hamilton Papers, National Archives, Washington, DC.

49. Harvey, *"A Few Bloody Noses,"* pp. 397–98; Clark, *All Cloudless Glory*, p. 505; Tonsetic, *1781*, p. 129; Mackesy, *War for America*, pp. 412, 414; Shachtman, *How the French Saved America*, p. 236; Cook, *Long Fuse*, pp. 342–44.
50. Harvey, *"A Few Bloody Noses,"* p. 398; Tonsetic, *1781*, p. 129; G. de Bertier de Sauvigney and David H. Pinkney, *History of France* (Santa Ana: The Forum Press, 1983), p. 201.; Cook, *Long Fuse*, pp. 342–343.
51. Carpenter, *Southern Gambit*, p. 234.
52. Cook, *Long Fuse*, p. 339.

Chapter IV

1. Thacher, *Military Journal*, pp. 268–69.
2. Agniel, *South in the American Revolution*, p. 124.
3. Clark, *All Cloudless Glory*, p. 528; Robert Hanson Harrison, Valley Forge National Historic Park, Pennsylvania, https://www.nps.gov/vafo/learn/historyculture/roberthansonharrison.htm; "Robert Hanson Harrison," *Baltimore Sun*, Baltimore, Maryland, December 31, 1990; Agniel, *South in the American Revolution*, p. 124; Freeman, *Washington*, pp. 465–66; Donald A. Moran, "George Washington's Militay Family," Liberty Tree Newsletter, (December 1998); Tonsetic, *1781*, p. 4; Shreve, *Tench Tilghman*, pp. 122–23.
4. "Robert Hanson Harrison," *Baltimore Sun*, December 31, 1990.
5. Kline, *Alexander Hamilton*, p. 97.
6. Abraham A. Davidson, *The Story of American Painting* (New York: Harry N. Abrams Publishers, 1974), p. 29; Moran, "George Washington's Military Family"; Irma B. Jaffe, *Trumbull: The Declaration of Independence* (London: Penguin Books, 1976), pp. 19–25; Vail, *Rochambeau*, p. 107.
7. Johnston, *Yorktown Campaign*, p. 112.
8. Vail, *Rochambeau*, p. 58.
9. Shachtman, *How the French Saved America*, p. 233.
10. Harvey, *"A Few Bloody Noses,"* pp. 398–99; Tonsetic, *1781*, p. 129; Randall, *Alexander Hamilton*, p. 237; Clark, *All Cloudless Glory*, pp. 523, 542; Chadwick, *George Washington's War*, p. 434; Johnston, *Yorktown Campaign*, pp. 87–88; Morrissey, *Yorktown 1781*, p. 35.
11. Johnston, *Yorktown Campaign*, p. 95.
12. Mitchell, *Alexander Hamilton*, pp. 253–54.
13. Ibid., p. 255; Randall, *Alexander Hamilton*, p. 237.
14. Mitchell, *Alexander Hamilton*, p. 255.

15. Chernow, *Hamilton*, p. 73.

16. Randall, *Alexander Hamilton*, pp. 237–38; Kline, *Alexander Hamilton*, p. 99; Mitchell, *Alexander Hamilton*, p. 250.

17. Mitchell, *Alexander Hamilton*, p. 250.

18. Johnston, *York Campaign*, p. 94.

19. Mitchell, *Alexander Hamilton*, p. 256.

20. Harvey, *"A Few Bloody Noses,"* p. 399; Randall, *Alexander Hamilton*, p. 238; Thacher, *Military Journal*, p. 271; Tonsetic, *1781*, pp. 135–36; Mitchell, *Alexander Hamilton*, p. 256; Mackesy, *War for America*, p. 414.

21. Thacher, *Military Journal*, pp. 269–70.

22. Ibid., p. 270; Carpenter, *Southern Gambit*, p. 234.

23. Randall, *Alexander Hamilton*, p. 237.

24. Mitchell, *Alexander Hamilton*, p. 256.

25. Johnston, *Yorktown Campaign*, p. 101.

26. Thacher, *Military Journal*, p. 271; *Maryland Gazette*, September 13, 1781; Charles Bracelen Flood, *Rise, and Fight Again: Perilous Times along the Road to Independence* (New York: Dodd, Mead & Company, 1976), p. 406; Chartrand, *French Army in American War*, p. 20; Morrissey, *Yorktown 1781*, p. 49.

27. *Maryland Gazette*, September 13, 1781.

28. *New York Gazette and Weekly Mercury*, September 10, 1781.

29. Morrissey, *Yorktown 1781*, p. 49.

30. Thacher, *Military Journal*, pp. 265–66.

31. Tonsetic, *1781*, p. 129.

32. Vail, *Rochambeau*, pp. 45, 130.

33. Ibid., p. 135.

34. John U. Rees, *"They Were Good Soldiers": African-Americans Serving in the Continental Army, 1775–1783*, (Warwick, UK: Helion & Company, 2019), pp. x-xi, 20-41, 36-41, 68, 72-81, 83, 86; Geake, *From Slaves to Soldiers*, pp. 79–80.

35. Rees, *"They Were Gold Soldiers,"* pp. x-xi, 20-41, 36-41, 68, 72-81, 83, 86; Mitchell, *Alexander Hamilton*, p. 231.

36. Randall, *Alexander Hamilton*, p. 238.

37. Morrissey, *Yorktown 1781*, pp. 19, 37, 39.

38. Harvey, *"A Few Bloody Noses,"* pp. 399–400; Tonsetic, *1781*, pp. 137–38; Vail, *Rochambeau*, p. 97; Cook, *Long Fuse*, pp. 344, 346.

39. Thacher, *Military Journal*, p. 274.

40. Desmarais, *America's First Ally*, p. 223; Vail, *Rochambeau*, p. 173; Shachtman, *How the French Saved America*, p. 234.

41. Chernow, *Alexander Hamilton*, p. 160.

42. Mitchell, *Alexander Hamilton*, p. 258.

43. Shachtman, *How the French Saved America*, p. 248.

44. Ibid., pp. 248–49; Philbrick, *In the Hurricane's Eye*, pp. 150–51. Vail, *Rochambeau*, p. 147.

45. Philbrick, *In the Hurricane's Eye*, p. 151.

46. Thacher, *Military Journal*, p. 274.

47. Mitchell, *Alexander Hamilton*, p. 259.

48. Randall, *Alexander Hamilton*, p. 238.

49. Joseph Plumb Martin, *A Narrative of a Revolutionary War Soldier: Some of the Adventures, Dangers, and Sufferings of Joseph Plumb Martin* (New York: Penguin Putnam Publishers, 2001), pp. vi, 196; Tonsetic, *1781*, p. 138; Shachtman, *How the French Saved America*, p. 234.

50. *Pennsylvania Packet*, September 18, 1781.

51. Carpenter, *Southern Gambit*, p. 236.

52. *Pennsylvania Packet*, September 18, 1781; Carpenter, *South Gambit*, p. 234; Harvey, *"A Few Bloody Noses,"* pp. 399–400; Mackesy, *War for America*, p. 428; Tonsetic, *1781*, pp. 135–38.

53. Sauvigney and Pinkney, *History of France*, pp. 200–201; Mackesy, *War for America*, p. 414, Vail, *Rochambeau*, pp. 26–29; Cook, *Long Fuse*, p. 346.

54. Cook, *Long Fuse*, pp. 344–45; Randall, *Alexander Hamilton*, pp. 238–39.

55. Mitchell, *Alexander Hamilton*, p. 261.

56. Carpenter, *Southern Gambit*, pp. 235–45; Harvey, *"A Few Bloody Noses,"* pp. 400–403; Tonsetic, *1781*, pp. 138–39; Flood, *Rise, and Fight Again*, p. 406; Mackesy, *War for America*, p. 428; Cook, *Long Fuse*, p. 345.

57. Thacher, *Military Journal*, p. 275; Mackesy, *War for America*, pp. 429–30; Tonsetic, *1781*, pp. 138–39; Carpenter, *Southern Gambit*, pp. 244–45.

58. Thacher, *Military Journal*, p. 277.

59. Carpenter, *Southern Gambit*, p. 244.

60. Agniel, *South in the American Revolution*, pp. 125–26.

61. Cook, *Long Fuse*, p. 346.

62. Shreve, *Tench Tilghman*, p. 9.

63. Ibid., *Tench Tilghman*, pp. 3–5, 154.

64. Vail, *Rochambeau*, pp. 146.

65. Alexander Hamilton to Elizabeth Hamilton, September 15–18, 1781, Alexander Hamilton Papers, National Archives, Washington, DC; Knott and Williams, *Washington and Hamilton*, p. 101.

66. Randall, *Alexander Hamilton*, p. 239; Boatner, *Encyclopedia of the American Revolution*, pp. 991–992.

67. Mitchell, *Alexander Hamilton*, p. 250.

68. Tilghman, *Washington's Loyalist*, pp. 56, 124; Shreve, *Tench Tilghman*, pp. 10, 22.
69. Tilghman, *Washington's Loyalist*, p. 56.
70. Mitchell, *Alexander Hamilton*, pp. 2, 262–63; Randall, *Alexander Hamilton*, p. 239; Massey, *John Laurens and the American Revolution*, p. 186; Tonsetic, *1781*, pp. 142, 179; Mackesy, *War for America*, p. 414; Mitchell, *Alexander Hamilton*, pp. 258–59, 262–63.
71. *Pennsylvania Packet*, September 18, 1781.
72. Chernow, *Alexander Hamilton*, pp. 42, 159, 161; Tonsetic, *1781*, pp. 161, 163; Mitchell, *Alexander Hamilton*, p. 263; Morrissey, *Yorktown 1781*, p. 59; Francis Barber—Famous Americans.net.
73. *Maryland Gazette*, September 20, 1781.
74. *New York and Weekly Mercury*, October 22, 1781.
75. Martin, *Narrative of a Revolutionary Soldier*, p. 196; Burke Davis, *The Campaign That Won America, The Story of Yorktown* (Durham: Eastern Acorn Press, 1979), pp. 189–90; Tonsetic, *1781*, pp. 143–44; Randall, *Alexander Hamilton*, p. 240; Mitchell, *Alexander Hamilton*, pp. 267–68; Vail, *Rochambeau*, p. 45.
76. Thacker, *Military Journal*, p. 278.
77. Massey, *John Laurens and the American Revolution*, p. 183; John Shelby, *The Road to Yorktown* (New York: St. Martin's Press, 1976), p. 199; Moran, "George Washington's Military Family,"; Shreve, *Tench Tilghman*, pp. 211–12.
78. Chadwick, *George Washington's War*, p. 132; Kaplan, *Alexander Hamilton*, p. 26.
79. Louis-Francois Lejeune, *The Napoleonic Wars through the Experiences of an Officer on Berthier's Staff*, vol. 2 (2 vols., LEONAUR, 2007), pp. 116–17; Rakove, *Revolutionaries*, p. 403; Clark, *All Cloudless Glory*, p. 521; Rice and Brown, *American Campaigns of Rochambeau's Army*, vol. 2, p. 7; Tonsetic, *1781*, p. 131; Vail, *Rochambeau*, p. 44.
80. David G. Chandler, *On the Napoleonic Wars: Collected Essays* (Mechanicsburg, PA: Stackpole Books, 1999), p. 111; Chris McNab, editor, *Armies of the Napoleonic Wars, An Illustrated History* (Oxford: Osprey Publishing, 2014), p. 39.
81. Bertrand Jost, *Life and Death of a French Soldier in the American War of Independence 1778–1781* (Private Printing, 2020), pp. 1–3; Vail, *Rochambeau*, pp. 137, 253; Morrissey, *Yorktown, 1781*, p. 35; Geake, *From Slaves to Soldiers*, pp. 79–80.
82. Jost, *Life and Death of a French Soldier*, p. 110.

83. Norman Desmarais, translated and annotated, *The Road to Yorktown: The French Campaigns in the American Revolution, 1780–1783* (El Dorado Hills, CA: Savas-Beatie Publishing, 2021), pp. xiv–xv.
84. Ibid., p. 7.
85. Ibid., pp. 105–6.
86. Ibid., p. 106–7.
87. Shreve, *Tench Tilghman*, p. 87.
88. Kline, *Alexander Hamilton*, p. 77.
89. Alexander Hamilton to John Jay, July 13 1777, Columbia University Libraries, New York, New York; Chernow, *Alexander Hamilton*, pp. 160–61.
90. Carpenter, *Southern Gambit*, pp. 244–45; *Pennsylvania Packet*, October 9, 1781; Desmarais, *America's First Ally*, p. 223; Agniel, *South in the American Revolution*, pp. 127–28; Shreve, *Tench Tilghman*, pp. 143–44.
91. Chernow, *Alexander Hamilton*, pp. 39, 161.
92. *Maryland Gazette*, August 2, 1781; Desmarais, *Road to Yorktown*, p. 173.
93. Cook, *Long Fuse*, p. 326.
94. *Maryland Gazette*, October 25, 1781.
95. Desmarais, *Road to Yorktown*, p. 158; Vail, *Rochambeau*, pp. 38, 42.
96. Agniel, *South in the American Revolution*, pp. 127–28.
97. Johnston, *Yorktown Campaign*, p. 102.
98. Morrissey, *Yorktown 1781*, p. 7.
99. Ibid., pp. 7, 60; Carpenter, *Southern Gambit*, pp. 237, 245; Mark Urban, *Fusiliers: The Saga of a British Redcoat Regiment in the American Revolution* (New York: Walker and Company, 2007), p. 270; Tonsetic, *1781*, pp. 106, 187; Shelby, *Road to Yorktown*, pp. 188–89; Chernow, *Alexander Hamilton*, p. 161; Tonsetic, *1781*, pp. 132–33, 143, 167; Harvey, *"A Few Bloody Noses,"* pp. 392, 397–404; Desmarais, *America's First Ally*, p. 223.
100. Thacher, *Military Journal*, p. 279.
101. Pennsylvania Packet, October 22, 1781.
102. Shelby, *Road to Yorktown*, pp. 189–90; Tonsetic, *1781*, pp. 166–67, 172; Jost, *Life and Death of a French Soldier*, p. 134; Agniel, *South in the American Revolution*, p. 125; Shreve, *Tench Tilghman*, p. 145; Morrissey, *Yorktown 1781*, p. 35; Shreve, *Tench Tilghman*, p. 149.
103. Desmarais, *Road to Yorktown*, p. 161; Vail, *Rochambeau*, pp. 156–57.
104. Thacher, *Military Journal*, p. 279.

105. Tonsetic, *1781*, p. 170; Harvey, *"A Few Bloody Noses,"* pp. 405–6; Robert Leckie, *George Washington's War: The Saga of the American Revolution* (New York: Harper's Perennial, 1993), p. 654.

106. Johnston, *Yorktown Campaign*, p. 127.

107. Carpenter, *Southern Gambit*, p. 246; Shachtman, *How the French Saved America*, pp. 248–49.

108. *Pennsylvania Packet*, October 9, 1781.

109. Carpenter, *Southern Gambit*, pp. 246–49; Harvey, *"A Few Bloody Noses,"* pp. 400–406; Flood, *Rise, and Fight Again*, p. 407.

110. Harvey, *"A Few Bloody Noses,"* pp. 405–7; Johnston, *Yorktown Campaign*, p. 121.

111. Thacher, *Military Journal*, pp. 279–80.

112. Martin, *Narrative of a Revolutionary Soldier*, p. 198.

113. *Pennsylvania Packet*, October 9, 1781.

114. Urban, *Fusiliers*, pp. 270, 272, 274, 276; Tonsetic, *1781*, pp. 168, 172; Flood, *Rise, and Fight Again*, p. 407; Mackesy, *War for America*, p. 428; Cook, *Long Fuse*, pp. 344–45; Chernow, *Alexander Hamilton*, pp. 161–62; Johnston, *Yorktown Campaign*, p. 124; Shreve, *Tench Tilghman*, p. 3.

115. Desmarais, *Road to Yorktown*, p. 105.

116. Martin, *Narrative of a Revolutionary Soldier*, p. 199; Flood, *Rise, and Fight Again*, p. 407.

117. Davis, *Campaign That Won America*, pp. 213–16; Harvey, *"A Few Bloody Noses,"* p. 408.

118. Morrissey, *Yorktown 1781*, p. 66; Tonsetic, *1781*, p. 179; Shelby, *Road to Yorktown*, p. 200.

119. Jost, *Life and Death of a French Soldier*, p. 109; Vail, *Rochambeau*, pp. 177–78, 187.

120. Jost, *Life and Death of a French Soldier*, p. 114.

Chapter V

1. Shachtman, *How the French Saved America*, p. 273.

2. Jost, *Life and Death of a French Soldier*, p. 140; Flood, *Rise, and Fight Again*, p. 408; Kline, *Alexander Hamilton*, pp. 58–59, 104; Morrissey, *Yorktown 1781*, p. 66; Tonsetic, *1781*, p. 179; Kaplan, *Alexander Hamilton*, p. 37; Miller, *Alexander Hamilton*, p. 68; Randall, *Alexander Hamilton*, p. 87; Davis, *Campaign That Won America*, p. 216; Philbrick, *In the Hurricane's Eye*, p. 208; Geake, *From Slaves to Soldiers*, pp. 79–80;

Vail, *Rochambeau*, p. 130; Shachtman, *How the French Saved America*, pp. 272, 277; Chernow, *Hamilton*, p. 73.

3. Tonsetic, *1781*, pp. 179, 229; Morrissey, *Yorktown 1781*, p. 66; Davis, *Campaign That Won America*, p. 216; Hugh Sheer and George F. Rankin, *Rebels and Redcoats* (New York: Mentor, 1987), p. 558.

4. *A List of Officer's and Men's Names Who Have Received One Month's Pay in Colonel Hamilton's Battalion*, Papers of Alexander Hamilton, Editor, Harold C. Syrett. Charlottesville: University of Virginia Press, Rotunda, 2011; Geake, *From Slaves to Soldiers*, pp. 79–80.

5. Morrissey, *Yorktown 1781*, p. 66; Tonsetic, *1781*, pp. 154–55, 179; Randall, *Alexander Hamilton*, p. 214; Davis, *Campaign That Won America*, p. 216; Johnston, *Yorktown Campaign*, p. 106.

6. Scheer and Rankin, *Rebels and Redcoats*, p. 558; Morrissey, *Yorktown 1781*, p. 66; Miller, *Alexander Hamilton*, p. 77.

7. Vail, *Rochambeau*, pp. 188–189.

8. John C. Hamilton, *The Life of Alexander Hamilton*, vol. 1 (2 vols., Charleston: BiblioBazaar, 2009), pp. 176–80; Harvey, *"A Few Bloody Noses,"* p. 407; Charles Royster, *A Revolutionary People at War: The Continental Army and America* (Chapel Hill: University of North Carolina Press, 1996), pp. 205–6; Stinchcombe, *American Revolution and French Alliance*, pp. 134–38; Morrissey, *Yorktown 1781*, p. 66.

9. Vail, *Rochambeau*, pp. 69–73, 130.

10. Miller, *Alexander Hamilton*, p. 77.

11. Morrissey, *Yorktown 1781*, pp. 66–67; Davis, *Campaign That Won America*, p. 216; Tonsetic, *1781*, p. 179.

12. Davis, *Campaign That Won America*, p. 216; Morrissey, *Yorktown 1781*, pp. 66–67.

13. Tonsetic, *1781*, p. 170; Davis, *Campaign That Won America*, p. 198; Thacher, *Military Journal*, pp. 280–81; Desmarais, *America's First Ally*, p. 224; Desmarais, *Road to Yorktown*, p. 117; Mitchell, *Alexander Hamilton*, pp. 270–71; Johnston, *Yorktown Campaign*, p. 123.

14. Desmarais, *America's First Ally*, p. 224.

15. Thacher, *Military Journal*, pp. 164, 266, 280.

16. Ibid., p. 281.

17. Desmarais, *Road to Yorktown*, p. 158.

18. Kline, *Alexander Hamilton*, p. 104.

19. Johnston, *Yorktown Campaign*, p. 174.

20. Ibid., p. 123.

21. Ibid., p. 175.

22. Morrissey, *Yorktown 1781*, pp. 66–67.
23. Tench Tilghman, *Memoir of Lieutenant Colonel Tench Tilghman* (Whitefish: Kessinger Publishing, 2010), pp. 31–32, 61.
24. Desmarais, *Road to Yorktown*, p. 163; Mitchell, *Alexander Hamilton*, pp. 272–73.
25. Vail, *Rochambeau*, p. 97.
26. Chernow, *Alexander Hamilton*, p. 162; Desmarais, *America's First Ally*, p. 228; Martin, *Narrative of a Revolutionary Soldier*, pp. 200–201; Harvey, *"A Few Blood Noses,"* p. 408; Randall, *Alexander Hamilton*, p. 241.
27. Thacher, *Military Journal*, p. 283; Tonsetic, *1781*, p. 180.
28. Randall, *Alexander Hamilton*, p. 241.
29. Harvey, *"A Few Bloody Noses,"* p. 408.
30. Carpenter, *Southern Gambit*, p. 252.
31. Shreve, *Tench Tilghman*, p. 155.
32. Carpenter, *Southern Gambit*, p. 252; Mitchell, *Alexander Hamilton*, p. 274.
33. Carpenter, *Southern Gambit*, p. 252.
34. Cook, *Long Fuse*, p. 347.
35. Desmarais, *Road to Yorktown*, p. 155.
36. Alexander Hamilton to Elizabeth Hamilton, October 12, 1781, Alexander Hamilton Papers, National Archives, Washington, DC.
37. Ibid.
38. Ibid.
39. John Ferling, *Jefferson and Hamilton, The Rivalry That Forged a Nation* (New York: Bloomsbury Press, 2013), pp. 9, 11; Lomask, *Alexander Hamilton*, p. 77.

Chapter VI

1. Shelby, *Road to Yorktown*, pp. 191–92; Harvey, *"A Few Bloody Noses,"* p. 407.
2. Morrissey, *Yorktown 1781*, p. 72; Chernow, *Alexander Hamilton*, pp. 162–63; Shelby, *Road to Yorktown*, pp. 189, 192; Urban, *Fusiliers*, pp. 274–75; Harvey, *"A Few Bloody Noses,"* p. 407; Randall, *Alexander Hamilton*, p. 241; Tonsetic, *1781*, pp. 170, 185–86; Robert A. Mayers, *The War Man: The True Story of a Citizen-Soldier Who Fought From Quebec to Yorktown* (Yardley, PA: Westholme Publishing, 2009), p. 166; Agniel, *South in the American Revolution*, p. 130.

3. Martin, *Narrative of a Revolutionary Soldier*, p. 201.

4. Thacher, *Military Journal*, p. 284.

5. Chernow, *Alexander Hamilton*, p. 162; Shelby, *Road to Yorktown*, pp. 192–93; Kline, *Alexander Hamilton*, p. 89; Leckie, *George Washington's War*, p. 360; Thomas J. Fleming, *Beat the Last Drum: The Story of Yorktown 1781* (New York: St. Martin's Press, 1963), pp. 273–74; Randall, *Alexander Hamilton*, p. 220; Boatner, *Encyclopedia of the American Revolution*, p. 433; Miller, *Alexander Hamilton*, p. 78; Vail, *Rochambeau*, p. 235; Lomask, *Alexander Hamilton*, pp. 10, 77; Desmarais, *Road to Yorktown*, p. 119.

6. Chernow, *Alexander Hamilton*, pp. 73, 162–63; Fleming, *Beat the Last Drum*, pp. 273–74; Ray Raphael, *Founders: The People Who Brought You a Nation* (New York: The New Press, 2010), p. 383; Davis, *Campaign That Won America*, p. 225; Tonsetic, *1781*, p. 188; Miller, *Alexander Hamilton*, p. 78; Mitchell, *Alexander Hamilton*, pp. 274–75.

7. Randall, *Hamilton*, p. 242.

8. Chernow, *Alexander Hamilton*, p. 163; Mitchell, *Alexander Hamilton*, p. 275.

9. Philbrick, *In the Hurricane's Eye*, p. 216.

10. Mitchell, *Alexander Hamilton*, p. 230.

11. Chernow, *Alexander Hamilton*, p. 163.

12. Johnston, *Yorktown Campaign*, p. 175.

13. Mitchell, *Alexander Hamilton*, p. 279.

14. Raphael, *Founders*, p. 383; Chernow, *Alexander Hamilton*, p. 162; Fleming, *Beat the Last Drum*, p. 272; Geake, *From Slaves to Soldiers*, pp. 79–80.

15. Urban, *Fusiliers*, pp. 270, 277; Flood, *Rise, and Fight Again*, p. 408; Kline, *Alexander Hamilton*, pp. 99–101; Chernow, *Alexander Hamilton*, pp. 9, 151–53, 159, 162–63; Wright, *Continental Army*, p. 167; Lomack, *Odd Destiny*, pp. 3–6; Leckie, *George Washington's War*, p. 657; Tonsetic, *1781*, p. 186; Fleming, *Beat the Last Drum*, pp. 272–74, 280; Christopher Ward, *The War of the Revolution* (New York: Skyhorse Publishing, 2011), p. 892; Shachtman, *How the French Saved America*, p. 277; Knott and Williams, *Washington and Hamilton*, pp. 231–36; Vail, *Rochambeau*, pp. 130, 135; Mitchell, *Alexander Hamilton*, pp. 274–76; Philbrick, *In the Hurricane's Eye*, pp. 216–17; Geake, *From Slaves to Soldiers*, pp. 47, 79–80; Alexander A. Lawrence, *Storm over Savannah: The Story of Count d'Estaing and the Siege of the Town in 1779* (Athens: University of Georgia Press, 2021), pp. 97, 108.

16. Mitchell, *Alexander Hamilton*, p. 274; Kline, *Alexander Hamilton*, p. 100; Fleming, *Beat the Last Drum*, p. 273.

17. Randall, *Alexander Hamilton*, p. 87.

18. Ibid., pp. 239, 243, 245; Chernow, *Alexander Hamilton*, pp. 42, 161; Johnston, *Yorktown Campaign*, p. 113; Mark Edward Lender and James Kirby Martin, editors, *Citizen Soldier: The Revolutionary Journal of Joseph Bloomfield* (Yardley, PA: Westholme, 2018), pp. 37n3, 106n2.

19. Massey, *John Laurens and the American Revolution*, pp. 89–92, 198; Lawrence, *Storm over Savannah*, pp. 97, 108.

20. Massey, *John Laurens and the American Revolution*, p. 127.

21. Randall, *Alexander Hamilton*, p. 233.

22. Massey, *John Laurens and the American Revolution*, p. 71; Fleming, *Beat the Last Drum*, p. 276; Lawrence, *Storm over Savannah*, pp. 97, 108.

23. Davis, *The Campaign That Won America*, p. 227; Mitchell, *Alexander Hamilton*, p. 275.

24. Vail, *Rochambeau*, p. 254.

25. Thacher, *Military Journal*, p. 285; "Jean-Joseph Sourbader de Gimar," National Park Service, Yorktown Battlefield, Yorktown, Virginia; Wright, *Continental Army*, p. 167.

26. Wright, *Continental Army*, p. 167; Tonsetic, *1781*, p. 187; Knott and Williams, *Washington and Hamilton*, pp. 90–92; Geake, *From Slaves to Soldiers*, p. 79.

27. Flood, *Rise, and Fight Again*, p. 408; Mitchell, *Alexander Hamilton*, p. 278; Fleming, *Beat the Last Drum*, pp. 276–77; Wright, *Continental Army*, pp. 133–34, 170; Tonsetic, *1781*, p. 187; Desmarais, *Road to Yorktown*, pp. x-xi.

28. Vail, *Rochambeau*, p. 251.

29. Martin, *Narrative of a Revolutionary Soldier*, pp. 183–84, 201; Tonsetic, *1781*, p. 163; Fleming, *Beat the Last Drum*, p. 280; Morrissey, *Yorktown 1781*, p. 34.

30. Martin, *Narrative of a Revolutionary Soldier*, p. 201; Scheer and Rankin, *Rebels and Redcoats*, p. 562; Tonsetic, *1781*, p. 190; Kline, *Alexander Hamilton*, pp. 100–101; Johnston, *Yorktown Campaign*, p. 145.

31. Chernow, *Alexander Hamilton*, pp. 73, 163; Flood, *Rise, and Fight Again*, p. 408; Shelby, *Road to Yorktown*, p. 193; Clark, *All Cloudless Glory*, p. 544; Martin, *Narrative of a Revolutionary Soldier*, p. 202; Kline, *Alexander Hamilton*, pp. 100–101; Tonsetic, *1781*, pp. 187–88, 190; Fleming, *Beat the Last Drum*, pp. 280, 283; Burke, *Campaign That Won America*, p. 227; Randall, *Alexander Hamilton*, pp. 15–16; Desmarais, *Road to*

Yorktown, p. 165; Johnston, *Yorktown Campaign*, p. 145; Massey, *John Laurens and the American Revolution*, pp. 195–98; Mitchell, *Alexander Hamilton*, pp. 246–47, 275–76; Morrissey, *Yorktown 1781*, p. 34.

32. Kline, *Alexander Hamilton*, p. 101; Tonsetic, *1781*, p. 189.

33. Thacher, *Military Journal*, p. 285; Desmarais, *Road to Yorktown*, p. 154.

34. Thacher, *Military Journal*, p. 285; Martin, *Narrative of a Revolutionary Soldier*, p. 202.

35. Carpenter, *Southern Gambit*, pp. 252–53; Flood, *Rise, and Fight Again*, p. 409; Martin, *Narrative of a Revolutionary Soldier*, p. 203; Kline, *Alexander Hamilton*, pp. 100–101; Randall, *Alexander Hamilton*, p. 243; Fleming, *Beat the Last Drum*, p. 283; Agniel, *South in the American Revolution*, p. 131.

36. Chernow, *Alexander Hamilton*, p. 163.

37. Ibid., p. 164.

38. Ibid., pp. 163–64; Royster, *Revolutionary People at War*, p. 220; Martin, *Narrative of a Revolutionary Soldier*, p. 202; Philbrick, *In the Hurricane's Eye*, pp. 216–17; Randall, *Alexander Hamilton*, p. 274; Fleming, *Beat the Last Drum*, pp. 280, 284–85; Randall, *Alexander Hamilton*, p. 243; Tonsetic, *1781*, p. 191; Knott and Williams, *Washington and Hamilton*, p. 102; Agniel, *South in the American Revolution*, p. 131; Mitchell, *Alexander Hamilton*, pp. 274, 276; Johnston, *Yorktown Campaign*, p. 146; Geake, *From Slaves to Soldiers*, pp. 79–80.

39. Chernow, *Alexander Hamilton*, p. 164; Kline, *Alexander Hamilton*, pp. 100–101.

40. Mitchell, *Alexander Hamilton*, p. 277.

41. Thacher, *Military Journal*, p. 285; Scheer and Rankin, *Rebels and Redcoats*, p. 255.

42. Massey, *John Laurens and the American Revolution*, p. 199; Kline, *Alexander Hamilton*, p. 101.

43. Martin, *Narrative of a Revolutionary Soldier*, p. 203.

44. Thacher, *Military Journal*, p. 285; Kline, *Alexander Hamilton*, pp. 100–101.

45. Randall, *Alexander Hamilton*, pp. 15–16, 241.

46. Thacher, *Military Journal*, p. 285; Tonsetic, *1781*, p. 192; Lomask, *Odd Destiny*, pp. 10–13; Fleming, *Beat the Last Drum*, p. 286.

47. Tonsetic, *1781*, pp. 187, 190; Flood, *Rise, and Fight Again*, p. 409; Chartrand, *French Army in the American War*, p. 22; Carpenter, *Southern Gambit*, pp. 252–53; Kline, *Alexander Hamilton*, p. 100; Jost, *Life and Death of a French Soldier*, p. 147.

48. Desmarais, *America's First Ally*, p. 166.
49. Ibid., p. 231.
50. Kline, *Alexander Hamilton*, p. 101.
51. Mitchell, *Alexander Hamilton*, p. 277.
52. Kline, *Alexander Hamilton*, p. 101; Tonsetic, *1781*, p. 192.
53. Kline, *Alexander Hamilton*, p. 101; Thacker, *Military Journal*, p. 285.
54. Alexander Hamilton to Marquis Lafayette, October 15, 1781, Alexander Hamilton Papers, National Archives, Washington, DC.
55. *Maryland Gazette*, October 25, 1781.
56. Fleming, *Beat the Last Drum*, p. 291.
57. Chernow, *Alexander Hamilton*, p. 164.
58. Ibid.
59. Mitchell, *Alexander Hamilton*, p. 277.

Chapter VII

1. Chernow, *Alexander Hamilton*, p. 164; Fleming, *Beat the Last Drum*, pp. 291–92; Royster, *Revolutionary People at War*, pp. 205–6; Lomask, *Odd Destiny*, pp. 10–12; Tonsetic, *1781*, pp. 192–93; Scheer and Rankin, *Rebels and Redcoats*, p. 565; Morrissey, *Yorktown 1781*, p. 71.
2. Scheer and Rankin, *Rebels and Redcoats*, p. 565.
3. Ibid.
4. Chernow, *Alexander Hamilton*, p. 164.
5. Thacher, *Military Journal*, p. 286.
6. *Maryland Gazette*, October 25, 1781; Harvey, *"A Few Bloody Noses,"* p. 392.
7. Clark, *All Cloudless Glory*, p. 543.
8. Kline, *Alexander Hamilton*, p. 81.
9. Hamilton, *Life of Alexander Hamilton*, vol. 1, p. 386; Kline, *Alexander Hamilton*, p. 93.
10. Randall, *Alexander Hamilton*, p. 244.
11. Chernow, *Alexander Hamilton*, pp. 164–65; Holger Hoock, *Scars of Independence: America's Violent Birth* (New York: Crown, 2017), pp. 326–27.
12. Carpenter, *Southern Gambit*, pp. 254–55; Harvey, *"A Few Bloody Noses,"* pp. 410–12; Chernow, *Alexander Hamilton*, p. 164; James Kirby Martin and Mark Edward Lender, *A Respectable Army: The Military Origins of the Republic, 1763–1789* (Arlington Heights, IL: Harlan Davidson,

1982), p. 178; Tonsetic, *1781*, pp. 197–98, 201–2; Jost, *Life and Death of a French Soldier*, p. 152; Leckie, *George Washington's War*, p. 656; Vail, *Rochambeau*, p. 74; Morissey, *Yorktown 1781*, pp. 73, 76; Shreve, *Tench Tilghman*, pp. 157, 159.

13. Geake, *From Slaves to Soldiers*, p. 81.
14. *New-York Journal*, November 12, 1781.
15. Johnston, *Yorktown Campaign*, pp. 177–78.
16. Jost, *Life and Death of a French Soldier*, p. 155.
17. Mitchell, *Alexander Hamilton*, p. 282.
18. Carpenter, *Southern Gambit*, p. 254; Johnston, *Yorktown Campaign*, pp. 19, 111.
19. Thacher, *Military Journal*, p. 288.
20. *Maryland Gazette*, October 25, 1781.
21. Thacher, *Military Journal*, pp. 289–93; Leckie, *George Washington's War*, p. 657.
22. Newton Martin Curtis, *From Bull Run To Chancellorsville: The Story of the Sixteenth New York Infantry Together with Personal Reminiscences* (New York: G. P. Putnam's Sons, 1906), p. 155; Carpenter, *Southern Gambit*, p. 254; Johnston, *Yorktown Campaign*, p. 158.
23. Curtis, *From Bull Run To Chancellorsville*, p. 155.
24. Chernow, *Alexander Hamilton*, p. 165; Harvey, *"A Few Bloody Noses,"* p. 412.
25. Morrissey, *Yorktown 1781*, pp. 76–77.
26. Alexander Hamilton to Vicomte De Noailles, November-December 1781, Alexander Hamilton Papers, National Archives, Washington, DC; Chernow, *Alexander Hamilton*, p. 165.
27. Chernow, *Alexander Hamilton*, p. 165.
28. Desmarais, *Road to Yorktown*, p. 173; Shachtman, *How the French Saved America*, p. 234.
29. *Maryland Gazette*, November 15, 1781.
30. *New-York Journal*, November 12, 1781.
31. Roche, *Alexander Hamilton*, p. 151; Tonsetic, *1781*, pp. 211–12; Ward, *War of the Revolution*, p. 895; Tilghman, *Washington's Loyalist*, p. 1.
32. Tilghman, *Washington's Loyalist*, pp. 17, 107.
33. Ibid., pp. 1, 18.
34. Hamilton to Vicomte De Noailles, November-December 1781, NA.
35. *New-York Journal*, November 12, 1781.
36. Carpenter, *Southern Gambit*, p. 260.
37. Cook, *Long Fuse*, p. 348.

38. Benton Rain Patterson, *Washington and Cornwallis: The Battle for America, 1775–1783* (New York: Taylor Trade Publishing, 2004), p. 329.

39. Mark Edward Lender and James Kirby Martin, *Citizen Soldier: The Revolutionary War Journal of Joseph Bloomfield* (Yardley, PA: Westholme, 2018), p. 38.

40. Kline, *Alexander Hamilton*, p. 92.

41. Chernow, *Alexander Hamilton*, p. 165.

42. Miller, *Alexander Hamilton*, p. 20.

43. Lomask, *Alexander Hamilton*, p. 78.

44. Chernow, *Alexander Hamilton*, p. 165.

45. Miller, *Alexander Hamilton*, p. 79; Knott and Williams, *Washington and Hamilton*, pp. 101, 113.

46. Chernow, *Alexander Hamilton*, pp. 163, 165.

47. Ibid.; Randall, *Alexander Hamilton*, p. 244.

48. Kline, *Alexander Hamilton*, pp. 101–2, 113; Randall, *Alexander Hamilton*, p. 245.

49. Kline, *Alexander Hamilton*, p. 102; Randall, *Alexander Hamilton*, p. 245.

50. Knott and Williams, *Washington and Hamilton*, pp. 113–14; Randall, *Alexander Hamilton*, p. 245; Mitchell, *Alexander Hamilton*, p. 284.

51. Randall, *Alexander Hamilton*, p. 245.

52. Ibid., p. 246.

53. Ibid., p. 250; Lomask, *Odd Destiny*, p. 79.

54. Hamilton to Vicomte De Noailles, November-December 1781, NA.

55. Puls, *Henry Knox*, pp. 170–71; Knott and Williams, *Washington and Hamilton*, pp. 117, 129–31.

56. Massey, *John Laurens and the American Revolution*, pp. 226–29.

57. Ibid., p. 230.

58. Randall, *Alexander Hamilton*, p. 247; Knott and Williams, *Washington and Hamilton*, pp. vii–257.

59. Kline, *Alexander Hamilton*, p. 71.

60. Massey, *John Laurens and the American Revolution*, pp. 173, 177–78, 186.

61. Fleming, *Beat the Last Drum*, pp. 281–86; Davis, *Campaign That Won America*, pp. 198–220; Morrissey, *Yorktown 1781*, pp. 66–77; Joanne B. Freeman, *Affairs of Honor* (New Haven, CT: Yale University Press, 2001), pp. 281–82; Chadwick, *George Washington's War*, pp. 138–40, 426; Nathan Schachner, *Aaron Burr, A Biography* (Hartford: Alfred Smith Barnes and Company, 1961), pp. 44–45, 252–53; Miller, *Alexander Hamilton*, pp. 36–37; Randall, *Alexander Hamilton*, pp. 176, 184–85, 247–48, 412–24; Knott and Williams, *Washington and Hamilton*,

pp. vii–257; Kline, *Alexander Hamilton*, pp. 49–102; Lomask, *Alexander Hamilton*, pp. 162–66; Chernow, *Hamilton*, pp. 73–166, 651–54.

62. Stephen F. Knott, *Alexander Hamilton and the Persistence of Myth* (Lawrence: University Press of Kansas, 2002), pp. 2–232; Raphael, *Founders*, p. 436; Chadwick, *George Washington's War*, pp. 38–140, 426; Miller, *Alexander Hamilton*, pp. 21–67; Clark, *All Cloudless Glory*, pp. 247, 251–52; Randall, *Alexander Hamilton*, p. 234; Fleming, *Beat the Drum*, p. 75; David T. Zabecki, editor, *Chief of Staff: The Principal Officers Behind History's Great Commanders, Napoleonic Wars to World War I* (2 vols., Annapolis, MD: Naval Institute Press, 2008), vol. 1, pp. 29–39; Shreve, *Tench Tilghman*, p. 118.

63. Mitchell, *Alexander Hamilton*, p. 75.

64. Francis Rufus Bellamy, *The Private Life of George Washington* (New York: Thomas Y. Crowell Company, 1951), p. 318.

65. Randall, *Alexander Hamilton*, p. 149.

66. Ibid., p. 121.

67. Kline, *Alexander Hamilton*, p. 102.

68. Randall, *Alexander Hamilton*, p. 421.

69. Marcus Cunliffe, *George Washington: Man and Monument* (New York: Mentor Books, 1958), p. 137; Miller, *Alexander Hamilton*, p. 67; Randall, *Alexander Hamilton*, pp. 119–421; Knott and Williams, *Washington and Hamilton*, pp. vii–257; Tilghman, *Washington's Loyalist*, p. 1.

70. Lomask, *Alexander Hamilton*, pp. 171–72; Knott and Williams, *Washington and Hamilton*, pp. 239–42.

71. Kline, *Alexander Hamilton*, p. 89.

72. Robert C. Baron, editor, *Soul of America: Documenting Our Past, 1492–1974* (Golden, CO: Fulcrum Publishing, 1989), p. 102; Shreve, *Tench Tilghman*, p. 118.

Epilogue

1. Rakove, *Revolutionaries*, p. 441.

2. Mitchell, *Alexander Hamilton*, p. 282.

3. Ibid., pp. 125–26; Philbrick, *In the Hurricane's Eye*, p. 271; Rakove, *Revolutionaries*, p. 441.

4. Philbrick, *In the Hurricane's Eye*, p. 236; Geake, *From Slaves to Soldiers*, pp. 79–80.

Index

About the Author

Phillip Thomas Tucker, PhD, is the award-winning author of more than eighty books in many fields of history and, in total, more than 180 works in history, including scholarly articles. He received his PhD in History from St. Louis University, St. Louis, Missouri, in 1990. Tucker has long specialized in producing groundbreaking history in multiple fields of study, including Women's history and African American history. He has been recognized as "the Stephen King of history," after more than three decades of authoring important books of unique distinction.